The Stuff Dreams Are Made Of

Housing Provision in Australia 1945–1960

Alastair Greig

MELBOURNE UNIVERSITY PRESS
1995

First published 1995

Typeset by Mark Peel in 11 pt Goudy
Printed inMalaysia by
SRM Production Services Sdn. Bhd. for
Melbourne University Press, Carlton, Victoria 3053

National Library of Australia Cataloguing-in-Publication entry

Greig, Alastair Whyte, 1960– .

The stuff dreams are made of: housing provision in Australia 1945–1960.

Bibliography.
Includes index.
ISBN 0 522 84621 1.

1. Housing—Australia. 2. Housing policy—Australia.
I. Title.

363.50994

The Stuff Dreams Are Made Of

To my parents

Bob and Jessie Greig

Contents

Figures

between pages 114 and 115

Acknowledgements

The original idea for this project came from Patrick Troy, who suggested a study on post-war housing production in Australia. Without his encouragement, guidance and support this book could never have been written. To him I owe an enormous debt.

I also benefited from the collegial atmosphere of the Urban Research Program in the Research School of Social Sciences at the Australian National University. My ideas have benefited greatly from my discussions with members of the program. In particular, the help I received from Mark Peel was invaluable. Not only was he a ready listener and a constant source of suggestions, he also performed heroics at the typesetting stage. For his multidimensional talents, I will always be grateful. In addition, I would like to thank Max Neutze, Graham Holland, Kevin White and Steven Bourassa for reading earlier drafts of the manuscript.

Other members of, and visitors to, the Urban Research Program and the Administration, Compliance and Governability Program participated in numerous seminars where I presented my ideas. I would like to thank Jane Marceau, Glenys Harding, Rita Coles, Stephen Little, Wendy Riemens, Barbara Norman, Heather Grant, Coralie Cullen, Janine Bush, Penny Hanley, Bette O'Brien, John Weaver, Richard Weatherley, Ann-Mari Jordens, Don Lamberton, Peter Self, Clem Lloyd, Val Braithwaite, Peter Grabosky and Tim Bonyhady. Other forums where these ideas were expressed included the Sociology Department, The Faculties, ANU, and the Federated PhD Scheme–Urban and Housing Studies. I especially benefited from comments from, and discussions with, Janelle Brown, Patrick Mullins, Frank Stilwell, Bronwyn Hanna and Glenn Maggs.

My opportunity to study the process of housebuilding started when I was commissioned to write a number of reports for the Commonwealth Department of Health, Housing and Community Services' National Housing Strategy. These were published under the title *Structure, Organisation and Skill Formation in the Australian Housing Industry*. Compared with the present book, those reports were more broadly framed historically and more narrowly focused on production. However, that experience convinced me that the story of the 1950s was worth telling. I would like to acknowledge the help I received from Meredith Edwards, Shelley Cooper, Gavin McCairns, Chris Paris, the numerous building firms and self-employed builders I interviewed, and the people who kindly gave me their time from the Building Workers' Industrial Union, the Housing Industry Association and the Royal Commission into Productivity in the Building Industry in New South Wales.

I would also like to thank John Iremonger and Brian Wilder for their support. For careful and informed editing and innumerable improvements in presentation and style I am indebted to Sarah Brenan. Lindy Coverdale saw the book through to completion. I am also indebted to Sophie Ducker for her encouragement and kind support.

My thanks go to the following for the use of illustrations: Time/Life Incorporated, the Australian National Gallery, Michael Leunig, Bruce Petty, the *Australian Women's Weekly*, *Australian Home Beautiful*, the New South Wales Chapter of the Royal Australian Institute of Architects, the Liberal Party of Australia, William Buckle Snr, Southcorp White Goods (Pyrox), Rocla, Pabco/Tremco (Ormonoid), ACI (Laminex Industries), CSR Wood Panels (Masonite) and the Commonwealth Department of Health, Housing and Community Services. While all efforts have been made to trace the copyright owners of the illustrations, I would be pleased to hear from anyone with further information. I am especially grateful to *Australian House and Garden*, not only for their permission to reproduce illustrations, but also for the inspiration I drew browsing through issues from the 1950s.

Others contributed more than they could know. They include Robert and Jessie Greig, Gillian Greig, Alan Greig, Rod Smith, Peter Lleonart, Graeme Regan, Rod Florence, Leighan Scurr, Phil Cohen, Sue MacMurtrie, John Mitchell, Ian Shepherd, Paul Kringas, Andrew Hopkins, Elizabeth Waters, Geoff Lee, John van der Velden, Paul Randalls, Klaus and Alison Ducker, Gail and Pete Slater, Marylou and Brooke Brazier, Tom Heinsohn and the Wanderers Soccer Club.

Finally, Sallyann and McCoist were always there. Thanks.

Introduction

Context

During the 1950s a solid sun-drenched house standing in the centre of a large and manicured suburban block was one of the dominant images of the 'Australian way of life'. This book explores this post-war 'Australian dream' and critically examines the ideas and theories surrounding post-war housing provision.

In the aftermath of World War II, the nation experienced its most severe housing shortage this century, estimated to be in the region of 300 000 dwellings. The magnitude of this housing crisis was inflated by an acute shortage of construction labour, a dearth of conventional building materials, high rates of new household formation and a mass immigration programme. The provision of housing was affected by a series of other unprecedented phenomena during the late 1940s and most of the 1950s. The Commonwealth and state governments embarked upon a large housebuilding programme: they aimed to provide housing for rental purposes and—especially after 1956—for owner occupation. In addition, during the fifteen years after the war more Australians than ever before assumed the responsibility for building their own dwelling. Furthermore, despite the growth in government rental housing, the nation experienced a dramatic rise in the level of owner occupation between 1947 and 1961. Between 1911—when the census first collected information on tenure status—and 1947, approximately half of all households owned or were purchasing their own dwelling. Between 1933 and 1947, the proportion remained at 52.6 per cent, although the number of mortgaged owner occupiers was declining, suggesting that fewer people had become owner occupiers during the fourteen intervening years. However, throughout the 1950s the percentage of owner occupiers climbed dramatically, to reach almost 70 per cent by 1961. Since the 1961 census, the level of owner occupation has stabilised at around 70 per cent of households.

This combination of unique circumstances coincided with an upsurge in modernist ideas in house design and planning. From the late 1940s onward, this philosophy struggled valiantly to meet the challenge of the post-war housing crisis, and to enter the hearts, minds and especially the homes of every household. However, by 1960 modernism was beginning to lose its dominant status and numerous proponents of the movement felt that the modernist revolution had been betrayed, misused or misunderstood.

This book sets out to establish that these series of exceptional circumstances and changes were interrelated. Furthermore, in order to explain how producers and consumers confronted the challenge of housing the nation it is important to appreciate that the form which post-war housing assumed was intricately connected with wider processes of social change. As the book unfolds it will become increasingly clear that any assessment of the nation's success in meeting the challenge to overcome the post-war housing crisis depends upon the ideas used to measure 'success' and upon the conceptual lenses through which reality and history are perceived.

Most previous research on post-war housing in Australia has been limited to specific aspects of housing provision. For example, Hill (1959) gave a detailed account of housing finance between 1945 and 1956 and Howard (1988) has explored the institutional politics of the early post-war period. Jones (1972) explored the role of state housing authorities between 1945 and the early 1970s and a number of histories on various state housing commissions have examined the production and allocation of government housing (see Howe 1988; Marsden 1986). A number of architectural historians have also examined post-war housing, although few, with the notable exceptions of Boyd (1968; 1991) and Freeland (1972), have examined the suburban landscape and its relationship to wider processes of change. However, more recently Powell (1993) has sketched an approach which added more intelligibility to the critique of post-war working-class suburban dwellings. The emerging interest in the post-war house was also reflected in Cuffley's (1993) study of post-war design as well as the Powerhouse Museum's exhibition 'The Australian Dream: Design in the Fifties' (O'Callaghan 1993).

These more recent studies on various aspects of post-war housing have adopted a relatively sympathetic approach to 1950s housing compared with earlier studies. Many who grew up in the post-war period have begun to search for and reinterpret the icons of their childhood or youth; a recent *Australian Magazine* (1993) issue was entitled 'The 50s: Why They Weren't So Bad'. A more reserved approach was illustrated in the *Bulletin*'s review of Cuffley which claimed that 'if ever a period was destined to avoid acquiring period charm, this was it' (Flower 1993). This latter view derives from a somewhat elitist—'mass cultural'—approach to cultural studies which assumes an undifferentiated consumption of mass-produced commodities, rather than a more 'popular cultural' emphasis on how people 'make do' with given resources (Fiske 1989). Thus, the early post-war era is an arena of potential conflict between mass cultural theorists and popular cultural theorists. The controversy over urban futures in the 1990s has also rekindled debate on the post-war built environment. Those demanding radical change in contemporary and future urban form have used the experience of the 1950s to highlight the problems associated with suburban 'sprawl'. However, the validity of this method is often weakened by a selective search for evidence. All too often those attempting to understand the present have changed the past in order to support a predetermined vision of the future. Ironically, this can often lead to an uncritical acceptance of the myth of the 'Australian way of life' during the 1950s.

This book is neither a nostalgic trip through the early post-war period, nor does it portray the 1950s as a disastrous era against which better futures can be measured. Its aim is to place housing provision, the form it assumed and the choices people made, within the context of existing material constraints and opportunities. Available housing opportunities were also influenced by the lenses through which post-war producers and consumers surveyed the surrounding social and economic landscape.

Concepts

My findings are consistent with the approach to housing provision adopted by Ball, Harloe and Martens (1988; Ball 1983 & 1988) which emphasises the importance of the interconnectedness of production, exchange and consumption in explaining change. Their theoretical concept of 'structures of housing provision' (SHP) rejects atomistic approaches which attempt to understand particular spheres of housing activity in isolation and stresses the interconnections between housing and wider social phenomena. As an 'operational' theoretical concept SHP is therefore both dynamic and empirically framed. Ball and Harloe (1992, 13) further qualify any grand theoretical pretensions by acknowledging Boudon's (1986) claim that theories of social change should be restricted to 'partial and local social processes firmly situated in time and in particular circumstances'.

The 'regulation school' of political economy has accepted similar qualifications to suprahistorical theories of social change, focusing on specific models of capitalist development, particular organisational forms of production and their corresponding forms of consumption. Given the importance of this framework for the understanding of post-war capitalism in general and housing in particular, it will receive more detailed attention in Chapter 1.

The interrelated concepts of modernity, modernisation and modernism are also crucial for understanding the wider theoretical framework I have used. Following Berman (1983) and Soja (1989), I have viewed modernity as a dynamic concept, in contrast to earlier definitions which tended to link it to a fixed set of social conditions and attitudes contrasted with those of a usually undefined 'traditional' society. Thus modernity in the 1950s is different from earlier or later forms of modernity.

Soja (1989, 26–7) linked modernisation to 'the many different "objective" processes of structural change that have been associated with the ability of capitalism to develop and survive, to reproduce successfully its fundamental social relations of production and distinctive divisions of labour despite endogenous tendencies towards debilitating crisis'. The advantage of this definition is that it liberates the concept from its earlier teleological strait-jacket, whereby modernisation was the process by which modernity replaces tradition. In development sociology, the term implied the transformation of 'backward' countries into 'advanced' capitalist countries through fostering Western attitudes and values. Within the housebuilding industry, 'modernisation' was used to describe a process of change whereby traditional craft production was replaced by 'more advanced', repetitive, mechanical—or Fordist (after Henry Ford)—processes of production. As in the case of development sociology, there was an assumption that the more 'advanced' example would show the more 'backward' one the image of its own future.

In this text, modernisation is discussed on two levels. In general terms, it refers to the consolidation of Fordist practices of mass production and their association with mass consumption in post-war Australian capitalism. In a more particular sense, modernisation also describes those changes within structures of housing provision which developed in an attempt to deal with the problems confronting post-war Australia.

The final concept, modernism, is described by Soja (1989, 29) as a 'response to modernisation'. He goes on:

> It encompasses a heterogeneous array of subjective visions and strategic action programmes in art, literature, science, philosophy, and political practice which are unleashed by the disintegration of an inherited, established order and the awareness of the projected possibilities and perils of a restructured contemporary moment or conjuncture. Modernism is . . . a conjunctural social movement mobilised to face the challenging question of what now is to be done given that the context of the contemporary has significantly changed.

In this text, modernism will be discussed as it arose in architecture and design, in connection with a range of theories associated with social and technological change.

Content

This study provides an historical description of some of the most important influences on housing provision between 1945 and 1960. The four interconnected realms explored are the socio-economic context, housing supply, housing demand and housing design.

Part I provides the socio-economic framework for an examination of post-war housing in Australia. Chapter 1 adopts the approach of the regulation school to interpret the specific forms which housing assumed during the period between 1945 and 1960 and maintains that the form of housing performed an important role in the ascendancy and reproduction of the post-war Fordist regime of accumulation in Australia. This approach to Australian post-war housing is supported by a synthesis of the more general theoretical propositions of the regulation school and a range of studies on Australian social and economic development. Chapter 2 contrasts earlier writers' emphasis on post-war 'prosperity'—the 'long boom'—with the austere housing conditions which faced many post-war Australians. Much was made of the post-war 'housing crisis', but it is clear that, to a large extent, the crisis was socially constructed. Once it ceased to affect the middle class it was assumed to have disappeared, although other groups (notably migrants) continued to be severely disadvantaged.

Part II focuses on the housebuilding process and technological change in the wake of World War II. The government joined numerous housing reformers and experts in the search for new techniques and processes which would deliver the nation from the housing shortage. This post-war environment enhanced the status of a modernist philosophy which promised to lift the housebuilding industry into the machine age. Chapter 3 discusses the nature of the housebuilding industry and the growing appeal of modernism. Chapters 4 and 5 explore the consequences of the post-war housing problem for the organisational and technological nature of the housebuilding industry. By 1960 numerous transformations had affected the structure and organisation of the industry, although few modernists would have recognised it as a fulfilment of their post-war ideals.

In Part III, the issue of post-war owner occupation—'the great Australian dream'—is reassessed in the contextual light provided by Parts I and II. After examining a range of social theories about post-war suburbanisation and owner occupation, Chapter 6 maintains that the explanatory burden which numerous theories have placed on affluence, ideology and government policy cannot be sustained in the light of empirical evidence. Although state sponsorship of owner occupation and the promotion of the 'dream' through various media certainly contributed, there are a range of other factors which make the post-war growth of owner occupation more intelligible. Although some households were 'pulled' by financial, security or image considerations into this form of tenure, many others were 'pushed' into owner occupation through lack of a viable alternative.

The circumstances which elevated the status of modernisation in housebuilding and which accelerated the rate of owner occupation were also exploited to promote modernist design. Part IV demonstrates the interconnections between post-war economic growth, housing austerity, housebuilding techniques and modernist design. Visions of technological modernisation, architectural modernism and a particular mood of post-war modernity coincided during the 1950s and invested the word 'modern' with substantial evocative power. Chapter 7 examines a wide spectrum of architectural and design features from the period. Many of these features were considered more than examples of the latest fashion; a scientific value was claimed for them, a value which, so it was said, transcended the vagaries of style. Alternatively, they could be viewed as an expression of the mood of post-war life, or as a practical contribution to the challenge of overcoming the constraints of post-war building shortages.

In the next two chapters the relationship between modernism, modernisation and modernity is subjected to further scrutiny to provide support for the argument that modernism was a multidimensional concept, with a variety of meanings dependent on context. In Chapter 8 modernism is investigated through the lens of one of Australia's most renowned architectural critics, Robin Boyd. Boyd was both a modernist and a vocal critic of the 1950s built environment, and his description of 'the Australian ugliness' soon became part of the Australian vernacular. Chapter 9 analyses modernism through an alternative medium, the *Australian House and Garden* magazine. This reading suggests that both conservative and radical functionalist theories on the role of popular magazines need qualification. The magazine began with the didactic mission of promoting modernism throughout Australia. While its content and tone occasionally betrayed an intellectual elitism, *Australian House and Garden* remained accessible to all classes and devoted considerable space to housing production as well as housing consumption. From the late 1940s until the mid-1950s it remained sensitive to problems associated with the housing shortage. By the end of the decade, however, the content of the magazine increasingly reflected the myth of the 'Australian way of life'. Features on housing production became less frequent and modernism was gradually relegated from a necessary accompaniment of post-war living to one of a number of possible lifestyle choices available from glossy catalogues. The magazine thus reflected the post-war journey which housing provision had ventured upon.

In the final chapter, I critically assesses this path which the nation took between 1945 and 1960, and conclude that even though the modernist compass had been lost somewhere along the track, it was remarkable that the nation had travelled so far. This final chapter also enjoys the retrospective luxury of pointing out the direction taken after 1960, revealing that the beginning of the 1960s marked an important fork in the road of post-war housing provision.

Part I

Laying the Foundations

1

Housing and Fordism in Post-war Australia

While post-war Australian society resembled inter-war society in many respects—the market economy continued to operate and the production of commodities remained largely in the hands of private companies—on another level significant changes were occurring, including a more interventionist role for the state, the emergence of patterns of mass consumption, the growth of local manufacturing, a large influx of foreign investment and the encouragement of mass immigration. Prevailing fears—based on a reading of inter-war economic dynamics—that the economy would sooner rather than later return to the recessionary conditions of the early 1930s proved unfounded, and the economy experienced boom conditions which lasted a quarter of a century.

This chapter provides some analytical tools for evaluating the role housing performed in the post-war economy. The conceptual framework adopted, based on the 'regulation school' or 'regulationist theory' and the concept of a Fordist model of development, helps explain the twin phenomena of systemic stability and conjunctural change within Australian society.

Regulation theory and Fordism

The concept of Fordism can be used to describe two separate yet interrelated phenomena (Lipietz 1988, 26). On a more restricted level, it is used to describe a particular techno-organisational system, one that depends on highly mechanised, repetitive techniques to produce standardised goods for mass consumption. This system can be analysed at the level of the individual enterprise, or within an industrial sector. However, the concept of Fordism can also be applied more broadly, and the 'regulation school' is linked with Fordism at this broader societal level. The intellectual origins of the school can be traced back to the break with 'rigid' or Stalinist Marxism during the 1960s by structuralist theoreticians such as Louis Althusser and Charles Bettelheim, who rejected a deterministic and linear model of capitalist development which predicted inevitable catastrophic contradictions and systemic revolution. However, regulationists went one stage further, in questioning these structuralists' stress upon 'reproduction'—the ability of capitalism to survive and periodically regenerate despite its seemingly inherent tendencies towards instability and crisis. The onset of the world economic downturn in the early 1970s further highlighted differences between approaches emphasising 'reproduction' and those examining 'crises' (Lipietz 1993, 101).

Regulation theorists replaced quasi-mechanistic structural relations stressing continuity with an emphasis upon significant epochal shifts within capitalist society. In addition, they allowed more scope for historical and spatial contingency. They observed that capitalism was capable of regenerating itself periodically through modification to both its techniques of production and key social and institutional relations. These modified relations are the *result* of a series of imposed or negotiated institutional compromises created—or 'discovered', or 'found'—during periods of crisis (Lipietz 1988, 19). An ever-evolving capitalist society continually generates economic, cultural and social change—'constructive destruction'—and this can alter the delicate balance on which historical compromises are based. This weakens its stability and tends to engender structural crises, 'during which the very functioning of regulation comes into contradiction with existing institutional forms, which are then abandoned, destroyed or bypassed' (Boyer 1988, 76).

Two fundamental concepts in regulation analysis are 'regimes of accumulation' and 'modes of regulation'. For Lipietz (1988, 19) a regime of accumulation 'describes the stabilisation over a long period of the allocation of the net product between consumption and accumulation'. The stability of a particular regime depends on a socio-institutional framework—or 'mode of regulation'—encompassing formal and informal rules, laws, norms, agreements, political practices, settlements, social contracts and conventions which codify behaviour and regulate relationships. These institutional mechanisms allow temporary solutions to the inherent instability of capitalist relationships.

The regulation school seeks to uncover the relationships between specific institutional forms, organisational procedures and techno-economic structures on the one hand and the structural stability, reproduction and transformation of regimes of accumulation on the other. This institutional focus remains sensitive to the peculiarities of local capitalisms and their specific political cultures. As Jessop (1991, 310) points out, the origins of a mode of regulation are 'historically contingent rather than capitalistically ordained'. The 'discovery' of stable regimes of accumulation occurs almost by accident and the corresponding mode of regulation performs a permissive or enabling role. When a crisis of regulation does occur, a state of social flux and experimentation emerges and it is possible—but not inevitable—that a new mode of regulation will arise.

The approach adopted by the regulationists strikes a balance between structure and agency, stability and change, reproduction and transformation, contingency and determinism, the specific and the general, and the local and the global. It focuses attention upon 'the complex interrelations, habits, political practices, and cultural forms that allow a highly dynamic and consequently unstable, capitalist system to acquire sufficient semblance of order to function coherently at least for a certain period of time' (Harvey 1989, 122).

The stability of the Fordist regime of accumulation, which dominated Western Europe (and Australia) from 1945 until the early 1970s, was premised upon a correspondence between mass-production techniques and institutions of mass consumption. This regime emerged in the late nineteenth century when a combination of technological innovation and organisational restructuring resulted in dramatically increased productivity in certain industries, but it became increasingly difficult to realise surplus value from commodities produced under these conditions due to limited demand, which in turn 'placed in question the social validity of the merchandise offered' (Lipietz 1993, 131). From another perspective, Beniger (1986) has labelled this non-correspondence 'the crisis of control' and has argued that a solution was discovered in the 'bureaucratic control of mass consumption'.

From a regulation perspective, the technico-organisational innovations (such as the moving assembly line) introduced by Henry Ford on the eve of World War I were only the latest developments within an emerging regime of accumulation. Of greater significance was Ford's decision to increase daily wages to $5; Ford recognised that exponentially expanded output required significant growth in buying power as well as a radical shift in wage-earners' consumption norms. Although a mass market began to emerge during the 1920s—especially in the United States (Beniger 1986)—a disequilibrium persisted. In regulationist terms, the economic crisis of the 1930s is interpreted as 'a new regime of accumulation in search of a viable mode of regulation' (Gunn 1991, 85). The depression of the 1930s provided further evidence that capitalist expansion on the basis of the productivity gains achieved through Fordist production methods could not be sustained without providing wage-earners with the means to consume mass-produced goods. A mature Fordist regime of accumulation required 'a growth in the purchasing power of wages in parallel with increases in productivity' (Lipietz 1985, 1–13).

The halcyon years of Fordism occurred during the long post-war economic boom, and one of the engines of Fordist development was the interventionist state. The post-war solution to the inter-war crisis of disequilibrium was found in the pursuit of 'Fordist-Keynesian' policies by core Western capitalist powers. Regardless of ideological predisposition, Western governments performed a crucial role in promoting high rates of growth and improving standards of living through a combination of 'welfare statism, Keynesian economic management, and control over wage relations' (Harvey 1989; Jessop 1991). This intervention occurred through direct state expenditure, through the management of conflict between capital and labour, and through patriarchal social welfare policies. Stabilisation of demand was also facilitated through the state's commitment to full employment, although it is questionable whether this commitment was a major cause of Fordist expansion. It should be noted that the system was premised upon internal demand rather than international expansion, even though the Third World was increasingly drawn into the production of mass commodities, primarily for core capitalist markets. This focus on regulation within national boundaries also enhanced the authority, or sovereignty, of the state within territorial boundaries (Camilleri & Falk 1992).

The first point which needs to be noted is that throughout the historical period which this book deals with—from 1945 until 1960—Western capitalist counties enjoyed historically high rates of economic growth. Fordist-Keynesian growth tended to build on its own success for a prolonged period: the post-war boom promoted employment, generated increasing tax revenue, improved public provision of welfare and services and thus provided greater security among consumers to spend today's and tomorrow's wages, and among investors to invest and employ (Jessop 1991, 89). High growth rates were bound up with the stability of the Fordist regime of accumulation which linked mass production with institutions promoting mass consumerism. Post-war Fordism was not simply a system of mass production—it was 'a total way of life' (Harvey 1989, 135). The relationship between Fordism and housing extends beyond attempts to employ Fordist techniques in the process of housing production (see Chapter 3). Housing also performed a significant role in ensuring the stability and reproduction of the Fordist regime of accumulation.

Fordism and housing

During the inter-war years, the most advanced experimentation with the Fordist regime of accumulation occurred in the United States, where a range of industrial complexes emerged in search of secure mass markets. The housing and home-based private consumption complex, the automobile complex and the development of mass communications were driving forces behind early efforts to create a bureaucratically controlled mass consumer market.

There was no determinist or functionalist logic operating behind this relationship: however, it so happened that the development corresponded with the technical and institutional logic of Fordism.

During the 1920s, the United States experienced a large suburban housing boom. Apart from its employment effects, suburban expansion was important for other reasons. The new houses became the 'functional containers' for new consumer items which poured into the kitchens and living rooms of suburbia (Gunn 1991, 86). It was also during this period that the home radio emerged as an important medium for mass advertising, further promoting the bureaucratic control of mass consumption (Beniger 1986). In addition, expansive suburban development facilitated the spectacular growth of the automobile complex, including the oil and petroleum, rubber, glass and steel industries.

This relationship between expansive urban form, the private 'residential container' for mass-produced goods, and the mass demand for commodities in key Fordist industrial sectors illustrates the importance of housing in the maintenance and reproduction of the Fordist regime of accumulation. Lipietz (1985, 1–14) has claimed that housing is the 'structuring motif of the Fordist way of life', despite the 'non-Fordist' form which the production of housing historically has assumed.

After the war, suburbia became a critical market for Fordist expansion, epitomised in the growth of stand-alone suburban and regional shopping centres. The process of suburbanisation also encouraged the interpenetration of a range of industrial complexes at the heart of Fordist accumulation (Roobeek 1987, 133). Suburban housing, the automobile and electrical appliances became the icons of Fordist consumerism, affluence and the long boom (see Figure 1).

Followers of the 'regulation school' were not the first to comment on the close relationship between suburbanisation and capitalist accumulation (Baran and Sweezy 1977; O'Connor 1973; Bassett and Short 1980; Checkoway 1986; Harloe 1981). However, while some of these authors have been careful to avoid implying any functionalist logic in this relationship between housing and capitalist development, others have presented suburbanisation as a social product of some general capitalist logic of reproduction.

In this vein, Castells (1977, 388) described the single-family home in the suburbs as 'the perfect design for maximising capitalist consumption'. The regulation school is more cautious, conceding the possibility that there can be historical epochs in which suburbanisation does not correspond with the dominant regime of accumulation.

Fordism and post-war Australia

There have been few systematic attempts to apply regulation theory to Australian development, let alone Australian housing (see Berry 1990; Low 1994). However, a wide range of existing historical, sociological and economic literature is available which can be used to demonstrate the utility of the regulation approach.

Mullins (1981a; 1981b, 1988) has provided one of the most useful studies of Australian capitalism and its relationship to urban form, drawing on the conceptual framework of the world systems analysis school of development studies to focus on the peculiarities of a group of semi-peripheral former colonial nations—labelled 'dominion capitalist' regimes.

Dominion capitalism was distinguished from other forms of development by eight principal features: the modern nation state was established through European colonisation of temperate or semi-temperate zones sparsely inhabited by indigenous people; the proportion of indigenous population declined relative to Europeans through genocide or assimilation and European culture quickly became dominant; rates of urbanisation, health and living standards were/are comparable to the core nations; in the share of GDP generated by primary, secondary and tertiary sectors they resemble 'core' rather than 'peripheral' nations; at least up until 1945, the working classes received wage rates comparable to those of western Europe; primary products extracted and/or refined using capital-intensive technology dominated export markets; secondary industries focus on early stages of processing, are sheltered behind comparatively high tariff barriers and serve a local rather than international market; and foreign multinational firms occupy a prominent position in many key industrial sectors (Ehrensaft & Armstrong 1978).

In analysing Australian dominion capitalist development, Mullins distinguished three stages of capitalist development, 'mercantile', 'industrial' and finally 'monopoly'. Corresponding with these three ideal types are specific patterns of urban settlement. While mercantile capitalism promoted an 'urban peasant community', industrial capitalism encouraged an 'occupational community' and monopoly capitalism give rise to a 'suburban community'. Between 1840 and 1940 Australian development was dominated by mercantile capitalism, and the existence of a relatively weak industrial base inhibited the development of a strong occupational community. While the mercantilist urban peasantry was characterised by 'individualism, privatisation and self-sufficiency', industrial occupational communities were marked by 'solidarity and cohesiveness'. Further, mercantilism promoted extensive settlement patterns, while industrial capital tended to group communities in an intensive pattern close to the place of work—usually within walking distance. Thus, there was 'no concentration of property capital in . . . rental dwellings and Australia's mercantile workers were more likely to be "abandoned" to provide their own accommodation directly from wages by buying [single family] housing' (Mullins 1981a, 68). In addition, members of the mercantile working class were forced to provide more of their own residential facilities (such as water, sewerage and energy) due to the less sophisticated infrastructural needs of mercantile capitalism (Mullins 1981a, 68).

Monopoly capital came to dominate mercantilism after World War II (Connell & Irving 1986). The characteristic urban form of monopoly capitalism—the suburban community—bore a greater resemblance to the mercantile/urban peasant community than to the industrial/occupational community. These similarities between the extensive urban patterns of settlement characteristic of both the urban peasant community and the suburban community makes the specific development of Australian suburbia appear more historically consistent than is actually the case. The traditional dominance of extensive development and owner occupation is in fact the result of two distinct periods of development, which were cross-cut by a weaker, subordinate intensive industrial/occupation community.

The cultural, institutional, economic and political forces promoting monopoly capitalism—and Fordism—gathered pace during the inter-war years. These forces were associated with modernism, mass production and mass consumption. Whitwell's study of the emergence of the mass market and mass consumerism in Australia also provides evidence in support of the regulationist perspective. A limited 'modern consumer society' began to emerge in Australia during the 1920s and was reflected in the expansion of the automobile market, the appearance of a range of 'labour-saving' household devices and an increase in hire purchase credit. However, the market for domestic appliances was limited until the latter part of the 1920s and most items 'remained expensive and certainly beyond the reach of most working class households' (Whitwell 1989, 14). The depression put a temporary halt to this process before World War II consumed the nation's attention as well as its resources.

These seeds of Australian Fordism—mass production plus mass consumption—planted during the 1920s reached maturity during the long boom after the war. The Bretton Woods agreement had stabilised international trade and exchange rates, foreign manufacturers seeking investment outlets saw an opportunity to satisfy pent-up local demand behind high tariff barriers and Australian primary exports were in high demand. The local economy was now more intricately linked with the global economy. In addition, innovations in communication increasingly alleviated the pre-war sense of global isolation (Davison 1993).

Although the mercantilist base remained important, post-war growth was premised on the expansion of industrial capital, often of foreign origin. The dominant monopoly form of foreign industrial capital and Fordist techniques and processes were transplanted from Europe and the United States. This combination of circumstances also promoted 'increasing metropolitan dominance' (Mullins 1981a, 1981b; McLoughlin 1993).

A robust Fordist regime of accumulation required a growing mass market for the expanding consumer goods base. During the long boom, this was facilitated through a massive immigration programme, an expanding labour force, high employment rates, high rates of household formation, rising living standards and political stability. Real consumption expenditure per person increased dramatically after the war and continued to expand rapidly until the early 1970s, although during the latter stages of the long boom households appear to have channelled more of their income into savings than consumer expenditure (Whitwell 1989, 25). While high employment and steady wages account for much of this growth, there were other institutional and psychological factors which must be taken into consideration. Whitwell (1989, 33) notes that 'the growing importance of automobiles and household durables in personal consumption expenditure can only be understood in terms of the ability and willingness of a large and growing number of Australians to borrow'. In contrast with the pre-war years, more and more consumers felt confident enough not only to purchase outright consumer durables rather than save, but also to part with future income in return for consumer items beyond the reach of their immediate savings.

Regulationists have stressed the role performed by Keynesian interventionism in the development and reproduction of the Fordist regime of accumulation. Whitwell (1989, 52) also adds the more interventionist state to the list of factors contributing to the advent of mass consumerism:

> World War I had ended with most people anxious to return to some idealised notion of what had existed before the war. There was no such desire after World War II. Instead, there was a pervasive determination to avoid the 1930s experience and create a new world in which economic insecurity was banished, income was more evenly distributed and shared prosperity would prevail. Prominent in this rosy vision was a much more active role for the state.

The Australian federal state was well placed to perform a central role in the advent of Fordism, as many of the institutions established in the infancy of federation coincided with the requirements of Fordist growth. Australia's post-war welfare state was 'differentiated' rather than 'integrated', in the sense that the economic and social aspects of state intervention were only loosely articulated (Jessop 1991). This occurred despite concerted pressure among elements within the post-war Labor government for a more comprehensive social-democratic model which would implement social planning through co-ordinated policies for welfare, housing and employment (see Howard 1987, Jones 1972). The prevailing view during the immediate post-war years within the Labor Party was that co-ordinated national planning was essential in order to avoid the repetition of another general recession. However, the post-war experience of a buoyant economy, high wages and high returns on investment undermined the perceived need for economic planning. The Liberal-Country Party attempted to woo voters during the 1946 and 1949 elections by promising to unfetter the economy from state controls reminiscent of wartime austerity (see Figure 2). By 1949, the population had grown 'sceptical about the merits of planning; it seemed too often like interference with the enjoyment of good things which were at last abundant' (Bolton 1993, 85).

Part of the failure to implement a more integrated vision of the welfare state was due to the maintenance and strength of the pre-war institutional compromises between labour and capital, which Castles (1987, 75) labels the 'politics of domestic defence'. This historical compromise, negotiated during the first decade of federation, prevented 'subsequent manifestations of economic vulnerability becoming the occasion of exacerbated class conflict and political crisis at a later date'. Its four pillars were (Castles 1988, 93):

> the protection of manufacturing industry through tariffs and other trade restrictions, the conciliation and arbitration of industrial disputes, the control of immigration, and a residual system of income maintenance for those outside the labour market. Each may be seen as interlocking components of a system of shock absorbers designed to defend and stabilise the existing structure of economic opportunities and rewards against any rapid or excessive disturbance from exogenous forces. Each simultaneously may be understood as elements of an 'historical compromise' which sought to guarantee some degree of social protection to all politically significant sectors of the Australian community.

This 'Australian settlement' was enshrined in a range of policies, laws and institutions, such as the Australian Conciliation and

Arbitration Commission, the White Australia policy and 'new protectionism'. The post-war Fordist boom was built on these regulatory foundations, which lasted intact for another quarter of a century. If the experience of the United States during the 1920s could be described as a Fordist regime of accumulation in search of a mode of regulation, then the Australian experience could almost appear as a mode of regulation waiting for a Fordist regime of accumulation.

Housing and Australian Fordism

The coincidence of an interventionist state, mass production, mass consumption and a belief in the powers of infinite technical and social progress permeated all areas of post-war social change, including urban development. Melbourne's experience of metropolitan growth has been described as being built on a 'seemingly unshakeable faith in Fordist growth, in the politics of Keynesian welfarism . . . in democratic capitalism, and in the overall project of modernity' (McLoughlin 1993, 25). In turn, the health of the Australian Fordist model of development depended to a significant extent on the promotion of suburban patterns of urban settlement and the extension of owner occupation, for housing demand had flow-on effects throughout the economy. It performed a vital role in the expansion of various industries linked to housebuilding and housing consumption, including the building materials sector, the design profession, a plethora of service industries—including finance, insurance and real estate—and encouraged or forced the post-war state to engage in the provision of infrastructure such as transport networks, water, sewerage and drainage facilities and power supply (Whitwell 1989, 61).

A number of commentators have observed a correlation between owner occupation, suburbanisation and the advent of a consumer society in post-war Australia. Between the end of the war and the early 1960s the number of owners and purchasers leapt by almost 20 per cent. Meanwhile, the proportion of households purchasing a dwelling—as distinct from outright ownership—almost trebled to 22.5 per cent. The suburban owner-occupied home was the 'container' for Fordist mass consumption. Whitwell

(1989, 38) called this pattern of consumer behaviour 'the suburban imperative' and said that it rested on a 'trilogy of compulsive needs': the suburban house, a range of 'labour-saving' household appliances and a private car. As mentioned earlier, post-war confidence facilitated the growth of the post-war credit industry and enabled households to obtain loans on a scale which had been inconceivable during the 1930s.

Berry's (1988, 114–16) assessment of post-war urbanisation is also consistent with the 'suburban imperative' although he placed more emphasis on 'the structural changes in the process of domestic capital accumulation'. Multinational capital penetrated the most profitable areas of Fordist accumulation—such as manufacturing and mining—while local savings tended to gravitate towards credit and the construction industry. Although these latter sectors were relatively less profitable, high demand ensured high returns. Chapters 4 and 5 show that residential construction, largely in the form of owner occupation, was profitable enough to attract a significant amount of foreign capital to Australia, especially during the early 1950s. Throughout the Western world, construction capital during this period was principally drawn from local sources, however, and Australia was no exception.

Despite the different weights which Berry and Whitwell attach to supply and demand, both emphasise the relationship between suburbia, owner occupation and Fordism. Mullins also noted that the post-war internationalisation of capital and the more tightly integrated world system pushed Australia towards a 'corporate monopoly stage' of capitalist development. This encouraged greater international uniformity in patterns of urban residential settlement, characterised by suburbanisation and owner occupation.

The post-war Fordist mode of regulation also fostered a privatised, individualised form of consumption similar to that of the urban peasantry. The crucial difference between the two epochs was the mass, bureaucratised and commodified nature of consumption during the post-war era. The 'politics of domestic defence' focused on providing adequate wage remuneration for workers on award rates, who would then be free to provide for their own individual requirements through the market rather than through publicly provided goods and services. Thus, despite a spirited defence of an integrated welfare policy—one which took account of housing needs among other needs— by some Labor Party members, post-war Australia had a residual welfare state.

The federal system of government and the organisation of independently run state housing commissions also hindered the development of an integrated public housing policy. Reformist tinkering with the welfare state came to an end with the victory of the Liberal-Country Party at the 1949 federal elections which initiated over two decades of conservative rule. Significantly, the Menzies era strengthened rather than weakened the institutions of the 'politics of domestic defence' (Capling & Galligan 1993, ch. 3). This institutional basis was augmented by the image promoted by Menzies of 'the home and the consensual symbols of the domestic sphere' (Brett 1984, 260). Thus, the regulatory institutions associated with the 'politics of domestic defence' were integral to the Australian Fordist model of development. The privatisation of mass consumption within suburbia not only ensured a steady market for consumer durables, but also tended to limit the effectiveness and accessibility of communal and public facilities.

Post-war suburban development was superficially similar to the extensive form of residential development which characterised pre-war mercantilism and the urban peasantry. Both are highly privatised and home-centred compared to the more intensive pattern of occupational community associated with industrial capitalism. Yet this post-war suburban development transformed and further commodified patterns of consumption. The urban peasant community was structured to facilitate the household production of goods and services. The vegie garden, the fruit trees, the chook run and the rabbito all reflected the productive household activities of the urban peasantry. Modernist hygiene and health concerns contributed to the erosion of this form of community from the turn of the century onwards, as did the growth of monopoly capitalism and the suburban community (Reiger 1986; Mullins 1981b, 40). Thus, the post-war suburban community promoted the generalised consumption of serially produced consumer durables and encouraged the commodification of productive activities previously conducted within the domestic economy.

The growth of a more sophisticated, modern, advertising industry during the 1950s (van de Ven 1993) was also a reflection of changing patterns of production and consumption. The industry targeted the suburban community. Manufacturers needed 'a way to keep up the momentum of mass production that had been used to meet the pent-up consumer demand from the war' (Blackburn 1992). By the mid-1950s the advertising profession had clearly recognised that the maintenance of a strong market—initially strengthened by pent-up demand from wartime shortages—was dependent on the growth of suburban owner occupation and newly formed young households. Therefore, it targeted 'the new suburbs where many young families were building their homes and seeking to equip them with consumer durables and products' (Blackburn 1992). Advertisements for new homes, building materials, interior decoration and white goods frequently portrayed a newly married woman—sometimes still in her bridal wear—rejoicing over her new dream home and the appliances which lay over the threshold (see Figure 3). In addition, waves of commercial travellers and door-to-door salesmen beat against suburban doors, signing up clients on hire-purchase contracts or 'terms' (Powell 1993, 80–1).

Mass advertising and home magazines were conduits linking mass production with mass consumption and performed a crucial role in the reproduction of the Fordist regime of accumulation. To paraphrase Weber (1978), the consumer ethic fostered the spirit of Fordism. The irony in recalling Weber is that 'the habits of frugality and thrift' (Blackburn) or 'asceticism' (Weber) were unlearned through the efforts or 'the call' of the advertising world. This 'irony' has been identified as a key cultural contradiction of contemporary capitalism (Bell 1976, 21):

> In the early development of capitalism, the unrestrained economic impulse was held in check by Puritan restraint and the Protestant ethic. One worked because of one's obligation to one's calling, or to fulfil the covenant of the community. But the Protestant ethic was undermined not by modernism but by capitalism itself. The greatest single engine in the destruction of the Protestant ethic was the invention of the

> instalment plan, or instant credit. Previously one had to save in order to buy. But with credit cards one could indulge in instant gratification. The system was transformed by mass production and mass consumption, by the creation of new wants and new means of gratifying those wants.

Whitwell (1989, 5) also pointed to the rejection of the 'traditional, puritan-inspired attitude that marriage should be postponed until couples had sufficient savings to buy the essential household goods' as an example of the changed psychological state and sense of greater security which helped inspire mass consumerism. Prior to World War II the threat of unemployment 'often discouraged wage-earners from trying to build or buy their own homes' (Hill 1959, 6).

The automobile completed the trilogy of the 'suburban imperative'. Prior to the war, the spread of suburban development had been restricted largely to ribbon development along public transport routes. Although the car had become relatively less expensive during the inter-war years, only half a million vehicles were registered in New South Wales by 1950. Fifteen years later, one and a half million vehicles were registered. During this period, the national proportion of cars to people rose from one car for every nine persons to one for every three and a half. The spread of suburbia outpaced that of the public transport system and made private car ownership more important while, on the other hand, the growing affordability of the automobile increased its use, encouraged facilities designed for car transport, and allowed further 'spiralling' of suburbanisation and private car ownership (Fry 1972, 19–20; Connell & Irving 1986, 295–6; Rowley 1972, 284–5). The automotive industry rose from modest origins during the 1920s to become the most important industrial complex of the 1950s (Connell & Irving 1986, 272–4).

Some observers point out that the suburban container and its contents epitomised the local 'way of life'. Blackburn, for example, describes how the advertising profession during the 1950s linked consumer durables with identity formation. The notion of an 'Australian way of life' itself was a particular product of post-war social change and social tensions (Alomes, Dober & Hellier 1984).

White (1981) associates this 'myth' with a defence of the status quo and the search for stability, and traces intolerance, Cold War defensiveness and suspicion towards immigration and towards cultural diversity to the need to assert homogeneity. This mood was custom-made for mass production and mass consumption.

White (1981) also pointed to the break with rural mythology and its replacement with predominantly suburban imagery as another feature of the post-war Australian identity. As local manufacturing flourished and as consumer durables were brought within the reach of more households, the suburban image was upheld as the 'Australian way of life':

> The familiar picture of suburban family life, with its focus on home and garden, and on a catalogue of family possessions—such as refrigerators, washing machines, radiograms, television sets and, of course, the family car—was the basis of post-war affluence and the vast new consumer economy which the manufacturers and governments encouraged.

This image captured the post-war fusion of mass production, mass consumption and suburban owner occupation. Harvey's claim that Fordism was not just an economic system, but something like a total way of life, was as relevant for Australia as for any other post-war economy.

The conceptual tools employed by the regulation school place housing provision and housing consumption within a more general socio-historical context. Post-war Australian housing provision and urban settlement patterns interacted dynamically to maintain the strength of the long post-war boom. They were also integral to the stability and maintenance of the post-war Fordist model of development.

This regulationist perspective rejects any crude and simplistic relationship between the systemic development of capitalism and the development of suburbia and owner occupation, however. Mullins' analysis of Australian urbanisation emphasised the importance of historical specificity: while he pointed out the similarities between the suburban community and the urban peasantry, he saw these as the products of distinct social and economic forces. The underlying dynamics of different models of development—

or regimes of accumulation—are often neglected in historical comparisons. If the history of capitalism has been a series of models of development—as the regulationists argue and as Mullins' work suggests—then it is futile formulating a general relationship between capitalism, housing and urbanisation. There is no justification on *a priori* grounds for concluding that some general logic of capital accumulation will demand ever-expanding suburbanisation and owner occupation in the future.

This discussion on Fordism provides the context for my examination of the links between modernism and industrialisation in the housebuilding industry, which begins with the 'post-war housing crisis'.

2

The Social Construction of the Post-war Housing Crisis

The 'affluence' often associated with the emergence of post-war Fordism also coincided with a severe housing shortage. During the late 1940s, the Australian Department of Information (1946, 88) informed prospective migrants that there was no more immediate and pressing problem facing Australia at the end of the war than the 'housing shortage', save the rehabilitation of servicefolk. To a large extent the two problems were connected, as part of the housing problem consisted of large numbers of returning servicefolk forming new households. An ambitious large-scale programme of immigration taxed the nation's scarce housing resources further and contributed to a crisis of unparalleled proportions. This chapter illustrates how the acute shortage of housing during the early post-war years gradually faded from public attention, even though the crisis continued to affect significant subgroups of the population.

The housing problem and the solution

After expanding rapidly under the pressure of the suburban boom of the 1920s, housebuilding activity in Australia virtually ceased during the depression of the early 1930s. While the industry again experienced high levels of demand during the late 1930s and reached record levels of output in 1939, it was unable to alleviate the earlier shortfall of housing. In addition, during the 1930s slum-clearance movements heightened public awareness that many existing inner-city dwellings were unfit for habitation. By the late 1930s there was a growing recognition among town planners and civic reformers that the market did not provide reasonable and affordable housing for all classes of the population (Troy 1992, 230; Williams 1984; Bourke 1960; Jones 1972). However, World War II intervened before these issues could be addressed seriously. Japan's entry into the war virtually signalled a halt to all private housebuilding (Gawler 1963, 57), as building materials and labour were diverted towards the war effort.

Before the war, housebuilding firms were invariably small businesses (a sole proprietor, family business, partnership). By their very nature, these firms usually possessed sufficient flexibility to absorb macro-economic shocks such as war. With limited overheads, the average housebuilding firm could complete the contract on hand, suspend business for the duration of the conflict and redirect its activity to whichever civilian or military duty the state demanded. Larger firms, with higher overheads and more specialised staff, were often in a more precarious position, although A. V. Jennings, for example, which redirected its attention towards building barracks and wartime factories, showed it could be done (Garden 1992, ch. 2). However, there were few housebuilding firms of significant size in Australia prior to 1939.

The suspension of housebuilding activity had more adverse consequences for the reproduction of the built environment in the longer term. During the war, slum reformers such as Barnett and Burt (1942) had warned of the need to 'prepare and plan now for the post-war economy'. However, at this stage the authors' attention remained focused on the late 1930s issue of slum abolition and housing 'reclamation'. When Barnett, Burt and Heath published *We Must Go On* in 1944 the emphasis had shifted towards the future and the need to plan reconstruction, develop new towns and reconsider the relationship between town and countryside. As the war progressed, a recognition built up that the coming housing problem would be of a magnitude unforeseen before the war and would involve a broader range of concerns.

Barnett, Burt & Heath's 1944 essay could have been subtitled *But We Can't Go On As Before!* In particular, the authors questioned the capacity and willingness of the private sector to satisfy working-class housing demand (1944, 38):

> It is . . . futile to expect private enterprise ever to overtake the housing shortage, for the simple reason it does not pay sufficient profits. It is inescapable that the task must be undertaken by the community. State Governments, financed by the Commonwealth Government, must enter the housing field to a degree hitherto undreamed of, and erect dwellings to be sold or let at a price of rental within the capacity of the worker.

Some critics such as Mendelsohn (1945, 54) argued that the 'liberal' measures suggested in *We Must Go On* were unrealistic, even naive, in attempting to 'mitigate the harshness of a system which they believe has certain bad results, but without changing the fundamental character of that system'. Mendelsohn was also sceptical that values derived from 'Christianity', 'kindliness' and 'tolerance' alone could undermine well-entrenched and powerful interests. There was even a hint that only force could achieve these ends (see also Howard 1987, 88), and he sounded an apocalyptic warning that 'the tide of reaction is now flowing strongly'. Yet by the time Mendelsohn's critique was published in June 1945, the nation had already embarked on the most extensive reform of housing provision ever instigated by an Australian government.

The Commonwealth Housing Commission (CHC) had been appointed in April 1943 under the powers conferred by the National Securities (Inquiries) Regulations, and was responsible to the Director-General of Post-War Reconstruction. The Commission was asked to conduct a quantitative and qualitative stocktake of housing and report on Australia's post-war housing requirements (CHC 1944, 8; Gawler 1963). The Commission handed down its final report on 25 August 1944. It dealt with a comprehensive range of factors influencing the provision of housing, including the role of government, national, regional and town planning, residential land, the development of housing programmes, housing administration, the building industry, construction labour, the building materials sector, rural housing, slum clearance, community facilities, housing standards and dwelling types. A national review of housing provision was not undertaken again until the early 1990s (National Housing Strategy 1991, 1).

Supporters of state intervention had drawn encouragement from the role performed by the state in mobilising production for military ends during the war. They argued that there was no reason why this same instrument could not be employed to meet pressing community goals in peacetime. In August 1945, as war was drawing to a close, the executive officer charged with the task of drawing up the CHC report wrote (Bunning 1945, 40–1):

> During the war, a planned economy, in which goals are set by the agents of the people, has proved successful in developing the resources of this country for the purposes of war . . . In peace this planned economy, with goals set by the people through Local, State and National Governments, could be used for developing our resources for the benefit of all the people. Within this framework private enterprise and Governments should co-operate to reach these goals. This would eliminate unemployment and would result in rising standards of living.

Estimating that the nation faced a shortage of some 300 000 houses, the report boldly called for annual completion targets of 80 000 dwellings during the first decade after the war, with 50 000 completions during the first post-war year. The state would contribute half of the nation's new housing through housing commission contracts (CHC 1944, 11). Eventually, the Commonwealth government, the state governments and the building industry agreed to a target of 60 000 annual completions over the next ten years (Downing 1948, 72). The Commission believed that these ambitious targets could be met with a smaller labour force than before the war, through changes in the technological and organisational nature of the residential construction industry. In addition, the Commission called for higher levels of housing quality, affirming that 'a dwelling of good standard and equipment is not only the need but the right of every citizen' (CHC 1944, 8).

The government proposed to reach these targets through improving the productivity and the efficiency of the housebuilding sector. Taking advantage of its strength as the largest client of the industry, the state was now in a position to encourage and sponsor an 'industrial revolution' through asserting its influence on private firms tendering for government contracts. The report claimed that the scale of state housing projects would foster large, efficient building firms and facilitate rationalisation within the industry (CHC 1944, 76). The states would also promote new forms of mass residential construction through the use of production techniques developed in various war industries. In March 1944 the government had established the Commonwealth Experimental Building Station. Federal funds for state housing were to be provided through the Commonwealth-State Housing Agreements (CSHAs). The inaugural CSHA was signed in 1945 and advanced funds to the states primarily for the provision of rental dwellings (Pugh 1976, 27–33).

On the basis of the report, the post-war federal Labor government committed itself to an unprecedented level of intervention in housing provision. The proposals stirred debate about the desirable balance between planning and the market. Towards the end of the war, one official from the Department of Post-War Reconstruction spoke of the need to 'limit the rights of those with money, with land and with building materials' and noted the 'real divisions' involved in the process of implementing the government's post-war reconstruction programme (Ross 1944). Another speaker at the same Australian Institute of Political Science forum also warned of the need for strict government control over labour and materials and pointed to the difficulties in maintaining a 'virtuous' policy when weighing up the 'old conflict' between authority and freedom (Copland 1944, 138–9). Bunning (1945, 40) tried to circumvent these philosophical difficulties, stressing that the programme adopted by the CHC was 'a major social reform' within capitalism as well as a practical contribution to the elimination of poverty and unemployment. However, in the same breath, he conceded that the CHC represented 'a patching up which enables the system to carry on'.

There was broad acceptance of greater state intervention in the housing market, yet this consensus often hid a variety of motives and purposes. Jones (1972, 4–5) has identified three viewpoints. The first approach viewed public housing as a key component of an integrated welfare system aimed at poverty alleviation. Another approach supported state housing as a 'reward' for 'deserving families' who, for one reason or another, remained excluded from the ranks of owner occupiers. A third approach, probably the dominant one by 1945, saw state provision of housing as a necessary, through temporary, means of overcoming the acute post-war housing shortage and anticipated a time when these extraordinary measures would be reversed in favour of the private housing market. This latter approach made state provision contingent on socio-economic circumstances rather than underlying political or moral principles and failed to confront the structural causes of poverty. As Jones (1972, 7) commented:

> The CSHA in 1945 probably received widespread electoral support because it was not put forward as a solution to the more intractable problems of the slum dweller—the chronically poor who were the subject of the slum clearance movement of the thirties—but rather was directed at the group sometimes referred to as the "submerged middle class". This latter group had none of the attributes of the lower working class life style and were the victims of the rapid social change, much of it causing downward social mobility, that characterised Australian society from 1930 to 1940 and was aggravated by the dislocation of the war.

Sandercock (1977, 99) has also made a distinction between the CHC report which 'proposed a revolution in public approach to social policy' and the government's response—the signing of the 1945 CSHA—which fell short of a 'comprehensive' housing policy. Many of the measures recommended in the CHC report, such as the nationalisation of land and public participation in planning, never entered the legislative or policy stage (Sandercock 1977, 104–7). The CSHA was a compromise between what was 'considered desirable and what was feasible' (Pugh 1976, 28).

Prior to the war, the 'housing problem' was seen as belonging to impoverished inner-city areas: it lacked personal immediacy for much of the population and awareness that there was a problem tended to be filtered to the rest of the population through social reformers and 'slummer journalists'. As Jones implied, one of the major differences between pre-war and the post-war housing shortages was the fact that the latter reached into the middle class. It was a highly visible problem. The absolute scarcity of building materials and labour left its visual imprint on the early post-war landscape and altered people's expectations of what they realistically could aspire to build or rent. A number of architectural critics have labelled the housebuilding product of the period 'austerity housing', even though the fifteen years after the war are often described as a period of 'relative affluence' and full employment (White 1993, 11–24; MacIntyre 1991, 64).

Construction times increased dramatically in the immediate post-war years and housing commencements remained extraordinarily high relative to completions. Housing commissions, individual builders and owner-builders all faced long gestation periods between commencement and completion due to material shortages and declining labour productivity (see Chapter 4). One writer for *Australian Home Beautiful* in 1948 lamented that outside 'the application of atomic power or some remarkable improvement in production technologies, the prospect of increasing the supply of materials for housing appears grimmer than a Boris Karloff film' (quoted in Archer 1987, 189). In October 1949, W. Watson Sharpe predicted gloomily that there was little indication that a decline in house prices would occur from factors within the industry itself and that there was 'little, if any possibility that the lag will be overtaken within a generation . . . ' (*Australian House and Garden*). Chapter 9 will illustrate how home magazines offered design and decoration ideas appropriate not only for the 'small house' but also for converted garages and other forms of temporary shelter.

Another consequence of these early post-war shortages was escalating costs of residential construction. For example, the cost of a full brick home in Melbourne rose 269 per cent between 1945 and 1952. During the same period the cost of a brick veneer house rose 229 per cent while the price of a weatherboard house increased by 235 per cent (ANZ 1954, 30–1). These costs represented dramatic real increases for house purchasers (Boyd 1991, 82; Freeland 1972, 265). In May 1951, Frank Greenop summed up the bitter experience of many early post-war house-seekers:

> A good many folk thought between 1945 and 1947 that waiting a little longer before they built a house would save money, because costs were bound to come down. Where are those people today? Trapped by their own cunning, and out on a limb. If you happen to be one of them, you are not alone. (*Australian House and Garden* May 1951, 11)

Census information provides some indication of the state of the housing stock and its adequacy. In 1947, over 10 per cent of households were sharing dwellings and another 80 000 people were recorded as 'sleeping out'. Public housing still only accounted for one per cent of the total stock of occupied dwellings, a figure which was consistent across all states. Despite acute labour and material shortages, the housing industry experienced high growth rates during the immediate post-war period. The annual number of new dwellings constructed almost quadrupled from 15 400 in 1946 to 57 000 in 1950 (Jackson & Bridge 1987, 355), although activity had increased from historically low levels and the 1950 figure remained below the target originally set by the federal government, the state governments and the industry as part of their ten-year plan to overcome the housing crisis. By 1950 Australia was constructing 7.8 dwellings per 1000 people, second only to New Zealand in the Western industrialised world (ANZ 1954, 6). Until 1952, governments placed strict controls on all non-residential construction activity, restricted maximum house sizes, and to a lesser extent regulated building functions and controlled the price of building materials to ensure that scarce resources were used to meet the housing shortage.

As a result of these restrictions, housing production constituted approximately 80 per cent of all building activity between 1945 and 1952 (ANZ 1954, 29). The number of completed dwellings remained around the 80 000 mark between 1952 and 1956, before dipping to around 68 000 in 1957. The industry then experienced annual growth, reaching a peak of over 94 000 completions in 1961 (Jackson & Bridge 1987, 355). However, much of this latter increase was accounted for by the boom in flat construction which began in the late 1950s and early 1960s (Hall 1961, 4). Between 1945 and 1960 approximately 900 000 dwellings were completed in Australia, almost one-third of which were financed by state and federal governments.

The state housing commissions possessed 4 per cent of the national housing stock by the time of the 1954 census, although variations between the states had begun to emerge, ranging from 9 per cent in South Australia to 3 per cent in Queensland and New South Wales. Strict conditions imposed by the 1945 CSHA had ensured that the overwhelming majority of houses constructed through the housing commissions remained state property. Under 5 per cent of the houses built by the commissions had been sold by 1954–55 (Bethune 1978, 207; Whitwell 1989, 41–2). The renegotiated 1956 CSHA encouraged more state-built housing to 'leak' into the owner-occupied sector. This was achieved through boosting Commonwealth funds designated to the states for private home loans and limiting the growth of the state rental sector. During the ten years covered by the initial CSHA, the states constructed over 96 000 dwellings.

Despite the progress made, the CHC's aim of ensuring that every citizen occupied a 'good standard' dwelling remained difficult to fulfil throughout the 1950s. However, this problem began to slip out of the public consciousness during the latter part of the 1950s.

Crisis?—whose crisis?

Despite its commitment to reform, the early post-war federal Labor government had been criticised for initiating action on the housing problem only when worsening conditions began affecting better-organised and wealthier sections of the community. A. M. Ramsay, later general manager of the South Australian Housing Trust, pointed out that it was only since 'the flow of new houses has almost ceased and the higher paid craftsmen and the middle class have had to go without that the outcry has reached its present proportions' (1945, 88). Only when the problem of adequate housing extended beyond working-class overcrowding and slum clearances had the state been forced to intervene more directly in housing provision. Ramsay accordingly emphasised the 'social construction' of the housing problem.

The severity of the housing crisis remained a contentious issue throughout the 1950s and continues as a matter of dispute among historians. For example, Freeland (1972, 277) argued that post-war austerity was over by 1954 or at least the 'worst pinch' of the chronic housing crisis had passed. The reasons offered for this date are the more liberal financial conditions and the beginnings of the drive towards 'full prosperity'. However, it is not entirely clear how these two variables solved supply problems, when logically their combination could have exacerbated the housing crisis.

During the 1950s, the federal Liberal-Country party government was more cautious in declaring the end of the housing crisis. By the mid-1950s it considered that the nation was close to solving the problem. In December 1956 the Department of National Development (1956, 3–6) claimed that between June 1947 and June 1956 the deficit in housing (indicated by number of dwellings per 1000 households) had been reduced by 53 per cent, and that increases in a wide range of structural and finishing building materials between 1938/39 and 1955/56 demonstrated the nation had overcome its shortages of materials, although it was forced to admit that the 'majority of home seekers in most states today would, from their experiences, challenge any claim that the "housing problem" is well on the way to being solved or that the "housing shortage" is fast being eliminated' (1956, 11). The Minister for National Development, W. H. Spooner, predicted that if the industry could maintain annual production levels of 77 000 dwellings, then '4 or 5 years at this rate of progress would break the back of the problem'. Spooner adopted the 'minimalist' principle towards state intervention in the housing market. He regarded the ten years after the war as an extraordinary period which had necessitated state involvement in housing provision and argued that there was less justification for state rental housing now that the shortages had been overcome. This reasoning was reflected in the new CSHA signed in 1956, which earmarked 30 per cent of all Commonwealth funds for the purpose of promoting owner occupation and eased the conditions under which state housing could be sold. For example, the New South Wales Housing Commission sold four out of every five houses it built between 1956 and 1963.

Despite Spooner's optimism, shortages continued. In the period between 1946 and 1955 the nation constructed more than 591 000 dwellings; but this was over 100 000 short of the 1944 CHC report target. In addition, mass immigration combined with high fertility rates far surpassed the report's population predictions. Furthermore, after the lifting of building restrictions in 1952 a larger proportion of building materials, along with many building firms, entered the non-residential construction sector. In an article in *Meanjin*, Kelly (1957, 399) continued to doubt whether the 'unparalleled' housing shortage had 'eased to any extent', compared with a decade before, 'in spite of the assurances of Federal politicians'. In mid-1958, the *Australian House and Garden* magazine devoted an editorial to 'the housing shortage', which compared advances in other areas of the economy with those in housing:

> We have drive-in theatres, drive-in banks, and a drive-in appliance store. And we have regional shopping centres with facilities which would have taken our breath away a few short years ago. Yes, we have everything. Everything, that is, but the most important thing of all—housing. Housing is the only shortage still with us. It is the only shortage in the whole nation we haven't solved.

Three years later, the 1961 census revealed over 45 000 people living 'permanently' in occupied huts and sheds.

The reality of the housing crisis was confirmed by institutions close to the problem. At the end of the decade J. M. Bourke (1960, 17–18), from the New South Wales Housing Commission, drew the conclusion from recent state housing commission annual reports that it was important to resist a sense of complacency. These reports indicated that demand for state housing continued 'unabated'. The Victorian Housing Commission warned that it was 'falling further and further behind the demand for housing', and argued that it required more loan funds in order to increase its output of houses and begin to satisfy the backlog in demand. The Tasmanian Housing Commission also warned that the 'development of a spirit of complacency and a tendency to depict a scene glowing with colour must be resisted as far as there is any suggestion of a lessened need for housing'. Although the New

South Wales Housing Commission claimed that its position was more favourable than that of housing commissions in other states, it also pointed out that 'there is still a considerable backlog to be overcome, especially when regard is paid to the number of substandard dwellings requiring demolition, many of which are at present housing not one but two or more families'. A less optimistic description of New South Wales was presented by the Department of the Interior in 1961, which claimed it possessed the only remaining 'serious housing shortage' (Department of the Interior 1961, 63).

Housing *per se* was not the only problem. The rapid urbanisation of post-war Australia left in its wake an enormous backlog in infrastructural provision. By 1960, one-quarter of Sydney's residents were without mains sewerage and three-quarters of those lived in the outer suburbs. In these suburbs other amenities—such as public transport or sealed roads—often remained either nonexistent or inadequate well into the 1960s (Rowley 1972, 287–8).

Despite this evidence, many historical accounts continue to state that the housing crisis was over by the end of the 1950s. Bethune (1978, 184) argued that the housing shortage 'had been substantially alleviated' by the early 1960s, while Ward (1977, 328) claimed that it had been 'overcome'. Wilton and Bosworth (1987, 116) also stated that the housing and rental situation had 'eased' as the nation entered the 1960s.

One of the problems associated with an assessment of the post-war housing performance is that socio-economic and demographic change made the definition of the housing problem a moving target. The editor of *Architecture in Australia*, in a June 1962 review of housing since 1939, candidly admitted that the housing problem 'still exists but to what extent nobody knows' (1962, 51). In the same issue, Winston (1962, 56) warned that the situation was far more disturbing than most appreciated. Not only had the nation failed to catch up with demand, since the war it had fallen behind with its real needs:

> Since [the war] over a million new dwellings have been completed, but in the same period there has also been over a million marriages and new families formed. The grey ring of slums and semi-slums around the central areas of the capital

> cities remains virtually untouched and, partly because of immigration, there is more intense overcrowding in some of these areas today than in 1945, so that when we do start replacing the slums we may have to provide three new dwellings for every two knocked down: in short Australia, like every other country, has a vast housing problem on her hands which has not yet been seriously tackled.

He continued to push this message further into the 1960s. At the 1966 AIPS summer school, he addressed the issue of 'Housing: The Unsolved Problem' in the same terms as his earlier paper (Winston 1966, 6–8). At the end of the 1950s, Hill (1959, 142) also hoped that now the housing shortage appeared to have been 'largely overcome' governments would start to tackle the problem of slum-clearance which had been left almost unresolved since the Commonwealth Housing Commission had identified it as a major concern in 1945.

The burden of this problem fell most heavily on subgroups of the population such as migrants—especially newly arrived southern Europeans. An important element in the immigration debate was whether adequate housing should be prepared before immigration levels were increased substantially. The prevailing sentiment, although not without some Labor Party and trade union dissent (White 1981; Berry 1988, 109–11), was that this was not necessary or even viable. After all, the early white settlers had not waited for adequate dwellings to be erected for them (Wilton & Bosworth 1987, 107). Early post-war migration was an integral part of the government's programme to increase the labour force and overcome the pent-up demand generated by the war. Whitwell (1989, 60) pointed out that migrants were consumers as well as producers and in areas such as housing 'it is likely that the imbalance between demand and supply was accentuated rather than reduced' by migration. (However, it is important to note that migrants were often placed in hostels and other 'temporary' accommodation which few if any people would have chosen to live in.) In 1947, a Western Australian Country Party member of parliament stated bluntly that substandard living conditions for migrants were unfortunate but necessary, 'to break the vicious circle in regard to housing in order to provide some workers to go into foundries and other distasteful forms of employment to supply the baths, sinks and stoves necessary for the housing programme' (quoted in Jordens 1994). A 1951 survey conducted by the Department of Immigration found that housing was the largest problem faced by migrants in Australia. Furthermore, during the first post-war decade many states possessed legislation barring aliens from owning land.

Once migrants left hostels, they were often at the mercy of an extremely tight private rental market and numerous surveys revealed widespread exploitation of migrants by landlords (Jordens 1994). This issue was again raised in parliament by the Leader of the Opposition, H. V. Evatt, in 1955. Further to the left, the Communist Party of Australia was also concerned about the 'desperate competition among workers for the shocking inadequate amount of homes for their families', and it opposed the Menzies Government's 'full-scale, reckless immigration' as a menace to the working class—Australian-born and migrant alike (Brown 1954, 303).

Migrants continued to suffer greater housing stress than the rest of the population after the most serious bottlenecks had been overcome. During the 1960s over one-quarter of Greek migrants lived in shared accommodation and one-third of Greek households shared a bathroom (Collins 1988, 171). The corresponding figures for the Australian-born population were 2 per cent and 3.4 per cent. Burnley (1985, 190) found that while most Greeks and Italians tended initially to congregate within inner-city enclaves where low-cost housing was available, most British bypassed the inner city and 'went to the suburbs, including Housing Commission estates'. In Victoria, where most southern Europeans initially settled, the Housing Commission actively discriminated against non-British migrants throughout the 1950s (Jupp 1966, 30; Appleyard 1963; also see Jones 1972, 124–5 for the low proportion of southern Europeans in public housing at the 1966 census).

Migrant hostels, built to cater for the post-war housing emergency or reconverted from old army camps, often remained the first point of contact for many migrants well into the 1960s. Places such as Bathurst, Bonegilla, Williamstown, Endeavour, Fishermans Bend, Westbridge, Wacol, Pennington and East Hills often left a permanent scar on migrants' memories. The conditions within the hostels contributed to the Yugoslavian riots at Bonegilla during 1961 and influenced the subsequent rejection by the Italian government of a new assisted passage agreement with the Australian government. Appleyard (1963) maintained that 'the major difficulty still confronting the new settler usually relates to housing' despite the fact that there were more houses available than in the late 1940s, 'a condition which immigrant workers have helped to achieve'. Jupp (1966, 29) also argued that the housing situation remained one of the 'weak points in migration absorption', although the problem was less 'acute' than the 1950s. Stubbs' (1966) study of Australian poverty devoted the entire chapter on migrants to their housing experiences.

At a time when many Australians believed that 'the migrant hostels have been abolished or that the inmates live there free', and when the migrant was 'politically almost voiceless' (Jupp 1966, 26), it is less than surprising that many Australians looked back on the post-war housing crisis as a bygone memory. At the other end of the social scale, 'affluence' could render official aggregated statistics misleading. The government's measurement of dwellings per 1000 households as an indicator of the housing crisis ignored the fact that the number of unoccupied dwellings was increasing (see Hill 1964a)—it had risen from 47 000 to 194 000 between the 1947 and the 1961 censuses. In 1961, 63 000 of these houses were classified as 'holiday homes, weekenders, and seasonal quarters'. Hill (1964a, 47) interpreted these figures as 'an improvement in census coverage, but it also reflects the increase in holiday homes, the increasing tendency with higher incomes to spend holidays away from the permanent home, and almost certainly a rapid increase in the numbers of dwellings available for sale or renting'. The relationship between the housing stock and households was far more complex than the federal government figures indicated.

Winston's warning that the housing crisis remained unresolved reinforced the implications drawn from Ramsay's critique in 1945. To a large extent, a 'housing crisis' is a socially constructed phenomenon. The extreme shortages of the early post-war era applied to all sectors of the community: although stories of graft and corruption abounded, no amount of wealth could conjure up unobtainable materials. During the 1950s, however, as more households achieved the 'Australian dream', the crisis was assumed to be a thing of the past. Consciences could be appeased by the knowledge that migrants and others still experiencing housing stress had yet to assimilate into the 'Australian way of life'. After all, some sociologists claimed that Continental migrants had a predilection for dense urban living (Clarke 1970). Winston's warning arrived at a time when many Australians were congratulating themselves on overcoming the unprecedented post-war problems and were rewarding themselves with the fruits of affluence. However, as new groups arrived or emerged, their voices were not always heard or listened to. In *The Hidden People*, Stubbs (1966, 4–9) argued that Australians had been deluded 'with the encouragement of politicians' into accepting 'the dangerous lie' that their nation was one of the fairest in the world with abundant welfare provision. The failure to expand social welfare and social services and the failure to investigate thoroughly the extent of poverty in Australia was possible 'only because the poor have no voice, no unity, no political influence or power'. The few observers analysing poverty in the early to mid-1960s continued to refer to the 'housing shortage' (Stubbs 1966, 110), while Appleyard (1963) argued that 'consideration should be given to discouraging large Commonwealth-nominated families from coming to Australia until the housing situation improves'. It was some time before their voices were heard.

Within Australia, it was only during the late 1960s that recognition of the existence of disadvantaged groups 'began to penetrate through the mists of the propaganda of affluence, as intellectuals again began to talk of "the poor"' (Connell & Irving 1986, 303). In the early 1960s, however, this recognition had yet to penetrate the 'national conscience'. Whitwell (1989, 26) also noted that while the long boom is often remembered as a 'golden age', it failed to bring 'universal affluence': the 'widespread belief by the early 1960s that poverty had at last been conquered [was a] delusion'. The fact that most people thought the housing crisis was over shows how selective perceptions of social problems are, especially when people of other classes or cultures are involved.

In his discussion of the post-war long boom in Western market economies, Harvey (1989, 138) observed that 'the shock of the discovery of awesome poverty in the midst of growing affluence . . . spawned strong counter-movements of discontent with the supposed benefits of Fordism'. One of the supposed benefits of Fordism was the application of mass-production techniques and scientific management throughout all industrial sectors, simplifying work processes while abolishing many other arduous labour tasks. The 1944 CHC report had also relied on mass-produced housing to alleviate the post-war housing crisis.

The promise of Fordist housing excited many commentators and practitioners during the 1950s. However, seventeen years after the war, Winston (1962, 56, 58) could still deliver scathing attacks upon the post-war performance of the housebuilding industry. Comparing modernisation in other sectors of production with the housing industry, he stated that 'the slowness, high costs and inefficiency of normal house production is something that we should all be ashamed of'. To highlight his point, Winston illustrated his paper with quotations from modernist architectural giants such as Gropius, Le Corbusier and Mies van der Rohe. The spirit of the Cold War was also evoked in order to shake capitalist complacency: 'Our western way of life is on trial in the world today, and one of the cracks in our armour is the squalor and inefficiency of our urban areas that are so largely housing areas'.

Part II assesses the extent to which Winston's assertions were justified. To what degree had the structure of the housebuilding industry been transformed by the early 1960s? Furthermore, to what extent were modernist dreams built on realistic foundations? Part II therefore returns to the examination of the concept of Fordism, this time in the more restricted sense of a set of mass-production techniques.

Part II

Putting Up the Framework

3

Housebuilding: The Industry Time Forgot?

On the eve of World War I, the Russian modernist painter Kasimir Malevich began to break with Cubo-Futurism, using his non-objectivist technique labelled 'suprematism'. One of the early fruits of this revolutionary abstract method was his 1915 painting *House Under Construction*. It depicts constructive human activity, and conveys the optimistic mood of a revolutionary intelligentsia anticipating the demolition of an *ancien regime* and eagerly awaiting the building of a new social order (see Figure 4).

To many people familiar with the housing industry it would appear ironic that Malevich used the housebuilding process as a metaphor for modernist enterprise. In the imagination of many commentators, housebuilding was and remains a 'backward' or conservative industry which continues to apply techniques and methods of production long discarded by other industries. Rudyard Kipling's dictum on the archaic and timeless nature of the industry was still considered pertinent enough to be placed on the masthead of the Australian Commonwealth Department of Housing and Construction's magazine *Shelter* throughout the mid-1970s:

> How very little since things were made
> Things have altered in the building trade.

This chapter assesses Kipling's dictum and concludes that it reflected a popular misconception of the constituents of technological change. While Chapter 1 viewed Fordism's relevance to housing at a broad societal level and examined changing patterns of production and consumption as well as changing social institutions, this chapter and the following two chapters focus on the concept of Fordism in the more restricted sense of a specific organisational and technological process within individual units of production or sectors of production. The post-war era coincided with an atmosphere of optimism surrounding the industrial possibilities inherent within the building process.

The housebuilding process and modernisation

The claim that the housebuilding industry is 'backward' is premised on an assumption that all sectors of production necessarily pass through a linear continuum of development and that each productive sector can be plotted on a line which stretches from the archaic to the contemporary or from the traditional to the modern. According to Levy, the degree of modernisation is indicated by the 'ratio of inanimate to animate sources of power' (quoted in Berger 1979, 101). This universal model of development begins with the observation that over the past two centuries in advanced industrial nations there have been fundamental transformations in the nature of work and technology. The production of most goods and services has shifted from a stage of simple co-operation, to manufacture, then mechanisation and finally through to automation (Bonke & Goth 1982). Most industries, meanwhile, have progressed from craft-based and labour-intensive relations to manufacture-based and more capital-intensive relations associated with technological and organisational innovations such as Fordism and Taylorism (the subdivision of work tasks into many discrete functions requiring less skill). Within many industrial sectors craft-related skills have become increasingly irrelevant as work has become more highly standardised and subject to more automation and direct supervision.

The housing industry sits uneasily within this developmental overview of economic, organisational and technological change. Marosszeky (1982, 5) has developed a continuum to chart levels of manufacturing progress in housing production. His six-stage process of change in techniques of production progressed through craft building, inclusion of manufactured components, construction entirely of premade components, panel housing systems, module housing systems and fully manufactured housing. Marosszeky located current (1980s) practice at a lowly stage two: inclusion of manufactured components. Yet all such continuums tend to transfer to the building process techniques applied in 'mature' industries—such as metal fabrication or automobiles—and assume (to paraphrase Marx) that the more advanced industry merely shows the less developed industry the image of its own future.

From such a vantage point, housebuilding remains in a state of underdevelopment. This condition has been diagnosed since the birth of modernism at the turn of the twentieth century. However, while the universal remedy has been prescribed more than once, the industry appears unwilling to swallow the Fordist pill. The principal trades which were operative within the industry over a century ago have retained their importance in the contemporary housebuilding process (Marosszeky 1982, 5) and the industry has retained a relatively low organic composition of capital and has remained highly labour-intensive. What accounts for the longevity of these dominant methods of housebuilding?

The housebuilding process is a tightly integrated operation involving a high degree of co-ordination between a variety of independent business enterprises. Hilton (1968, 13) has claimed that the physical, social and organisational complexity of the process makes housebuilding unique compared to other types of production (see also Needleman 1965, 114–15):

> A complicated series of operations has to be married to a flow of materials and labour and often on sites which may themselves present special problems. Nor is the direct control over labour and production processes vested in a single management as would be the situation in a factory. There may be anything from one to a dozen or more autonomous building firms involved on one site, and they will take their place in the production queue to carry out work which has been subcontracted to them.

This complexity is heightened by the immobile nature of the product, which restricts production and assembly primarily to the place of consumption or the building site. A multi-storey office block cannot roll past an operative on an assembly line! As a consequence, the housing industry has been characterised by a lack of production concentration and by a dispersed labour force. The economies of scale found in mass manufacturing remain absent in the production of housing. While prefabrication and standardisation have significantly altered certain aspects of the housing industry since the turn of the century, the on-site process of assembly and production has remained essentially a craft process; hence a range of relevant skills have been retained within the industry. Successful changes have usually reduced the amount of time building workers spent on a particular task, reduced the need for additional unskilled labour, or increased labour productivity, rather than involved a process of deskilling for the principal tradesfolk.

There is a relatively high degree of autonomy over work tasks. While most building contractors and supervisors have received trade training, they rarely possess either the time or the skills necessary to supervise directly each specialist subcontracted task. Changes which involve either deskilling or specialisation are also rendered more difficult by the nature of the contract between the contractor and the subcontracted tradesfolk. Usually, these contracts are for 'one-off' short-term projects. This reduces the possibility of standardising work procedures and developing sophisticated supervisory systems.

Even in situations where subcontracted trades are employed on an ongoing basis by a single building firm, factors such as the type of dwelling under construction, regional climatic conditions, seasonal adjustments and site conditions can vary to such an extent that the standardisation of procedures remains problematic. The customised nature of the product introduces a high degree of uncertainty into the assembly process. Most mass manufacturing industries have been able to develop rigidly defined work tasks, a highly refined division of labour, clear decision-making roles and a system of work accountability. On the other hand, the house-building industry has always required a high degree of flexibility, adaptability and autonomy from contractors, supervisors and tradesfolk.

However, the nature of the physical process in itself cannot be regarded as an insurmountable barrier to structural and organisational change. As Ball (1988) pointed out:

> Together, the physical characteristics of the building product and its construction are central components distinguishing construction from other industries . . . But to suggest that the products of the building industry are physically unique only implies that there are physical constraints, not that those physical characteristics alone determine the nature of the industry and its output. Technological developments and new products, moreover, change the boundaries imposed on working practices by the physical characteristics of nature. So physical constraints should not be seen as eternal, but subject to continual historical flux and transformation . . . While the physical nature of building places limits on the types of products that can be produced and on the potential techniques used, it is the organisational structure of the industry which fixes within those limits, for particular historical moments, the nature of the product and how it is produced.

Many other industries have also faced constraints which have been overcome through innovation. Yet throughout this century, countless 'modern' building techniques hailed as the face of the future have failed to live up to their promise, because of prohibitive cost, lack of consumer acceptance, aesthetics or functional performance. Diffusion, not invention, has remained the key problem.

The most important external factor affecting the industry is its high level of volatility. Housebuilding remains one of the most volatile sectors of market economies, and the performance of the industry is regularly used as an indicator of macro-economic trends. Demand for housing has always been difficult to predict because of the durability of the product, which allows the consumer to defer demand. Annually, new housing adds only approximately 2 per cent to the existing housing stock. Demand is also strongly influenced by other variables or unpredictable factors such as fiscal policy, demographic changes and the amount consumers are prepared to spend on housing at a particular time (International Labor Office 1948; International Labor Organisation 1948; Anderssen & McEvoy 1990).

The volatility of the housing market, along with the lack of standardisation of the product, creates a climate in which small businesses have always flourished. Scase and Goffee (1982, 53) have identified a number of features which must be present within an industry sector for small entrepreneurs to prosper. There is a preponderance of tasks requiring skilled labour rather than more capital-intensive work. The majority of the work on a building site is conducted by skilled tradesfolk—such as bricklayers, a variety of carpenters, plumbers, electricians, floor, wall and roof tilers, plasterers, painters. While a variety of innovative tools and processes have lowered the labour-intensity of some trade tasks, they remain dominated by traditionally defined skills. Few clients would rest content knowing their timber frame or brick wall had been constructed by someone without rudimentary informal or formal training within the appropriate trade.

Small business formation is also fostered within industrial sectors where a 'refined division of labour' has not been established. Again, the house-building industry fits this criterion. Although the era of the 'master craftsman' had passed well before the turn of the century, and although Taylorisation has increased markedly since World War II, the independent subcontractors or tradesfolk that build a dwelling continue to perform a wide variety of tasks within their specialist field.

This culture of small business formation also tends to flourish in industries where 'experience' is considered a more appropriate prerequisite for management than 'meritocratic' academic training. Many trade subcontractors form their independent business solely on the basis of the trade skills they have acquired either as an apprentice or through informal training with another tradesperson. Moreover, many family businesses have passed from one generation to another. Lack of product standardisation and a market characterised by fluctuation and the vagaries of 'consumer preferences' also tend to encourage small business formation.

Traditionally, standardisation has been rejected by housing consumers. A variety of other factors—such as site, climate and sometimes the availability of materials—has further inhibited standardisation. However, since World War II promoters of industrialised housing have been more successful in standardising components without compromising the visual appearance of 'individuality'. Scase and Goffee (1982, 53) concluded that these features, together with the instability of the housing industry, promote 'an industrial subculture that serves to encourage the further formation and growth of small-scale entrepreneurs' and they claimed that the building industry possesses 'par excellence those features which are most conducive to the formation, growth and persistence of small, independently-owned private businesses'.

Consequently, in the 1990s as in the 1940s, the majority of Australian building firms and the majority of specialist trade subcontractors are small in size (CHC 1944; ABS 1991, 3). The market is highly segmented and most builders operate within a narrowly defined regional basis. The dominance of small firms has both costs and benefits. Many small companies survive the booms and busts of the volatile market through functional metamorphoses. Small builders often revert to subcontract status during lean periods, re-emerging as builders when the housing market inevitably swings upwards. These conditions do not promote an ethos of capital expansion. Riding the waves of the housing market, the small builder needs to be aware of its peaks and troughs. Builders who succeed or simply survive tend to be those that understand when to pull back from riding a rising wave and watch as the more adventurous souls are dumped. Under these circumstances it is unlikely that a small builder will obtain sufficient capital to experiment with alternative building methods. He will also be conscious of being caught with excess stock and being overcapitalised during an inevitable downturn. For many building tradesfolk, their skills and work routine represent a way of life which would be lost if they undertook capital expansion and business growth. It would be a mistake to assume that all small businesses aspire to grow, and the conditions existing within certain industries actively discourage such expansion (Scase & Goffee 1982).

Despite this preponderance of small firms, a small number of large-volume producers have been able to survive within the market. Many larger post-war firms took advantage of substantial housing commission contracts and, later, private estate building to achieve economies of scale. However, by the mid-1980s, large firms constituted only 1.1 per cent of total housebuilding firms, although they produced over one-third of dwellings (Bureau of Industry Economics 1990, 21).

Both high-volume builders and small builders act as organisers and co-ordinators of the building process and rely on independent teams of trade subcontractors to undertake the various stages of building construction. The production of detached dwellings is dominated by these individuals and 'independent' teams of subcontractors. Subcontracted relations differ from award relations in a number of important respects: rates of earnings are determined by prevailing market conditions; rates are negotiated directly between the building contractor and the subcontractor; the subcontractor is bound to the contract entered into with the main contractor, and payment is made according to the work task rather than the time spent on the task; the subcontractor works in a more self-regulatory work environment with a higher degree of autonomy over the work task; and subcontracting reduces the employers' supervisory and administrative overheads. This contractual relationship encourages 'numerical flexibility' (Atkinson 1987) over the short term, as a principal building contractor erecting a small number of houses at any one time cannot afford to keep a specialist tradesperson on the books. Subcontracting relationships can exacerbate the difficulty of challenging the underlying structure of the industry and, at best, allow the innovative builder to tinker piecemeal with innovations within separate trades. Furthermore, while the apprenticeship system has been the most important traditional formal source of new skilled labour within the housing industry, the small size of many firms and the volatility of the industry discourage individual firms from taking on apprentices. Small firms often find it difficult to carry the additional costs associated with a less productive apprentice throughout a lengthy indenture period, especially during economic downturns. The problem is compounded by the historical tendency for cyclical upturns in the housing industry to be shorter than the traditional four-year indenture period required to complete an apprenticeship.

Despite these constraints, the housing industry has often adopted innovative organisational forms and appropriate on-site and off-site technology to meet volatile demand for its product. For example, a growing proportion of building components are pre-assembled under controlled factory conditions. These processed products are then transported to the building site for final assembly. This has reduced the need for on-site labour and in certain cases has reduced skills requirements.

Furthermore, there has been a change in the mix of on-site skills within the building process. The percentage of labourers, carpenters and painters has declined, while the percentage of bricklayers, electricians, plumbers and others has increased. There has been a degree of standardisation of the product and standardisation of components. In addition, while the nature of the key components of the building process have remained trade-based, specialisation and deskilling has occurred within some trades through the subdivision of work tasks, or Taylorism. As a result, many tradesfolk, such as plumbers and carpenters, are rarely called upon to exercise the entire range of skills which they were initially trained to perform (Ball 1988, 29–30).

This description has focused on technological and organisational characteristics of the industry which were as relevant at the end of World War II as they are in the early 1990s. The key point to note is the relationship between external factors (such as industry volatility), the structure and organisation of the industry (size of firms, subcontracting) and technological change. Any attempt to assess potential for change must remain sensitive to the structural constraints and economic realities imposed upon individual building companies. The next section briefly introduces the philosophical and architectural forces of modernism which struggled to rid the housebuilding industry of its traditional ways.

The housebuilding process and modernism

A recent example of the close relationship between ideas on housing and social change is the Housing Industry Association's *Our Homes Towards 2000* (1990, 1). The introduction of this booklet stated that the home of tomorrow will be 'vastly different to the home our parents lived in'. By the year 2000 the needs of 'new and different' buyers will have led to the application of a range of new micro-electronic technologies within the home and in the housebuilding process. This new home will not only be a 'sanctuary' or a place of rest, but also a centre for leisure and entertainment. Consumer activities such as shopping will also be conducted from the home through electronic ordering. Smaller homes will be more multifunctional, with rooms capable of adaptation for a range of activities. Flexible interior walls will replace permanent walls so that homes will be transformed instantly from leisure centres to offices or workplaces with the flick of a control panel. Never again will citizens feel the need to leave the comfort of the home to fulfil simple routine tasks.

It is not difficult to uncover the influence of a variety of futurologists behind this vision. The function of the home in this scenario is derived from predictions relating to the social consequences of the 'information revolution'. The image is consistent with McLuhan's (1964) 'global village', Toffler's (1970) 'electronic cottage' and Daniel Bell's (1973) 'post-industrial society'. It can also be viewed as a reflection of the current phase of 'time-space compression' which Harvey (1989) associates with the 'condition of post-modernity'.

This desire for correspondence between social function and housing production reached its height in the works of the early modernists. One of the transformations predicted by the Bauhaus movement was the ascendancy of construction into the 'modern age'. According to Gropius (n.d., 30, 38):

> The elementary impulse of all national economy proceeds from the desire to meet the needs of the community at less cost and effort by the improvement of its productive organisations. This has led progressively to mechanisation, specialised division of labour, and rationalisation: seemingly irrevocable steps in industrial evolution which have the same implications for building as for every other branch of organised production . . . Building, hitherto an essentially manual trade, is already in course of transformation into an organised industry.

The underlying assumption was that building inevitably would follow the forces of technical progress charted by more advanced industries. Mies van der Rohe also saw industrialisation as the key issue in building during the 1920s: 'If we succeed in carrying out this industrialisation, the social, economic, technical and also artistic problems will be readily solved'. As Jencks (1978, 15) observed, the Modern Movement 'fetishised' the means of production. It also tended to ignore both the wide range of social agents involved in housing provision and the economic context within which housebuilding occurs (Ball 1988, 23–6).

Stripped of much of their original revolutionary content, modernist ideas took on a new urgency in advanced capitalist countries after World War II, as governments, manufacturers and consumers searched for means to overcome the pent-up demand for housing. The forces of industrialisation, modernisation and capitalist development were hailed as the engines of progress. Harvey (1989, 68) has captured the essence of the post-war modernist project in the industrialised West:

> Postwar politics, if they were to remain democratic and capitalistic, had to address questions of full employment, decent housing, social provision, welfare, and broad-based opportunity to construct a better future . . . While the tactics and conditions differed from place to place . . . the trend was everywhere to look to the war-time experience of mass production and planning as a means to launch upon a vast program of reconstruction and reorganisation. It was almost as if a new and revivified version of the enlightenment project sprang, phoenix like, out of the death and destruction of the global conflict. The reconstruction, reshaping, and renewal of the urban fabric became an essential ingredient within this project. This was the context in which the ideas of the CIAM, of Le Corbusier, of Mies van der Rohe, of Frank Lloyd Wright, and the like, could gain the kind of purchase they did, less as a controlling force of ideas over production than as a theoretical framework and justification for what practical-minded engineers, politicians, builders, and developers were in many cases engaged upon out of sheer social, economic, and political necessity . . . Within this framework all kinds of solutions were explored . . . Under the watchful eye and sometimes strong hand of the state, procedures were devised to eliminate slums, build modular housing, schools, hospitals, factories etc. through the adoption of the industrialised construction sys-

> tems and rational planning procedures that modernist architects had long proposed. And all this was framed by a deep concern, expressed again and again in legislation, for the rationalisation of spatial patterns and of circulation systems so as to promote equality (at least of opportunity), social welfare, and economic growth.

This passage illustrates how the transcendental zeal which inspired the early modernists had filtered through to the post-war reformers. Even at the heart of free enterprise—in the United States—the post-war housing crisis was severe enough for many legislators and commentators to concur that 'federal intervention would benefit both the housebuilding industry and the entire economy' (Checkoway 1986, 127). Developments such as Levittown, Long Island, adopted Fordist organising principles in an effort to transform production techniques and by 1954 Frank Lloyd Wright had developed an 'automatic' version of his 'Usonian' house which reduced costs because it 'eliminated the need for skilled labour by prefabricating all plumbing, heating and wiring' and delivering it on-site in a 'factory-made package' (Wright 1963; Schlesinger & Erlich 1986; Gunn 1991).

However, the housebuilding industry was still regarded as an anomaly. According to *Fortune* magazine, it remained 'the industry capitalism forgot' and the 'one great sector of modern society that has remained largely unaffected by the industrial revolution' (quoted in Schlesinger & Erlich 1986, 139). However, optimism still prevailed that housebuilding would follow other industrial sectors into the age of mass production, standardisation, rationalism and Fordism: the car industry was used as a comparison. US *House and Home Magazine* (quoted in Landis 1981, 46) predicted that the potent combination of standardisation and capitalism would change irreversibly the housebuilding industry:

> Until now, much of the new housing created has simply been Model-T, and the best builders admit that they have hardly scratched the surface of the economies of scale their mass production processes should make possible. Given a few more years of a reasonable stable volume of around 1,000,000 new homes a year, competition should cure most faults, force builders to figure closer profit margins, introduce more con-

> struction economies, and generally make the same kind of progress the automobile industry made when competition made its Model-T products unsaleable.

During the mid-1950s the US architect/designer George Nelson (1957, 124–5) applied the same metaphor:

> There is no doubt that the present trend in house building is taking us ever closer to full industrial production of houses and their contents. Last year prefabrication business accounted for roughly 10 per cent of all house production and this percentage has no place to go except up. The current prefab is not much more than a rationalised version of a hand-built house, but, as the business grows and competition increases, it is reasonable to expect that the consumer will get more and better housing for his money. In the meantime, manufacturers of major appliances are driving strongly toward the development of "packages" of all descriptions, from prefab storage walls and kitchens to double-duty units that heat or cool the house according to the season. Both trends indicate that we are moving toward the time when we will be buying Ford- or Cadillac-type dwellings—and loving it.

Despite the work of modernist pioneers earlier in the century, and despite the growing acceptance of modernism during the 1930s, the movement only began to gain a widespread audience in Australia during the 1940s and 1950s (Howells 1993, ch. 12; Taylor 1986; Hamann 1981; Boyd 1963, 3). The post-war housing shortage heightened the search for economies of scale and elevated the status of an architectural design and construction philosophy which demanded that 'form follow function'. It was no coincidence that dissatisfaction with prevailing construction practices became more vocal after the war. The seeds of Australian modernism had fallen on fertile ground. To paraphrase Harvey, this was the ground of 'sheer social, economic and political necessity'. Pre-war agitators for slum clearances and promoters of health and hygiene were now joined by reformist Commonwealth agencies determined to unleash the housebuilding industry from its traditional productive and organisational fetters. The Commonwealth Housing Commission (CHC 1944, 77) adopted the optimistic linear view on industrial progress when it claimed in 1944 that 'the stage is set for a radical change which might be described as similar to that which took place in the English textile industry at the time of the Industrial Revolution, or to that which took place in the course of the Australian munitions production program'. The November 1945 *Australian Home Beautiful* adopted Corbusian terminology when it described the post-war house as 'a machine for living' with higher efficiency (O'Callaghan 1993, 159).

Australian magazines—like their United States counterparts—also made comparison with the car industry and looked to a machine aesthetic. In the October 1950 *Australian House and Garden*, H. Dalton Clifford used the analogy to highlight the irrationality of local house-production methods:

> When you want a new car you go to a showroom and order the complete thing ready-made. You don't buy an engine here, a gear box there, wheels from a wheelwright, tyres from somewhere else, get the blacksmith to knock together a chassis, a coachbuilder to measure you and your family and build a body to fit, and then get your local garage to put all the bits together. It would be perfectly possible to do this, and you might not have to wait so long for your new car, but it would be hopelessly inefficient. And yet when we want a new house that is exactly the way we set about it, with the help of an architect, and a builder, we buy bricks, timber, cement, sand, doors, windows, switches, knobs, locks, tiles, a bath, a cooker, a sink and so on . . . (there are said to be 30,000 separate parts in a traditional house) . . . and put them all together. And consider the result! Is it not reasonable to suppose that if specialist firms designed and manufactured houses in huge factories, in the same way that cars are built, more efficient and economical houses might result?

The question was rhetorical. Of course it would be more efficient and economical to build houses in the same way that cars were built—although, as the passage intimates, obtaining a new car in Australia during 1950 was almost as difficult as constructing a new house, regardless of production methods! However, following earlier modernist approaches—which as Boyd (1967b) observed, were 'disproportionately moved by the beauty of the machinery' and 'dreamt of a time when all buildings could be stamped out by giant machines like Chevrolets were'—this 'commonsense' approach to housing the nation tended to abstract housebuilding from its economic and social context and underemphasised the wide range of conflicting interests which the industry's constituent agents brought into housing provision.

Nevertheless, it should be acknowledged that the modernist Fordist linear vision of technological development generated its own reality during the late 1940s and throughout the 1950s and represented a brave response to a pressing social problem. This vision continues to inspire many contemporary observers. The two examples presented below demonstrate how such a view can lead to a variety of readings of the housebuilding industry.

The first example is the study of post-war housebuilding in the United States by Schlesinger and Erlich. In a critique of the 'backward thesis', Schlesinger and Erlich (1986, 140) suggested that the housing sector's 'record of innovation and building materials, construction methods, and tools and equipment compares favourably with developments in any major industry'. In other words, the modernist vision was as good as realised! While this possibly overstated the extent of post-war change, it served as a useful rejoinder to Kipling's dictum that nothing ever changes. The authors observed that there have been numerous innovations in the form of the finished product, in the components which make up the product and in the organisational and technological processes involved in assembling the product.

The modernist faith in rationalisation, standardisation and functionalism has had a lasting impact on the building process and building product. However, Schlesinger and Erlich possibly responded to the wrong question. In their attempt to demonstrate that housebuilding was not 'the industry which capitalism forgot', they grabbed their opponents' linear sword by the blade and focused all their attention on discovering the industrialisation which more sceptical observers claim does not exist. An alternative approach would measure technological change, Fordism and industrialisation in the industry not only at the level of the individual firm, but in terms of the relationships between agents of production and consumption as well as the role of housing within broader regimes of accumulation and modes of regulation (Lipietz 1985; also see Chapter 1).

The second example is a recent Australian report on the potential for change within the Australian housebuilding industry (Johnston & Lepani 1993). Unlike Schlesinger and Erlich, the authors did not accept the view that the industry has a relatively good record on technological change. The report gauged the possibility of employing information-based technologies—such as 'flexible specialisation', 'smart houses', 'computer-related manufacturing'—in the housebuilding sector:

> There is . . . a significant potential for the establishment of a 'post-industrial' housing production capability. Because housing in Australia, other than high rise residential, is predominantly organised around small scale builders working with independent subcontractors on a craft basis, with almost no unionisation, its structure is in tune with emerging trends in the manufacturing and service industries emphasising the value of flexibility achieved through the greater use of contract labour. In simple terms, as the housebuilding industry has not developed along the industrialised factory-based model of organisation, it is now well fitted to move directly to a post-industrialised, flexible and decentralised model . . . The flexibility of IT allows a complete bypassing of the industrialised mass production route.

In other words, the industry could simply 'skip' a stage of history. The authors observed that certain practices which are considered archaic from the perspective of one regime of accumulation can suddenly reappear in another historical context as a possible solution to the contradictions or dilemmas of a particular mode of regulation. 'Tradition' has a funny habit of tapping the shoulder of 'progress' on the back (Smart 1993). However, the same linear, universal model of technological change is being applied and provides a ready-mixed theory into which concrete reality can be poured.

A more dynamic approach which acknowledges historical change as well as structural constraints has been adopted by Ball (1988, ch. 2) in his study of the British construction industry. Ball rejected the premise that 'something has either retarded [the housebuilding industry's] technological growth or prematurely brought it to a grinding halt, and the purpose of any explanation is to understand what inhibited the industry's development'. Any simple juxtaposition between different industry sectors based on a linear scale of progress is 'flawed both in practice and in principle':

> Why should the future technical development of construction necessarily be towards more and more factory production? An unwarranted idealisation of particular methods of production seems to be elided with a very essentialist view of technical change. Yet, without such a view of the perfect universal technology applicable to the production of everything, how can you compare technologies on a scale of backward and forward? . . . The backward view of the building industry is asking the wrong question.

The most that can be said from a relational perspective is that the building industry is 'different' from other industries. Neither the physical nor the social nature of the building industry alone can explain its characteristics. Research should focus on the way physical, social and economic aspects interact.

The description earlier in this chapter of the process of technological change within the housebuilding industry is also consistent with Soja's concept of modernisation as the adaptation to changing social conditions and circumstances. Housebuilding has undergone a continuous process of modernisation, but technological and organisational innovation in housing succeeds only when it corresponds with the unique socio-economic relations within housing production and remains sensitive to changing patterns of housing consumption. Innovation therefore tends to be incremental and evolutionary rather than abrupt and revolutionary.

The following two chapters describe a range of technological and organisational changes within the Australian housebuilding industry in the wake of World War II and explore the forces which promoted or inhibited these changes.

4

Austerity and the Structure of the Housing Industry

The post-war housing shortage in Australia appeared to provide reformers with evidence that the housebuilding industry was inefficient and that it lagged behind most other industrial sectors. At a time when the nation faced a deficit of some 300 000 dwellings and when traditional materials and skilled labour were in high demand, the structure of the industry was subjected to critical examination. The post-war Labor government confronted the housing problem armed with a social-democratic programme which included redistribution through economic progress and prosperity, planning and state intervention. Private enterprise had failed to provide what was needed. The housebuilding industry would serve as a socially useful source of employment during a period when many on the left predicted the recurrence of a severe recession. Economic progress also demanded more rational use of resources within the housebuilding sector. The Commonwealth Housing Commission confidently stated in its 1944 report that the time had arrived for housebuilding to join the industrial revolution (CHC 1944, 75–7). In an era that promised mass production of consumer durables and when technology had demonstrated its awesome capability in wartime, the days of 'hand-made' housing had to be drawing to a close.

The 1944 report devoted an entire chapter to the organisation of the industry and identified a number of inefficiencies: building firms operated on small contracts; small isolated business units practised defective supply and distribution methods; methods of construction were 'out-of-date'; organisational procedures used within and between firms were 'inefficient'; and all these factors resulted from—and resulted in—'poor management', 'poor training' and 'discontented labour'. The weather could be a problem, but climatic vagaries would become less relevant once standardisation and prefabrication became an integral part of a more controlled, factory-based production process.

The idea was that the Commonwealth Housing Commission and the various state housing commissions would perform a catalytic role in overcoming these inefficiencies through fostering the restructuring of the industry. The size of government contracts would facilitate the formation of large private-sector operators, and the competitive nature of the tendering process would promote innovation along industrialised lines. Armed with market clout, the state was in a position to deliver its housing pledge to each and every citizen, rationally plan urban growth and encourage economic progress. The linear perspective on technological development described in the last chapter also permeated government thinking. Again, this was nowhere more evident than in the comparisons between the progress witnessed in transport technology and the state of housing construction. At the end of the war, one senior Commonwealth government official expressed the state's mission in terms of taking 'housing from the horse and buggy era into the machine age' (quoted in Howard 1987, 80). The yawning gap between reality and the government's vision was starkly illustrated by Ramsay, who also compared the Fordist automobile complex to the housing sector (1945, 89):

> the building industry has not increased its efficiency nearly as rapidly as other parts of our economy. To see three or four men assemble on a suburban block to erect a house is to step from the age of Henry Ford to that of erecting a medieval cathedral. Some country brick fields go back further than that; I know one reminiscent of ancient Egypt.

These pleas for structural reform continued after the war as demand from returned servicefolk, migrants and newly formed households compounded the housing problems identified by the

CHC report. The economist H. W. Arndt (1949, 98–9) was 'startled' by the 'universal backwardness and inefficiency' of the housebuilding sector after reading R. I. Downing's monograph *Housing and Employment*. He also must have read *Fortune* magazine as he referred to the building sector as 'The Industry Capitalism Forgot'. Arndt supported Downing's argument that 'there is no reason, whether on technological grounds or because of the nature of its product, why the building industry should continue to muddle along as a handicrafts industry with small productive units and less capital equipment per head than any other industry of significance'. During an era of post-war confidence in the powers of technological progress and faced with acute shortages, few thought to ask why the industry couldn't simply 'muddle along'! Arndt also made a mistake characteristic of other modernisation theorists by failing to distinguish between capitalism and industrialisation. As Lipietz (1985) suggested, the form which housing assumed was integral to post-war capital accumulation.

Although government officials confidently diagnosed the industry's problems, it proved more difficult to apply a remedy. Industry associations were opposed to state interference and fought against heightened union presence within their industry. The conservative political parties were opposed to state intervention in principle and the more opportunistic could sense voters' growing weariness with government restrictions as memories of the war years faded. In addition, the technological breakthroughs predicted by many experts often failed to meet with consumer acceptance or else proved less economical than the 'horse and buggy'. The role eventually assumed by the state—even during the period of the more interventionist federal Labor government—involved the provision of 'incentives and assistance' to the housing industry rather than 'competition and regulation' (Howard 1987, 36).

This shift from 'wartime regulation' to 'peacetime co-existence' was not accomplished without some degree of friction. Even as the Labor government gradually relaxed its stringent wartime restrictions on supplies and dwelling size, there remained numerous pockets of resistance and pleas for the retention of government regulation. The contentious issue of equity remained unresolved (AIPS 1947; Howard 1987, 75). During the 1949 federal election, the more conservative Liberal-Country Party partners pledged to remove most of the remaining Commonwealth restrictions and presented themselves to the nation as the parties which looked to the future rather than the past. The Liberal Party also presented women voters with the choice between a socialist system which supervised all spheres of family life including housing, and a happy marriage 'to a man securely established in work of his own choosing' and an 'attractive house of your own' (quoted in Alomes, Dober & Hellier 1984, 27). Menzies presented a stark choice between the maintenance of Labor's wartime restrictions and the unleashing of the spirit of mass consumerism. The housing restrictions which proved most difficult to overcome involved rent control and this sphere of responsibility was handed back to the state governments in 1948. However, the ascendancy of the conservative coalition after 1949 undermined the reformers' rationale for structural housing reform in the name of necessity. Consumer preferences would now lead the market towards the goal of living in 'a dream home'.

The builders

Immediately after the war the structure of the private sector retained most of its pre-war characteristics and remained dominated by the traditional small operator (Ifould 1947, 30). The scarcity of building materials was hardly conducive to the growth of large building firms or a state-sponsored direct labour force. Tradesfolk were able to take advantage of high levels of demand and opt for self-employment, thereby accentuating the dominance of small firms and small contracts. There were exceptions, such as the company A. V. Jennings. Formed in Melbourne during the depression, Jennings had grown by 1950 to become the largest employer of building labour in Australia. During the 1930s, the company had pioneered innovative estate building for the lower middle-income market, but the company's metamorphosis into a housebuilding giant really began with its close relationship with the Victorian Housing Commission after the war (Garden 1992, 68). By 1950, Jennings was distinguished by its size, its selection of standard designs and its vertical integration of housebuilding with other upstream activities including road-making teams, timber mills, joinery shops and an architectural office. However, while Jennings can be cited as an example of a successful large operator in the industry, it remained one of the few exceptions to the rule. The company's relationships with state governments were so lucrative that it wound down its private housing contracts and only began considering moving back to private estate development during 1954 (Garden 1992, 119).

One means adopted by the state during the early 1950s to promote large-scale production was the importation of foreign firms and prefabricated buildings. This measure instantaneously provided skilled overseas tradesfolk, increased the supply of housing and provided examples of overseas technical solutions to the housing crisis. Although some firms remained in Australia afterwards, the scheme was wound down after three years in 1953. Private firms and governments combed western Europe in search of suitable labour. For example, A. V. Jennings had selected 150 German tradesmen from 2500 applicants for their expanding operations after trade testing and 'personal screening' for 'Nazi or Communist connections and venereal disease' (Garden 1992, 104).

Victoria and South Australia appear to have been more successful than New South Wales in attracting large contractors (Howard 1987, 87–90; Marsden 1986, 95). Mass production in South Australia pre-dated the CHC's 1944 report. Prior to the end of the war, the South Australian Housing Trust—founded in 1936—contracted all its housebuilding exclusively to E. F. Marshall & Son. According to Marsden (1986, 58), the Trust 'pioneered' mass production. She quotes A. M. Ramsay:

> The building industry, you see is a traditional industry and the concept of a contractor's work, and the very documents used, all relate to a single job, begun and finished as a unit. To adapt these factors to the flow concept of modern mass production with large contracts to achieve economies of scale, and yet avoid monotony, is, let me confess, my greatest satisfaction as a manager . . . And it has worked because it was started, as most new ideas are started, by an individual genius, one Frank Marshall. I sometimes long for the days when we negotiated contracts for 1,000 houses with Frank Marshall.

Ramsay would let out private contracts for over 1000 houses without specifying completion dates. Independent investigators auditing the Trust's activities gradually 'normalised' such unconventional procedures and scaled down contracts to much smaller quantities of between twenty and sixty houses (Stretton 1978, 95).

However, the grand vision of mass housing, prefabrication, standardisation and planning fostered by the CHC was obscured by the scale of demand created by post-war demographic and economic changes. One significant—yet unforeseen—feature which affected the structure of the industry during the early post-war period was the increasing number of owner-builders. While this tradition of building one's own house had persisted since the arrival of the First Fleet, labour and material scarcity stimulated its growth after the war (see Kelly 1957, 399–400; Holland 1988). During 1951/52, one-third of all houses constructed in Australia were owner-built. The proportion grew to 39.1 per cent in 1953/54, and remained over 30 per cent until 1958/59 (Holland 1988, 230) when the boom in flat construction began.

The category 'owner-builders' hid a variety of levels of involvement in the building process. Many desperate households did the tradeswork themselves. These were the heroic suburban pioneers who built their house while living in a temporary structure on site or in a hastily erected garage. Other less confident yet equally desperate households acted as their own building managers and subcontracted work requiring particular skills out to tradesfolk or friends. Some households simply asked a builder—if one could be found—to work to their specifications. Recognising the problems which migrant owner-builders experienced in coping with regulatory authorities, the Department of Immigration, the Royal Australian Institute of Architects and local government authorities jointly published a booklet in 1954 entitled 'Building a Home' (Jordens 1994). The playwright David Williamson (1993, 44) recalls the cultural imprint which early 1950s owner-building left on him:

> I still remember at the start of the fifties I had an extreme anxiety attack when I went out to my cousin's place at Niddrie in Melbourne's outer suburbs. I saw all these guys building

> their houses. It used to be the Australian pastime; they'd work all week and then spend the weekends building these homes-to-be so they could get married. I thought this was a rite of passage and it was obligatory that every male had to build his own house. I was hopeless at carpentry and I had nightmares that when I reached 21 I'd have to go out to Niddrie and build my own house.

Under conditions of scarcity, many owner-builders emerged as the most innovative builders during the period, adapting whatever materials and techniques were available in their quest for construction. A number of owner-builders were also innovative in organisational terms (Cuffley 1993, 76–80). A range of collective self-help groups emerged in an effort to decrease construction time, reduce costs and to benefit from members' labour and diverse range of skills.

Magazines such as *Australian House and Garden*, *Australian Women's Weekly* and *Home Beautiful* as well as daily newspapers reflected and influenced this trend and took their architectural and trade mission very seriously (see Figure 5). Chapter 7 discusses the close relationship between necessity, austerity and modernism during the late 1940s and early 1950s as consumers made the most of limited resources (see also Pickett 1993, 83). While the process of modernisation in the housebuilding industry failed to be as comprehensive as government and industrial visionaries expected, this did not stop 'the modern' from becoming the catchword of advertisers and magazine editors in their attempt to capture the essence of life in the 1950s. If these magazines are any indication of reality, then every Australian had suddenly become vitally interested in new materials and building techniques. Never before or since have popular home magazines been so concerned with house production (see Chapter 9).

A variety of firms specialising in 'ready-cut' homes or in 'partial erection' also emerged to take advantage of the high proportion of owner-builders and the diverse talents and inclinations of the new breed of producer-consumers (Freeland 1972, 268; Kelly 1957, 400; see also Chapter 5). Advertisements in home magazines for these various forms of prefabricated houses and precut houses often stressed speed as well as ease of erection as a key advantage of the process (see Figures 6 & 7). A June 1952 feature on prefabrication in the *Australian House and Garden* was subtitled: 'A short survey of the pre-cut houses which do much to offset the long lag in home building'. Marketing of pre-cut homes was directed at the handyman and the aspiring owner-builder and many companies stressed that few if any savings would result from engaging a builder or subcontractor to assemble the components. However, these packaged products released the owner-builder from combing the land in search of a wide variety of scarce and overpriced building materials and from negotiating for scarce skilled tradesfolk. A similar phenomenon occurred in the United States, where one successful post-war 'shell housing' business run by Jim Walter grew to become one of the nation's largest building firms and material suppliers (Schlesinger & Erlich 1986, 147). However, this self-help building phenomenon failed to shorten significantly the lead times between housing commencements and completions.

There were calls for stricter controls over building in order to avoid lengthy lead times, the subsequent waste of partially constructed houses and the resemblance of new suburbs to permanent construction sites. Many of these outlying new suburbs could have benefited from Bukharin's warning to super-industrialisers in the late 1920s that 'it is not possible to construct today's buildings with "future bricks"' (Bukharin 1965, 71). However, increases in gestation periods were only partly a result of material shortages and bottlenecks. They were also a result of owner-builders' staging of construction according to their means and savings (Hill 1959, 135–7). Under conditions of scarcity many owner-builders were also prey to unscrupulous suppliers. The durability of the final product depended on the quality of materials available—such as good quality, seasoned, pest-free timber—as well as the ability of the amateur owner-builder.

This problem spread across the spectrum of building. As W. Watson Sharpe observed in the November 1949 issue of *Australian House and Garden*: 'If you build now, it will be with the certainty that no matter how conscientious your builder and your architect, or how skilled the tradesman, your home will be second-rate'. However, this consideration had to be weighed against the severity of the housing shortage: 'The house you build now will not be perfect in workmanship and materials—but it *will* be a house'.

The building worker

The problems raised by shortages of materials and building labour were compounded by the decline in the quality of building labour since the war. A 1947 CSHA report estimated that labour productivity had declined by 25 per cent since 1939, because of problems faced by workers in readjusting to peacetime conditions, delayed retirements of experienced workers which led to difficulties in maintaining apprenticeship standards, and the growth of small inexperienced opportunistic building firms in an expanding market (Howard 1981, 45). This latter problem was a constant source of concern in home magazines. The January 1950 *Australian House and Garden* warned that 'unscrupulous contractors have duped hundreds of homemakers in Australia today. In a housing shortage, desperate citizens are easy game'. The 'house-hungry' citizen could ill afford to be fussy, and if a contractor's methods and materials were questioned he could easily retort, 'Well, get someone else to do the job'.

The Australian Institute of Political Science devoted its 1947 winter forum to 'The Housing Problem in Australia'. One speaker, W. H. Ifould, the former deputy director of War Organisation of Industry in New South Wales, used the opportunity to describe his personal housing crisis. He had been unable to get a plumber to visit his house to repair leaking gutters for eighteen months and water was falling from his roof through his leaking gutters onto his flower-beds and paths. He also commented on declining labour productivity. In response to this criticism of his members, the national president of the Building Workers' Industrial Union (BWIU) of Australia, Mr E. W. Bulmer, tried to place productivity decline in perspective. Without refuting the claim, he turned attention to the failure of the state to control building and speculation. Despite the inadequate supply of building materials, the government had failed to control the allocation of materials or to control the number of dwellings commenced according to available resources; the quality of building materials had also declined and this also led to productivity problems beyond the control of labour; some employers were 'hoarding' labour beyond their immediate requirements in anticipation of future contracts, and the lack of state controls also contributed to this problem; some firms were employing unskilled or semi-skilled labour in tradeswork to take advantage of 'the promise of abnormal profits'; and finally, workers were dissatisfied with their existing conditions and wages (AIPS 1947, 54–5). The shortage of building labour was so marked by the end of the 1940s that the government directed 75 per cent of 'displaced persons' under its control into work directly associated with housing (Jordens 1994).

The force of circumstances also had a direct effect upon housebuilding production relations. Before the war many small housebuilders retained tradespeople, especially carpenters, tilers, painters and bricklayers, as direct employees. Traditionally, the more regulated plumbing and electrical trades had been subcontracted. Howard (1987, 50) claimed that 50–60 per cent of the Victorian building workforce was covered by Commonwealth awards immediately after the war, although he stresses that this coverage was not uniform across states. Although evidence is sketchy, most commentators view the immediate post-war period as an important step within the housebuilding industry along the subcontracting path. According to Freeland (1972, 265):

> With so much work to do and high wages being offered on all sides, employed tradesmen were assured of a fat living for a minimum return of quality and quantity. If the contractor objected to either there were plenty of others ready to snap up their services. A bricklayer who before the war laid at least 900 bricks a day now felt he had done a day's work when he had laid 500 or even less. Individual or small groups of tradesmen took to subcontracting for the work of their trade. They worked quickly but not cheaply. With their own time being money they did the work quickly and roughly. Working seven days a week they made three or four times their award trade wage.

The situation was similar in the United States: the 'insatiable demand for housing prompted hired hands to strike out on their own and become independent subcontractors' (Schlesinger and Erlich 1986, 158). Murphy (1984, 9) claims that successful union pressure for better conditions in a favourable market encouraged overtime and moonlighting and, as a consequence, many skilled tradesfolk converted to subcontracting. W. B. Burnett defined moonlighters as 'week-end specialists' and 'those tradesmen ever anxious to get their hands on some easy off-the-record money from you on Saturday and Sunday'. The building trade was a bitter game of 'dog-eat-dog completely ruthless and not one for the faint-hearted' (*Australian House and Garden* June 1949). While subcontracting had existed in the housebuilding industry prior to World War II, post-war conditions accelerated the practice.

The private sector and various housing commissions also began employing labour-only subcontracting (for New South Wales see Burns Commission 1981, 55; for South Australia see Marsden 1986, 97) and the union movement tended to look darkly upon this form of contract. According to evidence presented by the deputy general manager of the New South Wales Housing Commission, Mr V. Helby, to a commission of inquiry into the nature and terms of employment in the state's housing industry, the 'long-standing dispute within the industry over the rates payable to labour-only subcontractors' originated from this period (Burns Commission 1981, 55). In South Australia, there were also claims made by some builders and tradesfolk that the increased use of subcontracting reduced the quality of Trust houses and inhibited the training of apprentices (Marsden 1986, 97–9).

There were 'push' and 'pull' factors involved in this process of labour restructuring. While commentators such as Freeland, Murphy and Helby have emphasised workers' decision to take advantage of higher wages and self-employment, there is also evidence that private building firms—as well as some housing commissions—preferred this form of contract. A. V. Jennings was involved in a number of disputes with the BWIU during the late 1940s and early 1950s in Tasmania and Canberra over the firm's use of subcontracted labour rather than day labour on housing commission projects (Garden 1992, 73, 102; Burns Commission 1981, 56). Moreover, it was difficult for smaller firms to retain tradesfolk as direct employees under conditions where material supply was unpredictable and workers were left idle 'on the books'.

Although the growth of subcontracting can be labelled an organisational innovation, it failed to promote the forms of technological innovation sought by housing reformers and tended to reinforce the small average size of housebuilding firms. It was also the antithesis of the Fordist forms of organisation prevalent in more 'advanced' sectors of industry.

An era of hybrid forms

Once the building activity of state governments, owner-builders and large builders are combined, the residual activity remains significant. By the mid-1950s government housing accounted for around 21 per cent of all commencements and this level gradually declined throughout the next three decades (Commonwealth of Australia 1990). The few large firms which did exist in the early post-war era were enticed by the states into producing government housing and found this sphere of activity secure and profitable enough to suspend large-scale private building. The government was content to farm out its contracts to large firms in the expectation that their economies of scale would encourage more efficient Fordist practices of standardisation and prefabrication. However, although the government's intentions were clear, large firms were more interested in the advantages of security of contract than exploring new techniques and methods of production. There were certain areas—such as rural housing—where the government found it extremely difficult to find local tenderers for projects (Walsh 1972, 63). Under these conditions prefabrication was the only solution (for South Australia, see Marsden 1986).

If large firms operated mainly within the state sphere and owner-builders never accounted for more than half of all private starts during the 1950s, then who produced the remainder of the nation's housing? Hutton (1970, 87) argued that during this period 'most dwellings were erected by small local builders on a speculative basis'. Although he fails to provide an explanation, he argued that the practice of speculative subdivision and building involved higher risks as 'total demand grew and the capacity of the industry expanded'. Freeland (1972, 265) also claimed that the housing shortage and state-sponsored owner-occupation schemes encouraged the formation of many small speculative building firms, some of which had dubious trade credentials and were merely exploiting the housing famine. With respect to the expansion in flat-building —which re-emerged at the end of the 1950s after an early post-war lull—Neutze (1968, 24–6) argued that most flat-builders were small firms also engaged in other forms of residential construction, although New South Wales seems to have possessed a more specialised industry (see also Commonwealth Department of Housing 1968). This is supported by evidence from a study of St Kilda in inner Melbourne where the most important transformation of the area was the provision of private rental flats after the mid-1950s. According to Johnson (1979, 87) these dwellings were 'constructed by small firms in response to the demands for rental accommodation'. Most of these ventures appear to have been speculative.

On the other hand, Pickett (1993, 81) has claimed that speculative housebuilding by small firms declined during the period of austerity and shortages:

> In the decade from 1945, spec building declined as rent control and high building costs reduced the attractiveness of building investment. Its demise was most evident in the decline in the construction of flats, which all but ceased in NSW until the end of the decade, despite the contribution of the Housing Commission . . . Not until late in the decade, when labour and materials shortages eased, did spec building revive, although in the 1960s its place was taken partly by project home building.

Unfortunately there is nothing more than anecdotal evidence to back up these claims.

Much of this confusion over the changing structure of the industry during the late 1940s and 1950s can be attributed to the combination of scarcity and growing state involvement: they fostered the existence of a range of hybrid organisations which did not fit the usual categories. Large private firms were attracted to state contracts due to their volume and their relative security, so the distinction between 'state' and 'private' faded; owner-builders suddenly became principal contractors and hired builders and tradesfolk as needed and as building supplies became available;

and speculative building in such a secure market was almost a contradiction in terms. However, these hybrids were unstable phenomena dependent on the state of the building materials market, labour market forces, the level of state commitment to housing provision and relative prosperity, among other factors. They were the result of the unstable social compromise created by the post-war Fordist-Keynesian state as well as peculiar economic and demographic circumstances. These contingent circumstances in the production and consumption of the residential built environment promoted a partial, albeit significant, withdrawal from market relations.

The government's vision of transforming the structure of the industry and encouraging large-volume producers was less successful than originally anticipated. The supposition that 'more advanced' Fordist industries would show the 'less developed' housebuilding industry the image of its own future proved to be based on shaky underlying assumptions about the dynamics of technological and organisational change.

5

Austerity and Innovation

If necessity is 'the mother of invention' then it is reasonable to expect that the acute housing shortage during the post-war era and the 'age of austerity' would have provided an unprecedented volume of experimentation in process techniques and product design. Chapter 3 outlined the broader social forces behind this move towards technological progress within the housing industry. It could be argued that the high levels of post-war demand for housing and the distress which many families experienced as a result of inadequate housing provided a suitable environment for either the market or a committed state to transform the provision of housing. During the 1940s and throughout the early 1950s there was more experimentation than in the inter-war years or the period after 1960. However, the inventiveness demonstrated by both local and international firms was not translated into the innovative processes which reformers believed necessary if the housebuilding industry was to enter the ranks of the industrial revolution.

Innovative products and processes

A Masonite advertisement from the *Australian Women's Weekly* in May 1942 depicts a woman embracing a disembarking soldier. He appears to be imparting some vital information to her, but she interrupts him impatiently with 'yes . . . yes . . . Johnny Dear. I know . . . but must you talk about Masonite?' One could be forgiven for assuming that the soldier was consumed with a passion to erect his own dwelling. Indeed, the advertisement informs us that 'the modern fighting man' could easily become 'obsessed' with Masonite. After the war, the desire for any building material became insatiable and in many cases frustration lingered for years. Even though the military demand for Masonite declined with the cessation of the war, supplies of the product—along with most other building materials—were difficult to procure (see Figure 8). One typically wordy 1951 advertisement informed readers that 'in spite of trebled production, it is difficult to get Masonite immediately, you might be tempted to accept a "substitute". If you do so, do it with your eyes wide open because "a board by any other name isn't Masonite"'. Shortages also provided incentives for other entrepreneurs to test the undersupplied building market. Some, like Masonite and Caneite, had been introduced prior to the war, but the post-war climate eased their entry—or heightened their acceptance—into the market. Others, like Durabestos building sheets by Wunderlich, found a new lease of marketing life (Bures 1987, 139–40).

Scarcity combined with high employment levels encouraged experienced builders and owner-builders alike to shake off their oft-quoted conservatism with respect to external cladding and structural materials and try on anything new as long as it did the job (Allport 1985, 53; Walsh 1972, 63–66; Marsden 1986, 99). Freeland (1972, 280) captured the innovative mood of a market flooded with new materials in this 'age of austerity'. Products ranged from the genuinely innovative to 'old materials in new forms'—or the ersatz:

> Spray-on plastic roof covering or screwed-on baked-enamel metal panels, extruded aluminium sections and curtain walling, rubber-based paints and pressed straw panels, pressed sheets in all sorts of metals for all sorts of jobs and plastics that were said to be the perfect answer for anything from sealing openings to finishing floors—these and a thousand others claimed to have wonderful properties which made them the perfect answer to particular situations.

Anything that could be pulled from the ground and reshaped was experimented with. Ifould (1947, 47) could not understand why the nation still imported white asbestos and why the industry 'appears curiously averse to the use of blue asbestos, of which we are just beginning to work enormous deposits in north-west Australia'. During the 1940s CSR diversified further away from its sugar base into building products derived from cane. The company had broken into the wallboard market with Caneite and by the mid-1950s its building materials division boasted over a dozen products: Caneite wallboards, ceiling batts, lino-bases, plasters, floor tiles, plaster acoustic tiles, asbestos-cement sidings, flat sheets, corrugated roofing, Timbrock hardboards and Gyprock wallboards. A bewildering variety of wallboards, ceiling boards and laminates entered the market during the era.

Apart from CSR's successes with alternative material sources, Australia was foremost among the world's leaders in factory-mixed concrete, again introduced immediately before the war, and the Australian Aluminium Company and Trimview—a division of A. V. Jennings—among others had adapted the US technique of manufacturing pre-made aluminium windows (Garden 1992, 137). Famous fasteners such as Rawlplugs also entered the market during the early post-war period. The growth in variety did not necessarily result in wider consumer choice during a period of shortages. Location began to assume more importance. Commenting on the wide range of available roofing materials on the market, W. Watson Sharpe noted: 'If any one particular roofing material is manufactured in the vicinity of the house to be roofed, that material is invariably used, whether it is suitable from an aesthetic point of view or not' (*Australian House and Garden*, July 1951). In the late 1940s, Wunderlich Metal Tile Roofing's advertising slogan read 'Why let roofing delay your home plans'. Substitutes could reduce production times for housebuilders.

However, much of the innovation during the period could be described as ersatz and this was not what the modernists sought. Prefabricated steel roofs were designed to look like tile roofs, while concrete tiles were regarded as the poor relation of the terracotta tile. Decorative plastic moulded fireplaces replaced the brick hearth at a time when bricks remained in short supply.

Gilsto marketed 'strongly moulded prefabricated units for gas and electric fires' under the slogan 'Install a modern fireplace'. Freeland (1972, 266) maintained that these new products 'were not, in the main, aimed at finding really new materials but rather satisfactory substitutes for old ones which were in scarce supply'. On the other hand, the acute shortages of new materials and the shortages of skilled tradesfolk opened up new marketing possibilities for more traditional products well into the 1950s. For example, the Fibrous Plaster Association of New South Wales—whose members' market had been encroached upon by the wide variety of new wallboards and ceiling boards—pitched their advertising campaign during the mid-1950s at problems associated with inexperienced and unreliable labour and new products. The campaign pointed out that not only did members of the Association 'manufacture and supply Fibrous Plaster products but they also provide the skilled tradesmen to erect them on the job'. The advantage of this process over some other products was that it 'ensures both materials and fixing workmanship being to your entire satisfaction . . . from one responsible source'. In an era which worshipped 'the modern' and tended to ridicule the 'traditional', the Association felt more comfortable using the experience of 'older folk' and 'the older generation' to sell its members' products (see *Australian House and Garden*, April 1956, 70).

Innovative materials were only part of the process of modernisation urged and fostered by housing reformers. A related problem was the search for innovative methods of production. Throughout the industrialised world, the vision of adequate and affordable housing rested on a belief in prefabrication, factory production, standardisation, rationalisation—or Fordism. As pointed out in Chapter 3, this obsession with Fordism was not solely an Australian fetish but one which excited building and housing reformists throughout the world and one which formed the cornerstone of the modernist school (Gropius n.d., 19–43).

During the war, Barnett, Burt and Heath (1944, 44) had expressed faith that the 'successful prefabricated house will soon be with us'. The old-style contractor would soon be nothing more than a mass assembler following the process of deskilling which had occurred within other more 'advanced' sectors of industry. In a moment of syndicalist inspiration they predicted that this breakthrough would provide 'opportunity for groups of workers to undertake as contractors a considerable proportion of the mass production building of the post-war period' (1944, 65). The syndicalist afterthought suggested a hint of concern over the inevitable process of deskilling which would accompany prefabrication. However, faith in the prefabricated house and linear progress remained strong throughout the Western world well into the 1950s. George Nelson informed the readers of the US *House and Garden* that

> the problem today is not whether to prefabricate or not to prefabricate. This question has already been settled. The simple, observable fact is that the building of homes is becoming an industrial affair. The problem is how, through these industrial methods, to bring the house up to the technical level of the refrigerator, the automatic machine tool, the automobile, and to use this technique to enhance human values. We are entitled to this kind of performance in our dwellings simply because we have demonstrated so abundantly elsewhere that we know how to achieve it. But not with carpenters or masons. For us, 20th Century people who have made an irrevocable commitment to the machine, there is only one choice. The swift growth of prefabrication in building means that again—as in transportation, food and clothing—we have already chosen.

The late 1940s were the halcyon years of experimentation with prefabrication. Never before had the choice been so broad! Wartime aircraft factories were converted and refitted for this purpose and every conceivable scheme was assessed. Both the Commonwealth and the state governments encouraged prefabricated solutions to the housing crisis. The Commonwealth Experimental Building Station engaged in a wide range of basic structural research. The state governments tended to focus on the more practical problems of housebuilding and house design—floor efficiency and the minimum size of rooms, for example. In Victoria, the Holmesglen factory built the prefabricated 'Beaufort' home made of annealed zinc for the Victorian Housing Commission

(Lewis 1985, 288). The more spacious privately sponsored Myer-Ansett home initially appeared to have vindicated the Commonwealth Housing Commission's belief that state initiatives would foster competition between innovative private firms. However, the Beaufort home project was abandoned shortly after the electoral defeat of the Labor Party in Victoria and the private initiative was buried soon after (Boyd 1991). The Public Works Department of New South Wales constructed a range of prefabricated prototypes at its Granville factory (Walsh 1972, 64). The chairman of the New South Wales Housing Commission, Mr Gallup, informed the 1947 winter forum of the Australian Institute of Political Science that the Commission had examined over 200 designs and erected twenty-five test houses. However, he claimed that most of these had proved more expensive than 'orthodox' dwellings (AIPS 1947, 26; see also Walsh 1972, 66). The South Australian Housing Trust also opened a factory for prefabricated housing for country, mining and Aboriginal housing (Marsden 1986, 101).

Apart from these state initiatives, numerous private firms saw an opening in the housing market for quickly and easily installed prefabricated dwellings. An early 1950s feature in *Australian House and Garden* by R. M. Roberts, entitled 'Facts About Factory-Made Homes', provided a review of a range of private firms in the Sydney region engaged in different forms of prefabrication (although other states possessed an equally impressive variety of prefabricators: see Cuffley 1993 for an analysis of the more Melbourne-oriented *Australian Home Beautiful*). Roberts distinguished three main forms of prefabrication, ranging from the more traditional to the more industrial: the pre-cut house, the pre-assembled house and the completely prefabricated house.

For pre-cut houses the traditional components were factory-cut into standard lengths and transported to the client's land where they were erected using 'ordinary site methods'. Other items—such as doors and windows—were also pre-cut at the factory or workshop ready for the next phase of installation. This process greatly simplified the work of the 'unskilled homebuilder' who might otherwise waste valuable and scarce timber in the learning process. It was then the client's responsibility to organise the wiring and the plumbing—which were regulated trades—and also choose and install the prime cost (p.c.) items, such as baths, sinks and basins.

At the other end of the spectrum, the completely prefabricated house, fitted with electricity and plumbing, was assembled at the factory before being hauled to the clients' land in a number of sections and placed on top of footings built prior to delivery. Between these extremes of prefabrication lay the pre-assembled house. According to Roberts, these houses were 'prefabricated in panels with linings in position but individual variations and traditional methods are allowed for in finishes, prime cost items . . . and the like'. These variations remained the responsibility of the client, although Roberts noted that more and more manufacturers were putting together 'packages' of finishing and p.c. items. There were also firms such as Cemac Pty Ltd which offered 'build them yourself' cupboards, tables and panelling. The standard procedure for pre-assembled dwellings was for the customer to erect the panels before the company arranged for the fibrous plaster and the roof tiles to be supplied and fixed.

Ready-cutting—or pre-cutting—was the most prevalent form of prefabrication within the Sydney region and participating firms included Hudson's—which had been pre-cutting for almost a century and also produced a prefabricated home—A. H. Pikett of Sydney and Springwood, Norwoods of Auburn, G. E. Brown & Sons of Auburn, Campbell and Dening of Lawson, Granville Ready Cut Homes, Leask Timber and Hardware of Waitara (see Figure 9), J. A. Letchford & Co. of Peakhurst (see Figure 10) and Cooper's Ready Cut Homes. While most firms aimed at the owner-builder market and stressed labour savings, Hudson's frequently supplied its product to builders. Some could supply pre-assembled houses, although they preferred to simply pre-cut. A number of pre-cutters could accommodate their clients' specifications. Pre-assembly specialists included N. R. Smith, Hutcherson Bros of Sydney, Woodall and Montague of Peakhurst—who worked solely to clients' designs —and the Ridley New Australian Home of Manly Vale. Prefabricated house manufacturers included Vandyke Bros of Villawood, F. R. Wolstenholme of Kogarah and Leichhardt Constructions of Auburn (the prefabricated division of G. E. Brown & Sons).

Almost without exception, these homes were timber-framed, with either asbestos-cement or weatherboard external lining. One exception was the pre-cast house produced by Monocrete—a division of Concrete Industries (Aust)—which consisted of hollow concrete wall panels with steel door and window frames (see Figure 11). One important advantage of the Monocrete structure was that it was acceptable to most councils with 'brick-only' areas. It was also 'vermin-proof'. In addition, the Monocrete house required no internal lining and the panels were only four inches thick compared to eleven inches for a cavity brick wall. This increased the internal dimensions of the dwelling.

Once the client had built the piers, Monocrete transported and erected the wall panels. The company also produced Monier bricks, Monier tiles and Hollowbeam flooring and other building products. In the early 1950s Monier's concrete tiles came in a range of colours—red, grey, brown, yellow, green and orange, single-tone or mottled—and immediate delivery for Monocrete homes was guaranteed. By 1955 Redland Monier Roof Tiles offered thirteen 'wonderful contemporary colours' in its range, which was produced in Sydney, Adelaide, Brisbane and the Causeway in Canberra.

Between 1950 and 1953, as housing demand remained strong, another prefabricated option was tested. Over 18 000 prefabricated houses were imported from Europe. The majority were imported by state housing commissions under a £300 per house subsidy from the federal government, while over 4000 prefabs were imported directly by the Commonwealth for the Department of Works and the Snowy Mountains hydroelectric scheme. The construction giant Lend Lease/Civil and Civic owed its modest origins to this scheme as a joint venture between two Dutch companies erecting 200 Finnish prefabricated houses in Cooma for the Snowy Mountains Hydro-Electric Authority. The contract stipulated that the firm recruit its workers from overseas and the successful Dutch applicants endured the same rigorous screening process as the Jennings Germans (Murphy 1984, 2–3). The British construction firm George Wimpey & Co. also entered the 'contract construction' market in 1951. It soon moved into estate house-building in Sydney and Melbourne and by the end of the 1950s was active in the Canberra market (George Wimpey & Co. Ltd 1965, 1). Another successful contractor, the German firm Wender & Duerholt, built prefabricated houses for the South Australian Housing Trust and remained in Australia serving the Trust after the suspension of the import programme (Marsden 1986, 110–12). The scheme was suspended at the end of 1953 (Department of National Development 1956, 6). In addition, imports of most building materials declined as local suppliers gradually increased their production capacity and after the federal government imposed heavier import restrictions in March 1952 due to a temporary trade deficit.

Assessing prefabrication

Despite the excitement it generated, prefabrication failed to ignite the building revolution which modernists, industrialists and the Commonwealth Housing Commission had expected. Boyd (1991, 197–8)—a disappointed modernist—placed the blame for the failure of prefabrication squarely at the feet of conservative political interests suspicious of any attempt by the government to interfere with the dynamics of the private housing market. He berated the building trade for its retention of methods 'which were old when Governor Phillip landed' (1991, 96) and painted a picture of building stagnation against a background of progress: 'Six years after World War II, with all attempts at mass production shelved, it faced a new half century of unlimited technical potentialities with little more than a trowel, a saw and a hammer'. McDonell (1956, 34) also questioned how far the industry had progressed since the war. Comparing Australian and US housing he pointed out that an average US tradesperson could buy a house for half the price paid by his Australian counterpart. Australians needed to be shaken out of their complacency.

Freeland (1972, 266) adopted a more structural approach. He maintained that the local market could not provide the scale demanded by prefabrication. The result was inevitable: 'As overseas prefabricated houses, designed without due awareness of Australian conditions and economic factors, were unsuitable and there were no other industries in Australia large enough or equipped properly to undertake large-scale factory production of houses the idea of prefabrication came to nothing more than a few odd prototypes'. However, this comment underemphasised the substantial interest generated in prefabricated solutions to the post-war housing crisis and the variety of firms engaged in the process (see Walsh 1972, 66).

Winston (1962, 56) also saw the size of the market as a key factor:

> Modern industrial production necessarily involves large scale organisation as opposed to the small scale operations of the typical house builder, it also presupposes intensive technical research and experiment as well as searching investigation into the real needs of the situation . . . The assurance of a sizeable and continuing market is one prerequisite of the re-organisation and modernisation of the house building industry.

A sizeable and continuing market could have been achieved through reasserting the role of the state in housing provision. However, by the early 1960s government housing was beginning to decline in proportion to total commencements from their historically high early post-war levels. Although a number of private firms such as A. V. Jennings became 'volume builders' during the 1960s, they showed little interest in industrial building. The only other means of securing a sizeable and continuing market would have been through exports, and this option would remain quixotic until prefabrication and modular standardisation were taken seriously. The issue of exports has been taken up by a number of commentators in the 1990s as a means of improving housing provision and to help 'spread market risk, increase economies of scale, reduce the impact of cyclical variations and improve competition' (Wilson 1993, 2; see also Johnston & Lepani 1993).

Howard's (1987) history of the relationship between the state, the building industry and the union movement during this period concluded that while 'social democratic technocrats' within the state apparatus—motivated by what Jones (1972, 6) labelled 'paternalistic altruism'—were capable of generating policies which conflicted with the interests of fractions of private capital, they found it far more difficult to implement these policies. The defeat of the federal Labor Party in 1949 helped relieve some of this conflict. Howard suspended judgement on the issue of the failure of technological innovation: 'Whether market dormancy was due solely to technical and economic problems in design or also to builder attitudes and organisational manoeuvring has not been ascertained' (Howard 1987, 122).

Whatever the reason, it is clear that prefabrication was seen by many as a stopgap. Despite periodic review of prefabrication processes (see Burkitt 1974), numerous commentators have never considered it a serious permanent solution except in rural areas where it reduced transportation and labour costs and allowed housing commissions to erect dwellings where private tenderers feared to tread (Marsden 1986; O'Callaghan 1993, 174; Burkitt 1974). There were contemporaries such as Ifould (1947, 42) who adopted this position and viewed prefabricated solutions as 'emergency houses to assist in tiding over the worst period of housing shortage'. Garden's account (1992, 61) of A. V. Jennings' experience with prefabrication also suggested that it was seen as a passing phase washed in by the tide of contingency:

> Mass production became the rage in the 1940s and 1950s. Though it served a short term purpose in helping to overcome the housing shortage, it was not until Jennings threw off its interest in prefabrication in the early 1960s, and abandoned the unappealing houses it produced, that the company again became a successful private home builder.

Perhaps a more useful approach is to recognise that although the modernist dream of producing housing in the same manner as Henry Ford produced automobiles was not matched by reality, experimentation with the housing product did have flow-on effects which in time helped in the standardisation and pre-assembly of the components which constituted the final product. In addition, the structure of the housebuilding industry is not an absolute constraint to innovation and 'progress'. Although certain features of the industry could inhibit change, other features encouraged change. As a July 1952 *Australian House and Garden* article noted, many housing reformers in their hurry to catch up with other industries had ignored the substantial progress which the industry had already made:

> Towards the end of the war we expected prefabrication to solve all our problems. Houses, we used to say, will be stamped out in so many seconds, they will be streamlined like motor cars and scrapped every ten years. Well, the war was over, the housing shortage was tremendous but prefabrication was not much apparent. Houses were still being built in the old slow hand method, in fact their building had even become considerably slower than before the war. And people began to forget about prefabrication. They forgot also that dozens of components of houses were indeed prefabricated already (such as steel windows, lavatory basins, door locks).

In this incremental manner, it would be possible to enjoy the advantages of prefabrication while 'retaining the flexibility and individuality obtained by traditional methods of construction' (*Australian House and Garden*, October 1950).

Landis' (1982, 52) study of post-war changes in the United States housebuilding industry also noted the 'combination of ingenuity, inventiveness, enthusiasm, and entrepreneurial spirit which characterised the homebuilding industry after World War Two' and identified five institutional or structural barriers through which this spirit was weakened. These barriers included the devaluing of innovation through excessively long payback periods for innovators; the volatile market conditions which deterred even the few large housebuilders from investing in research and development; growing costs, for example, rising land prices, which lessened the financial importance of technical innovations in the total house package; the growing reliance on subcontractors; and the growing fragmentation of the market which inhibited economies of scale. On the other hand, Landis also identified three significant forces fostering innovation and technological change during the same period. These included: the ability of large upstream material suppliers to invest, invent and innovate; the opportunity for small housebuilders to introduce new technologies and products; and the existence of 'starter home' builders with an incentive to keep costs to a minimum. The Australian experience described in this chapter lends support to Landis' claims regarding the importance of countervailing trends against innovation.

The verdict

There are a number of factors which explain why modernisation excited reformers within the housebuilding industry during the period immediately after World War II. There was a pressing need to solve the housing shortage and the capacity and willingness of the private sector to do so was in doubt. The fresh forces of modernism combined with social democracy appeared to have transformative potential. The organisational role of the state and technological advances during the war further encouraged the belief that the housebuilding industry was ready for its technological 'take-off'. A religious fervour was attached to the prophecy that a Henry Ford—clad in fibro—would return to lift the industry into the twentieth century.

However, the modernisation project trundled along a sticky runway. The industry was hampered by severe shortages of labour and building materials. Although this encouraged innovation, the 'new' was often considered inferior to conventional materials, processes and practices. However, while many innovations failed to make a significant impact upon the market at the time or were viewed simply as temporary substitutes, other innovative methods were gradually refined over the next two decades and became more competitive relative to traditional products and processes, such as wallboards, metal window frames and concrete roofing tiles. The state also succeeded in encouraging the growth of a few large firms through its role as the industry's largest client, but failed to induce large firms to experiment seriously with prefabrication. By the middle of the 1950s, as the size and number of government housing contracts tapered off, these firms found their feet in the private housing market or commercial construction. However, while these firms had the advantage of economies of scale, they still preferred using more conventional techniques of production. Innovation since 1960 has remained incremental (Marosszeky 1991), failing to shake the foundations of the structure which obstructed the early post-war reformers' vision of mass production.

The facilitating role of state contracts was more important in the case of post-war Britain, where many large-scale construction firms emerged from social housing programmes (Harloe 1981, 40). Even within the United States, where public provision of housing remained more residual (low-standard housing targeting the most marginalised sectors of the population), Checkoway (1986) has argued that post-war suburbanisation functioned not only as a 'built form' but also as a federally facilitated 'economic instrument for production'.

Housebuilding was not the industry which capitalism forgot. Essentially, capitalism and petty commodity production found innovative means of weathering the post-war storm without seriously adopting the ideas of the industrial housing reformers. One significant structural change which the industry adopted during this era was the more intense use of the practice of subcontracting, especially labour-only subcontracting. Studies on the building industry (Austrin 1980), as well as studies on industrial restructuring and new production systems (Phizacklea 1990; Greig 1992b), show that subcontracting clearly is compatible with capitalist modernisation while at the same time endangering trade unionism. Aspects of modernisation were exploited eagerly by building firms where they were perceived to be in their interest.

Commentators are divided about why the modernist dream failed. Some stress structural factors—the size of the local market, the structure of the industry, industry concentration, technical problems, Commonwealth/state friction, etc.—while others stress purposive factors—the influence of private interests, lack of state commitment, management and planning weaknesses, etc. This experience holds lessons in the contemporary environment where 'flexible specialisation', 'computer-related manufacturing', 'smart houses' and other post-Fordist concepts and practices provide opportunities to modernise or post-modernise the housebuilding industry. Both structural and purposive factors influence change. The most productive terrain for understanding innovation in the housebuilding industry remains somewhere between transformative ideas and a detailed understanding of existing structures and particular socio-economic circumstances.

Part III

Buying the Dream

6

Falling into the Dream: The Growth of Owner Occupation

Affluence, suburbia and owner occupation

Although the industrial revolution in the domestic built environment was far less comprehensive than most housing reformers expected, patterns of housing consumption experienced more radical change. Between 1945 and 1960 Australia was transformed from a society possessing almost equal numbers of owners and renters to one dominated by owner occupation. In 1947, 52.6 per cent of the population were owners or purchasers. The rate climbed to 62.9 per cent in 1954 and to 69.9 per cent in 1961. By 1966, 70.8 per cent of the population either owned or were buying their own house. Rates of owner occupation traditionally had been higher in rural than in urban areas. However, during this period owner-occupation levels in the state capitals outpaced national rates. Contemporaneously, the proportion and absolute numbers of houses available for private rent declined.

The dominant theories within Western social science in the 1950s and 1960s looked upon the growth of owner occupation as a natural part of the process of social modernisation. According to these evolutionary and linear theories, owner-occupation rates tended to increase as societies become more affluent. For example, Rostow (1960, 78) saw owner occupation and suburbanisation as part of an affluent 'age of high consumption'.

In explaining this tenure shift, many commentators placed significant emphasis on the role of changing values and attitudes.

'Embourgeoisement'—the process whereby people who were 'objectively' working class acquired or aspired to a middle-class income, adopted middle-class consumption patterns and assumed the values, attitudes and psychology of the middle class (Hindess 1971, 20; Kemp 1978)—went hand-in-hand with growing levels of affluence, high rates of owner occupation and suburbanisation (Checkoway 1986, 132). Many novels of the period—including Braine's *Room At The Top* in Britain and Yates' *Revolutionary Road* in the US—explored the themes of working-class affluence and invariably the symbolic site of social mobility was suburbia (Martin 1970, 306). The 'affluent worker' became an object of intensive sociological examination and a crude form of materialism was used to explain a range of social phenomena from changing voting patterns and the decline of class conflict to the privatised individual.

Owner occupation, suburbia and 'home-centredness' were also seen as integral components of the material and psychological conditions for post-war affluent modernity and the 'end of ideology' (Butler & Rose 1960; Bell 1958). During the mid-1950s, Premier Gair of Queensland claimed that owner occupation 'encourages a sense of responsibility in the individual and is an antidote to any of the "isms" that may exist here' in Australia (quoted in Jones 1972, 120). Kemp (1978) translated the 'end of ideology' as the 'ending of political cleavages'. In the post-war 'affluent society' (Galbraith 1970) the problem of 'blocked social mobility' could be alleviated through 'compensatory consumption', the accumulation of 'appliances, automobiles and the dream of a home of their own' (Caplovitz 1963).

Conservative and radical writers placed different values on owner occupation. Conservatives argued that owner occupation provided workers with a stake in their nation, helped to tie the social fabric together and promoted respect for private property among the masses. On the other hand, from a less conservative position, Crisp (1973, 187) maintained that two decades of 'prosperity and expansionary economic policies, extensive housing and rehousing programmes, and more plentiful housing finance' had encouraged the descendants of the pre-war Australian working class to move to 'the newer, outer suburbs' where, lacking the inner-city feelings of working-class solidarity, the identify less strongly with socialist politics and be 'politically footloose'. The old pre-war Labor 'image' wa appropriate in 'the new suburbia'.

Connell and Irving (1986, 300) also noted how '..uburbia' and 'affluence' were often cited by Australian intellectuals as the reasons for the demise of political Labor during the 1950s. Rowley (1972, 284–9), in his analysis of post-war Australian political economy, entitled his section on the working class 'Suburbia Forever', although he attacked the concept of embourgeoisement and argued that it would be 'foolish to see working class suburbia as an affluent utopia'.

Attitudes towards the alleged 'middle-classing' or embourgeoisement of Australia depended on one's political allegiance. Other left-wing commentators, like Strachey (1956, 238) pointed to owner occupation and affluence as a demonstration to the more 'intransigent' left that capitalism could be tamed and that Marxist revolutionaries 'neglected the power which contemporary democracy had developed to raise the standard of life of the masses of the highly developed last stage of capitalism'. In addition, reformist housing policy demonstrated the virtues of the post-war welfare state in overcoming the imperfections of the private housing market. In sum, owner occupation could be interpreted in a variety of ways to explain political behaviour.

Post-war affluence is one of the most commonly cited reasons for the growth of owner occupation in Australia. Fry (1972) linked the rise of owner occupation with affluence and the 'pent-up hunger for material things and a freer way of life' during the first twenty years after World War II. In this form of prosperity, 'marked enough to be called affluence, most city dwellers have been able to satisfy wants: for a home of their own, a home for each family; a home which one owns, or is buying; a detached house or alternatives for the interested minority; in a better suburb; with a car, comforts, the job that provided these and the hope of improvement'. In other accounts, post-war affluence is viewed as the moment of opportunity which households had been waiting for in order to satisfy their natural predisposition towards owner occupation. For example, Bolton (1981, 148), writing of the options facing Australian house-seekers in the wake of the war—in a chapter entitled 'Affluent Society'—claimed that 'the value of owning one's own home was a belief entrenched in far too many Australians to be overthrown by economic theorising'. Too often, statements purporting to explain owner occupation imply an irrational or subconscious urge driving the population towards this tenure preference (McGregor 1966, ch. 5).

Other social scientists have refused to reduce tenural changes to simple causal connections. Tenure is intricately linked with a wide range of social variables, such as class, wealth, income and security (Paris 1993, 74–6). The political, social and cultural conservatism of the era was the result of a unique blend of historical circumstances which included fear and instability as well as greater material contentment (see Alomes, Dober & Hellier 1984). These included the memory of depression-era insecurities, war or post-war scarcity and the subsequent fear of any force, however nebulous, which threatened to undermine the advent of more prosperous times; the fear of communism and the perceived threat to national security generated by the Cold War, the Chinese revolution and post-colonial Asia; the insecurities created in the wake of Britain's decline and the ascendancy of the United States in the region; the fears generated by mass immigration and 'aliens'; the perceived threat to an entrenched 'British' way of life which intensified the search for the essence of the post-war 'Australian way of life' and the promotion of cultural homogeneity; and the reassertion of the male in the public domain and within the 'traditional' family after the experiences of the war (Alomes, Dober & Hellier 1984). This list undermines any attempt to construct simple causal relationships between post-war suburbanisation, owner occupation, affluence and political conservatism. The work of Mullins and the regulation theorists discussed in Chapter 1 also suggests that suburban aspirations and the meaning of owner occupation can possess quite different meanings during different historical periods.

Many Marxists also adopted 'functionalist' explanations of the post-war decline in revolutionary politics, maintaining that suburbia and owner occupation were contemporary manifestations of alienation (Baran & Sweezy 1977, 292; see also Westergaard &

Resler 1977). However, Marxists tended to focus less on the attitudinal aspects of affluence and more on the pattern of life and the material ties which mass consumption, suburbia and owner occupation brought in its wake. In the Australian context, Connell (1977, 216) claimed that these manifestations of affluence bound the working class to the prevailing economic system. The purchase of a suburban house surrounded by a garden, the need to fill the dwelling with appliances and the growing requirement of a car all burdened most families with debt for the duration of their working life. In addition, the 'routines of interaction that in the interwar years had provided a basis of working class solidarity, mutual aid and sometimes mobilisation were altered and mobilisation correspondingly made more difficult' (Connell 1977, 216). These changes most directly affected the 'occupational community' (Mullins 1981a; 1981b).

The use of concepts such as affluence suggests that the nation was 'pulled' irresistibly towards owner occupation during the immediate post-war years. However, there are grounds for doubting whether the growth of owner occupation was as 'natural' as many commentators assume. Far too often, unquestioned assumptions have been made concerning the Australian post-war predisposition towards owner occupation, suburbia and the 'great Australian dream', despite the significant advantages which the tenure holds (for a critique, see Troy 1991). In response to the argument that the population was drawn or pulled irresistibly towards owner occupation, either naturally or through affluence, other theorists have bent the theoretical stick in the opposite direction and have claimed that the shift to an owner-occupier nation was imposed upon the population rather than a reflection of innate desires. Connell (1977, 215) has argued that the pattern of suburban living adopted by large sections of the working class after World War II needs to be placed in the context of the forces that 'persuaded or pushed' the population to the city fringes. Connell rejected the 'natural predisposition', 'national character' and 'affluent worker' arguments and maintained that 'there was no lemming-like rush to spiritual death beyond the reach of the sewerage'. In other words, people weren't drawn towards home ownership; they were pushed!

The state, ideology and owner occupation

The claim that the nation was 'pushed' into owner occupation is often associated with the work of Jim Kemeny. Kemeny has questioned the relationship between material wealth, the Australian character and high rates of owner occupation. Dismissing the significance of such explanations, he focused on the role which the state and capitalistic interests performed in promoting and sponsoring owner occupation after World War II. He maintained that after the mid-1950s, the intervention of the state in housing affairs was directed primarily at supporting owner occupation and this action transformed consumer behaviour in the housing market. There was also a bipartisan unwillingness to challenge the dominance of this tenure. Williams (1984, 182–9) also pointed out that the similarities between post-war Labor Party policy and Liberal-Country Party policy on tenure were more pronounced than the differences and that 'both party differences and electoral impacts seem to have been exaggerated' by commentators.

While 'Dedman's dictum' (the statement by a federal Labor Party minister that Labor was concerned 'to provide adequate and good housing for the workers; it is not concerned with making the workers into little capitalists') was used by the Liberal Party as a weapon to question the Chifley government's commitment to owner occupation, tenure never became a major political or electoral issue throughout the 1950s. Kemeny associated this bipartisan monotenural housing policy with such social ills as the neglect of the public rental sector and the welfare state, the dependence on foreign capital and other social inequities which make up the 'great Australian nightmare' (Kemeny 1983).

Challenging many assumptions about Australian owner occupation, Kemeny (1983, ch. 1) claimed that there was an 'underlying trend' away from owner occupation during the inter-war era. While the rate of owner occupation remained relatively stable during the inter-war years, the number of new mortgagees was declining, especially from the late 1920s onwards. Fewer households were entering owner occupation and if this trend had continued then the rate eventually would have fallen. Some factor must have intervened to reverse this trend away from owner occupation. Kemeny (1983, 22) stated that after a brief bitenural policy under the Chifley Labor government in the late 1940s, government housing policy became 'aggressively interventionist, and has been marked by extremely high levels of expenditure on private housing which have been sufficient to determine the pace and nature of the development of the owner occupied sector'. Kemeny dismissed the view that the growth in owner occupation was 'inevitable' and 'natural' or a result of affluence. The popularity of the tenure was influenced by 'heavily interventionist' and 'tenure-biased' state policies. Kemeny focused attention on the historical role which owner occupation has performed in capital accumulation and deepening existing social inequalities.

However, Kemeny's argument should be qualified in a number of respects. First, it is misleading to focus on the period between 1933 and 1947 and suggest that there was an 'underlying' trend away from owner occupation during the later inter-war years. As Chapter 2 demonstrated, the effects of the depression during the early 1930s combined with the effects of World War II severely constrained households' choices. Any assessment of tenure preference during this period must be made with qualification. Second, while Kemeny's point that the state encouraged people to enter the ranks of owner occupation can easily be verified through a cursory examination of housing legislation and parliamentary speeches, he tended to ignore other factors. The severe housing shortage combined with shortages of labour and materials for new housing, lack of rental accommodation—or its conversion into owner-occupied stock—and rent control all influenced the scope of tenure options. Furthermore, while post-war affluence has been overemphasised by some commentators, it cannot be ignored totally. Third, Kemeny does not explain why rates of owner occupation accelerated most dramatically in the intercensal period 1947–54, that is, *before* the 1956 CSHA when the Menzies government altered funding arrangements in order to ease the restrictions on selling housing commission dwellings and allocated more federal funds to the promotion of owner occupation.

These gaps in Kemeny's argument suggest that he assigned to the state a causal significance for owner-occupation rates which in reality were the result of a combination of factors. Recently, Beer

(1993, 152) claimed that post-war government policy 'triggered' the growth in owner-occupation rates. However, commentators adopting a more multivariate approach to owner-occupation rates have claimed that the state, at the most, acted as an 'accelerator' for owner occupation.

Connell (1977, 215)—who also maintained that the nation was 'pushed' and also stressed the role of ideology—qualified his argument by noting that there were 'good reasons why people moved'. These included the government's drive to populate the nation, which raised population pressures within the inner-city working-class areas; the explosion of private motor traffic that made these areas less pleasant places in which to bring up children; and rent control measures, leading to a decline in maintenance standards by landlords. Although this list was far from exhaustive, it pointed to the need to look beyond post-war government housing policy as an explanation.

Other commentators have noted Kemeny's failure to demonstrate the causal link between government policy and post-war owner occupation. Morris and Winn (1990, 228) stated that Kemeny only offered an 'assertion' that a symbiotic relationship exists between power, ideology and the construction of tenure. Other commentators have claimed that the causal connection ran in the opposite direction to that assumed by Kemeny: 'that is, the emergence of a monotenural housing policy may have been the result, rather than the cause, of the rapid growth of post-war owner occupation' (Berry 1988, 113). Berry located the underlying dynamics of this process in the global and local patterns of capital accumulation during the 1950s. Rising levels of domestic savings were directed towards the (re)production of the built environment. The magnitude of this investment was illustrated by the almost sevenfold increase in outstanding housing advances by major lending institutions between 1945 and 1956 (Hall 1959, 7). Lending institutions financed approximately 55 per cent of new dwellings, governments 17 per cent, and the remainder was financed by other means—principally owners' own funds (Hill 1959, 133–7).

Berry (1988, 117) has maintained that the perceived benefits of owner occupation and its universality led to a 'political ratchet effect' for the Menzies government, locking it into defending the monotenural policy not because of any ideological disposition (although that clearly existed) but because of the 'structural forces' underpinning the tenure. Berry has identified an impressive range of macro-economic structural factors involved in the growth of owner occupation during the 1950s. However, his analysis tended to focus on a more abstract set of forces which set the global and national context for housing provision. With the exception of state provision, he left unidentified the context within which housing consumers operated. The analysis below attempts to make this context and consumer options more intelligible.

Castles' (1988) concept of the 'politics of domestic defence' lends further support to Berry's critique. By comparing Australia with certain European nations, Castles argued that the historical class compromise reached at the turn of the century aimed to defend workers' conditions through an individualistic wages system, rather than through an interventionist social-democratic welfare state. As a consequence, the Australian welfare state functioned 'as a residual safety net in the last resort' (Castles 1988, 108). With respect to housing, the state abandoned workers to fend for themselves. This undermines Kemeny's assumption that high rates of owner occupation led to a weak welfare state.

Hayward (1986, 215) has also criticised Kemeny's abstract treatment of the state as well as his tendency to 'overlook the more material constraints within which the state formulates and implements housing policies'. Hayward maintained that this leads to an oversimplified dichotomy between a voluntarist state 'free to do what it wants' and a socially controlled and manipulated mass which is the 'passive recipient of government decision making'.

Although it is not stated explicitly, Hayward rejected the perspective which assumes a homogeneous population and which views most cultural phenomena as imposed from above. Instead he stressed how subordinate groups (re)construct their own culture out of available or given resources. As Fiske (1989, 2) argued, there is always an element of popular culture which lies beyond the control of hegemonic interests. According to Hayward, the 'Australian dream' of home ownership was something the working class has struggled for rather than something which was 'foisted upon an unsuspecting public' (Hayward 1986, 215–17). He pointed to the high levels of owner occupation among working-class households since the late nineteenth century. The weakness of Hayward's argument lies in the flimsy evidence he offers as well as his failure to examine the historical peculiarities and contingencies of the post-war period.

The debate over the relationship between the state and the ideology of owner occupation often ends up in a discursive alley rather than examining the material structuring of the choices which were available to consumers in a particular place at a particular time. The power of ideology depends upon its ability to 'resonate with the material "lived" experience of the individual' (Hay 1992, 32). One question is what made the ideology of owner occupation—supported by the state—so 'commonsensical' to consumers? Only through operating on this less reductionist level is it possible to make intelligible the options open to consumers, and the decisions made by them.

Kemeny's argument provided a powerful refutation of the 'affluent worker' thesis and the 'natural' social development theses as they relate to owner occupation. However, Kemeny shared with his more conservative commentators a functionalist approach to this tenure. On one level owner occupation performs the function of maintaining and reproducing capitalist relations through reducing the state's welfare burden; on another level the ideology of home ownership maintains the quiescence of the working class. This second proposition has been repeated by radical and conservative thinkers alike for the best part of a century and it has been associated with a curious range of political and ethical values and beliefs—as well as a bewildering array of myths and concepts, from nationalism and patriotism to false consciousness. To paraphrase Abercrombie, Hill and Turner (1980, 3), the following evidence suggests that the importance of the ideology of owner occupation has been greatly exaggerated by radicals and conservatives alike and suggests that this ideology does not have the consequences which have been attributed to it.

A more qualified version of Kemeny's argument would state that government manipulation and ideological persuasion 'pushed' owner occupation. However, it is more difficult to find evidence to suggest that the behaviour of the working class was modified by an 'ideological state apparatus'. In other words, Kemeny has observed the coincidence of two phenomena but has failed to establish the causal relationship between them (Berry 1988). While Kemeny (1981, 117) acknowledged that the dominance of owner occupation rested on the absence of 'attractive alternatives', he focused attention on the 'stigmatisation' of public renting to the exclusion of more non-ideological factors.

Owner occupation and the alternatives

Whitwell (1989, 40–1) observed that most commentators have isolated direct and indirect government encouragement as the crucial variable affecting post-war owner-occupation rates. In contrast, he challenged any monocausal view and maintained that the rising rate of post-war owner occupation was the result of a number of interrelated factors. These included: an identification with the 'owner occupation ideal'; a favourable economic climate; demographic changes such as high rates of household formation and immigration; readily available cheap finance; relatively cheap land; and 'the strong direct and indirect encouragement to owner occupation provided by government'.

He pointed out that government initiatives often have effects opposite to those intended, and he cited the example of government instructions to saving banks to maintain low interest rates (Whitwell 1989, 43), which brought correspondingly low deposit rates, and resulted in lower volumes of funds being available for lending. Thus, Whitwell demonstrated that at least one of the policies cited by Kemeny as contributing to higher rates of owner occupation conceivably could have had the opposite effect.

Whitwell concluded that the success of government objectives was predicated on the economy's performance. However—like Kemeny—he rejected the simple reductionist argument that owner occupation was a consequence of growing affluence:

> Without denying the importance of government policies, the postwar rise in owner occupation depended heavily on the existence of a favourable economic environment. The amount

> which governments devoted to subsidising owner occupation was linked in the long run to the amount of governmental receipts. Likewise the volume of housing finance was tied to the volume of deposits. The growth of governmental receipts and of finance institution deposits were in turn determined ultimately by the growth of national income. Furthermore, the willingness of individuals to obtain and seek the large loans necessary to purchase homes was strongly influenced by the prevailing economic conditions. The full employment and sustained increases in household income which occurred during the long boom made borrowers feel more secure about taking on a heavy debt burden and made lenders more willing to provide loans. This is not to say that rising levels of home ownership follow automatically from the enjoyment of sustained and widespread economic affluence. It is simply making the point that without the appropriate economic conditions the ability of governments to increase the rate of home ownership would have been limited.

Although Whitwell also noted in passing that it is 'sometimes argued, with good reason, that many people were forced into owner occupation simply because of a lack of rental accommodation' and also that the growth of the rental stock was affected by rent control, he clearly placed emphasis on the demand side of the housing equation in order to explain the rising rates of owner occupation in the wake of World War II.

Hill's (1964a, 49–51) analysis, on the other hand, attempted to 'balance' supply and demand factors. The dramatic post-war increase in rates of owner occupation were the result of higher incomes, full employment, official policy, official encouragement and inducements, those 'forced into it by the lack of a suitable alternative', exacerbated by the number of owners—for a variety of reasons—quitting landlordism. The literature has tended to underemphasise the last two variables.

The dramatic growth of owner occupation was more the result of 'a desperate demand for shelter' than of a fundamental shift in 'values and economics' (Pickett 1993, 77). For many people—in the absence of sufficient state rental housing—owner occupation was simply the only feasible alternative to exposure! Owner occupation, in other words, 'was as much a reflection of the desperate shortage of housing at the beginning of the 1950s, and Australia's high rents, as it was of affluence' (White 1993, 19). Even the Menzies government—the official standard-bearer for owner occupation—was forced to concede that those who were unable or unwilling to purchase a home found renting shelter extremely difficult (Department for National Development 1956, 15; see also Hill 1964a, 49). Household decisions to commit to owner occupation often had more to do with the hardship and extortion involved in the alternative process of finding a place to rent—such as crowding, lack of privacy and the payment of key money—than it had to do with financial capacity.

Ironically, the rental supply problem was exacerbated by measures designed to alleviate the exploitation of tenants. Federal and state rent control policies were the focus of much political debate during the 1950s, although few historical and sociological commentators have given rent control the attention it deserves. While various states had introduced 'fair rents' legislation during the depression of the 1930s, and the Commonwealth had introduced limited federal legislation in March 1940, the incoming Labor government passed a more comprehensive Landlord and Tenant Act under National Security Regulations in 1941. This legislation was imposed upon all states—although Western Australian and South Australian state legislation was considered to be sufficiently similar to federal legislation to be left intact.

The key features of the legislation were eviction control provisions and a freeze on rent levels at their August 1939 levels unless otherwise determined by the Rent Controller. The legislation was extended in 1945 to include 'shared accommodation' and—with slight modifications—remained in existence until 1948 when the Commonwealth government lost a referendum for retaining price controls. The Commonwealth passed responsibility for rent controls over to the states in August 1948. However, the newly empowered states quickly passed their own legislation which effectively mirrored the previous Commonwealth powers.

While rent control during the post-war housing shortage was designed to stop landlords exploiting the scarcity of rental accommodation, the severity of the housing crisis encouraged a flourishing of illegal practices such as the demand by landlords for 'key money' and other extra-rental payments in return for tenant possession. Most states gradually watered down their rent control provisions throughout the 1950s. Between 1947 and 1965 there were thirteen amending bills on rent control passed in the New South Wales Parliament (Nelson 1980, 149). By 1960 only New South Wales retained significant rent control legislation, with two-thirds of privately rented dwellings remaining subject to controls (Albon 1980, 96–7). In that year, the state held a royal commission to inquire into the legislation. Its recommendations for a milder policy were rejected, and in 1975, nearly 36 000 New South Wales dwellings were still subject to rent control (Nelson 1980, 139). However, it remained a controversial political issue during the 1950s.

In June 1949, Heinz Arndt (1949, 99–100) noted that a decade of rent control combined with rising incomes and rising house prices had brought about a 'serious maladjustment' which would soon have to be confronted politically. Pointing out that rent control 'inevitably discourages private investment in houses for letting', he identified three possibilities: 'further injury to landlords, subsidisation of abnormally low housing expenditure out of the public purse, or a gradual stepping-up of controlled rents'. Arndt argued that the first two courses were difficult to justify, while the third, which he saw as the only sensible course, required 'unusual political courage'—the kind of path rarely ventured on by governments! His short discussion of rent control predicted the dilemmas which would face state governments throughout the 1950s.

In an April 1953 article in the Melbourne *Age*, a group of economists argued that the housing shortage had been artificially created by rent controls and called for their abolition (Albon 1980, 96). Two months earlier, the Bank of New South Wales had called for the abolition of state legislation in an article which highlighted the effects of control on private rental accommodation. It pointed out that of the 24 000 houses constructed during 1951/52, 20 000 had been occupied by owners or owner-builders and the overwhelming majority of the remainder had been constructed by the New South Wales Housing Commission. It claimed that 'rent control has rested more lightly on newly built houses, but of all the houses privately constructed since the war an insignificant number were available for rental, and even then in most cases the letting has been due to a change in circumstances of the owner' (Bank of New South Wales 1953, 130). The article concluded by calling for a relaxation or repeal of the legislation based on the observation of 'relatively slack conditions in the building industry' which could 'reopen the prospect of private building for rental' (Bank of New South Wales 1953, 131).

Nelson (1980, 144–5) has noted that the surprisingly subdued building market in the wake of the lifting of building restrictions in October 1952 led many to use rent control as a 'scapegoat' for housing shortages. By 1954, landlords had begun forming pressure groups such as the Home Owners' League and later the Landlords' Justice Association and the Flat and Property Owners' Association of New South Wales (Nelson 1980, 146–7).

In mid-1954, the Victorian chapter of the Institute of Public Affairs (IPA) issued a much stronger attack on rent control, arguing that it was 'a classic example of where government interference with the free price mechanism can do almost irreparable damage' (*IPA Review* 1954, 121). The IPA's attack was partly motivated by the fact that rent controls remained tighter in Victoria than any other state. Furthermore, the Institute helped formulate Liberal Party policy (Connell & Irving 1986, 290) and a critique of rent control represented an opportunity to attack the Labor state government. Although the IPA admitted that it might have been a necessary evil under emergency conditions, rent control legislation had outlived its usefulness and it now 'inflicted grave social injustice on a small minority, and delayed the provision of adequate housing facilities for the great majority'.

This small minority—lessors—had seen their share of national income reduced from 4 per cent in 1938/39 to less than 1 per cent in 1954. One of the dire consequences of their low rate of return was that tenanted houses were 'falling into disrepair for lack of proper maintenance' (*IPA Review* 1954, 121–4). In addition, the IPA pointed out that under existing legislation an owner had to offer first sale option to sitting tenants and a high premium was attached to vacant possession. Many owners had been forced to sell at well below market value to tenants who, in turn, resold the property with its newly acquired status at a substantial profit.

In a study of the New South Wales experience, Nelson (1980, 153–4) maintained that the principal beneficiaries of rent control legislation 'appear to have been those who bought controlled premises and had the means and the know-how, or the luck, to gain vacant possession'. The luckiest appear to have been sitting tenants. Johnson's (1972, 91) study of real estate agents' records in North Melbourne during the 1950s and 1960s revealed that 'most of the buying was by people who were sitting tenants of the landlord . . . '. This anecdotal evidence was supported in a later study of St Kilda, where 'rent control induced landlords to sell their property. Unless they could gain vacant possession they could only sell at a lower price. Therefore the sitting tenant was able to buy at a favourable price' (Johnson 1979, 104). Sales peaked around 1954, while the Victorian legislation was substantially amended through the 1955 Landlord and Tenant (Amendment) Act which came into effect in mid-1956 (Johnson 1979, 44; Albon 1980, 95). Similar effects of rent control were evident in Sydney (see Neutze 1972b, 96–8 for the Sydney suburb of Redfern).

Other case studies conducted by the Urban Research Unit at the Australian National University during the 1970s on changing post-war property and demographic profiles within selected Sydney and Melbourne suburbs also found that rent control tended to affect inner-city suburbs more than outer areas, as there were more owner-occupied dwellings built in the outer areas either immediately prior to the war, or immediately after the war (see Neutze 1971b and 1972a for Bankstown and Liverpool). However, in outer areas like Liverpool, which experienced 'the flat boom' beginning in the late 1950s, the proportion of private rented dwellings began to increase (Neutze 1972a).

The IPA (*IPA Review* 1954, 124–5) also maintained that rent control affected consumers' tenural behaviour. Moreover—in a passage which could have been lifted from the 'Building Better Cities' programme of the Keating Labor government in the 1990s—it claimed that rent control had delayed urban renewal and promoted 'urban sprawl':

> Rent control is bringing about a revolution in home ownership. The supply of privately rented houses is falling rapidly each year through sales to tenants and other owner occupiers. Thus many people seeking to rent a home are being forced against their wishes and, ultimately possibly against their interests, to purchase on heavy mortgages. These people are often obliged to erect cheap weatherboard homes on the outskirts of the metropolitan area, greatly adding to the community cost of providing sewerage, electricity and transport.

The Bank of New South Wales (1958) also pointed to the harmful effects of New South Wales legislation. First, it created a depressed market in rental housing. Second, it resulted in the 'virtual elimination of new investment in rental housing'. Third, it reduced maintenance and repair in rental dwellings and resulted in 'minimum modernisation'. A follow-on effect of this decline in private rental building was the need to greatly expand home building to cope with the growth in family formation.

Despite the growth of government housing, the number of tenancies fell slightly between 1947 and 1956 while the number of owner-occupied houses rose by 50 per cent. Nationally, there was an absolute decline in privately rented dwellings and the tenure only regained its 1947 level in the early 1970s (Bethune 1978, 158). As late as 1961, the Department of the Interior (1961, 66) commented that 'unfurnished houses or flats for rent are difficult to find'. In addition, the Department warned that current average rents were misleading because remaining rent controls dragged averages down. Those lucky enough to find rental accommodation in more recent times often were forced to pay prices well above the statistical average. The Bank of New South Wales took a rather ambivalent attitude towards this decline in rental accommodation and the growth of owner occupation:

> While socially desirable for many reasons, an expansion of private home building has some economic drawbacks. It has led young people into burdens of debt which they might well have preferred to avoid if rental homes had been available. The trend towards private home ownership has made demands on the banking system for a heavy proportion of longer-term housing finance, and so limited the loans available for other

> purposes. Investors who might have invested in rental housing but for rent control presumably directed their funds towards other avenues via the stock exchange, while those who owned rent-controlled property, found their asset virtually frozen. It might be said, therefore, that the forced movement towards more extensive home ownership has introduced greater rigidity into the financial structure. Possibly it has also brought about less mobility of labour, for people are less willing to move to new locations when, because of the absence of suitable rental accommodation, they are obliged to sell their own house and buy another.

This statement demonstrates that the relationship between capitalism and owner occupation is more complex than Kemeny suggested. The Bank's assessment was also supported by Bethune, who maintained that rent control had forced many landlords to sell their rental properties and—in the absence of other landlords entering the market—promoted owner occupation. The rental crisis 'made ownership almost mandatory for new households'.

Even in the capital cities, where a higher proportion of people rented, the owner-occupation rate rose from 46.4 per cent in 1947 to 61.5 per cent in 1954. Bethune (1978, 166) estimated that the combined effect of the fall in the number of private rental dwellings plus rental control between 1947 and 1961 increased the rate of owner occupation by up to eight percentage points. Hill (1959, 6–7) also attempted to measure the effect of rent control and concluded that the increase in owner occupation after the war was the result of high incomes, full employment and rent control. He claimed that the latter variable was 'the most potent'. He also pointed out that landlords had virtually stopped building houses for rent and that approximately 90 000 dwellings formerly for private rental—or one-sixth of the total—had entered the owner-occupied stock since 1947.

Thus, less conservative observers than the IPA and the Bank of New South Wales drew from the experience of the 1950s the conclusion that rent controls had major consequences for housing and urban development. Mendelsohn (1982, 167), in his review of Australian welfare policies, concluded that the imposition of blanket controls on private rents was 'self-defeating' and that

Figure 1 Filling the Fordist suburban container: Moving Day, Los Angeles, 1953
(J. R. Eyerman, Life *magazine)*

Figure 2 *'We Can't Live in a House of Dreams', Liberal Party advertisement, 1946*
(Australian Women's Weekly, *11 May)*

Figure 3 *Mass consumerism and domestic bliss: advertisement for Bendix automatic washing machine, 1955*
(Australian House and Garden, *March*)

Figure 4 House Under Construction *by Kasimir Malevich, 1915*
(Australian National Gallery)

FACTS you will face

if you take on the job of owner-contractor

By E. M. BERNARD

Before you decide definitely to be your own contractor read this article.

MANY home-builders feel that a contractor's fees—something like ten to twenty per cent of the cost of the building—are excessive. A home-owner who tries to save most of this amount (he will hardly ever save the lot) through doing his own contracting should have some experience in building, he must be capable of organising a fairly complicated business and he certainly needs a measure of free time during ordinary business hours. Another thing he needs is an extra amount of capital. Most lending institutions won't make their first payment on an owner-builder's job before the roof timbers are erected. Thus the owner has to lay out extra money in the beginning of the job which will later on be refunded to him.

The safest course for the owner-builder is to employ a good architect who will take the responsibility for technical problems leaving the owner the job of obtaining materials, labour, sub-contractors, carters and all the legal requirements such as permits, insurances, etc. It is wise, from the beginning, to keep axact amounts of all money spent in connection with the building. This way, excessive spending on any item can be spotted in time, overcharging can be checked and the owner will know at any time whether he is keeping within his budget. Accounts should show clearly the money spent on materials, labour, subcontracts,

(Continued on page 78)

Figure 5 *'Facts you will face if you take on the job of owner-contractor', 1952*
(Australian House and Garden, *July*)

Figure 6 *'Build Your Own Home', advertisement by* G. E. Brown *& Sons, 1952*
(Australian House and Garden, *July*)

Figure 7 *'Big home comfort at small home cost', advertisement by N. R. Smith, 1952*
(Australian House and Garden, *July*)

Figure 8 *'If your home is to be modern . . .', advertisement for Masonite, 1946*
(Australian Home Beautiful, *July*)

Figure 9 *Advertisement by Leask Timber & Hardware Pty Ltd, 1955* (Australian House and Garden, *May*)

Figure 10 *'Your home by Letchford'*, *1952* (Australian House and Garden, *September*)

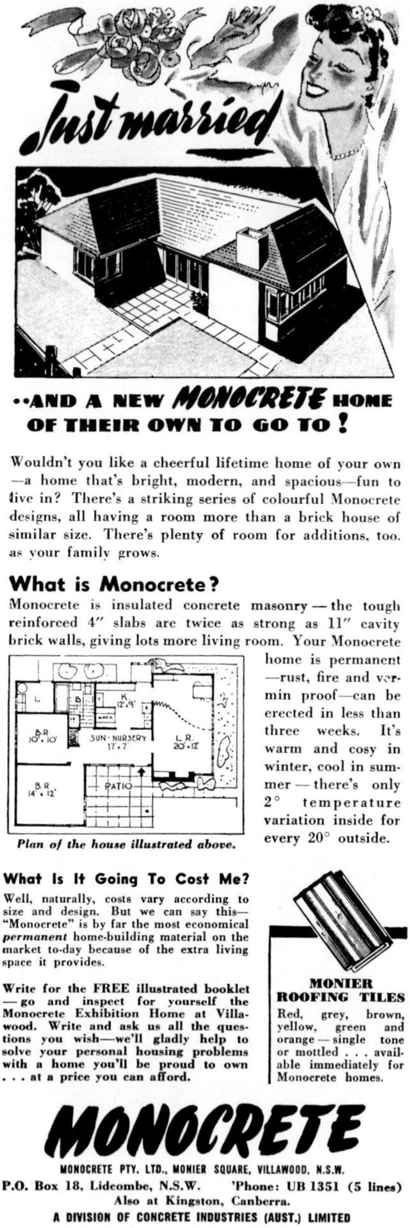

Figure 11 *Advertisement for Monocrete, 1949* (Australian House and Garden, *June*)

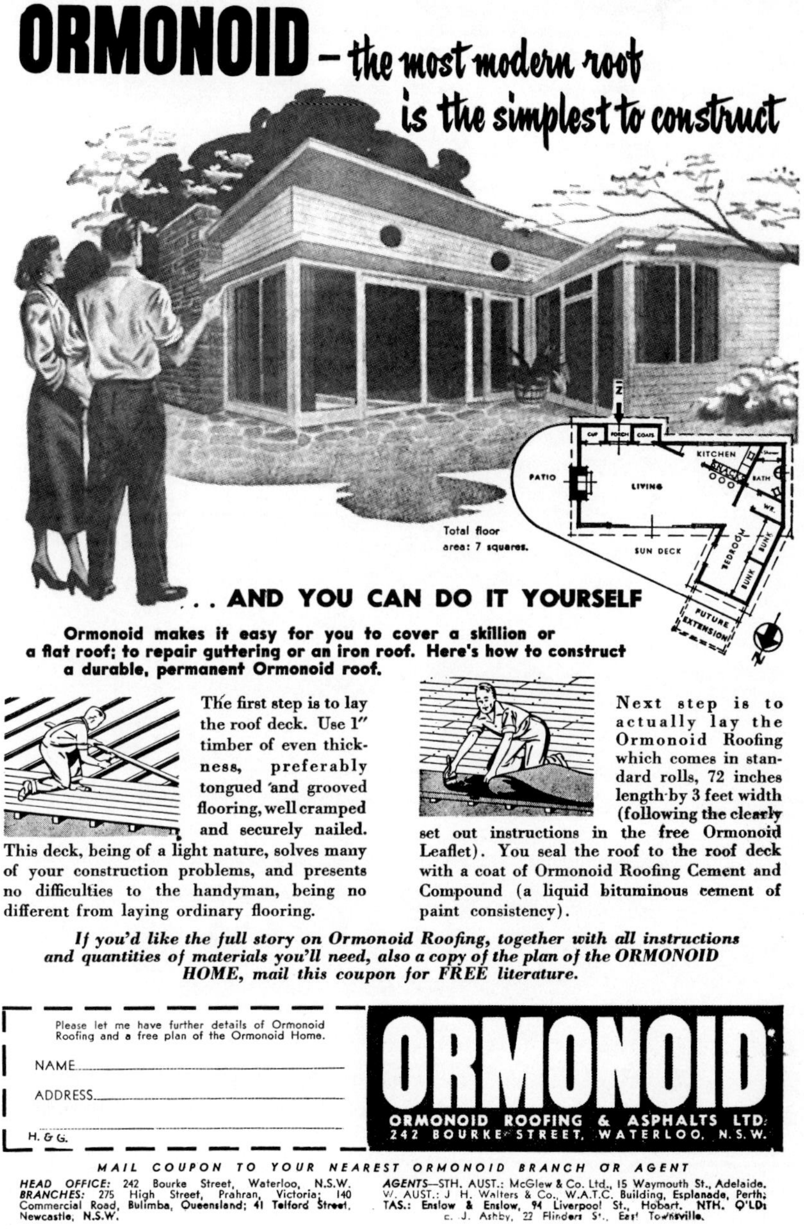

Figure 12 *Advertisement for Ormonoid, 1955*
(Australian House and Garden, *February*)

Figure 13 Louie Laminex escorts the bride around her new domestic workstation, 1952
(Australian House and Garden, *November*)

Figure 14 *The poverty of criticism: 'The Understandascope', Michael Leunig, 1984*

Figure 15 *'If we can stand the conditions, mate, you can stand the ugliness', Bruce Petty, 1966*
(Bruce Petty, The Best of Petty, *Sydney, Horwitz, 1968)*

What are we doing to our homes?

Who are the people who dictate your choice of furnishings? What about telling buyers what you want!

By PEGGY GAYNOR

WHY can't we build well-planned community flats or settlements with community gardens and amenities that have proved a success overseas? Because they apparently couldn't be built quickly enough —— remember it's an emergency!' All right —— let huts serve the emergency but let the people in them see the more permanent housing projects going ahead before their eyes. Let them feel their present quarters won't remain once the better buildings are built. Let the best architects and designers fuse their efforts in housing projects that consider the people as individuals not as animals. How can anyone feel civic pride —— or national pride —— if there is nothing in their immediate surroundings to foster it?

Utility designs invariably produce the best in design because cost demands that basic needs be served first with no allowance for extravagances. Well-planned utility projects could show the people quickly and clearly that good design, good planning, good interiors, aren't a matter of money but commonsense and taste. Demonstration is the best teacher. And we do need teaching.

We don't seem to have a national tendency for home planning or exploiting our natural advantages. Only encouragement of the men who do have this ability and appreciation will bring us even into line with building developments abroad.

What of our own ability to decorate the house, flat, or room we do live in Are we capable of stamping our own personality on it or do we abide by the stock formulae dished out by buyers for furniture stores and by advertisements Do we consider the outside view or the room's aspect or scale Do we consider anything but having what everyone else has and the time-honored safe color schemes we've seen repeated a thousand times Despite articles and magazine pictures, have we learnt anything Presumably. Why can't we bring a fresh approach into our own homes?

Personally, I think it's lack of courage. We can add a different belt or scarf to a dress but we can remove it easily if it doesn't fit in. It is more daring to introduce a new chair, a new color scheme and unless we could have everything home on approval first, much too permanent if we go wrong. ***(Page 54, please)***

Figure 16 'What are we doing to our homes?', 1951
(Australian House and Garden, *June)*

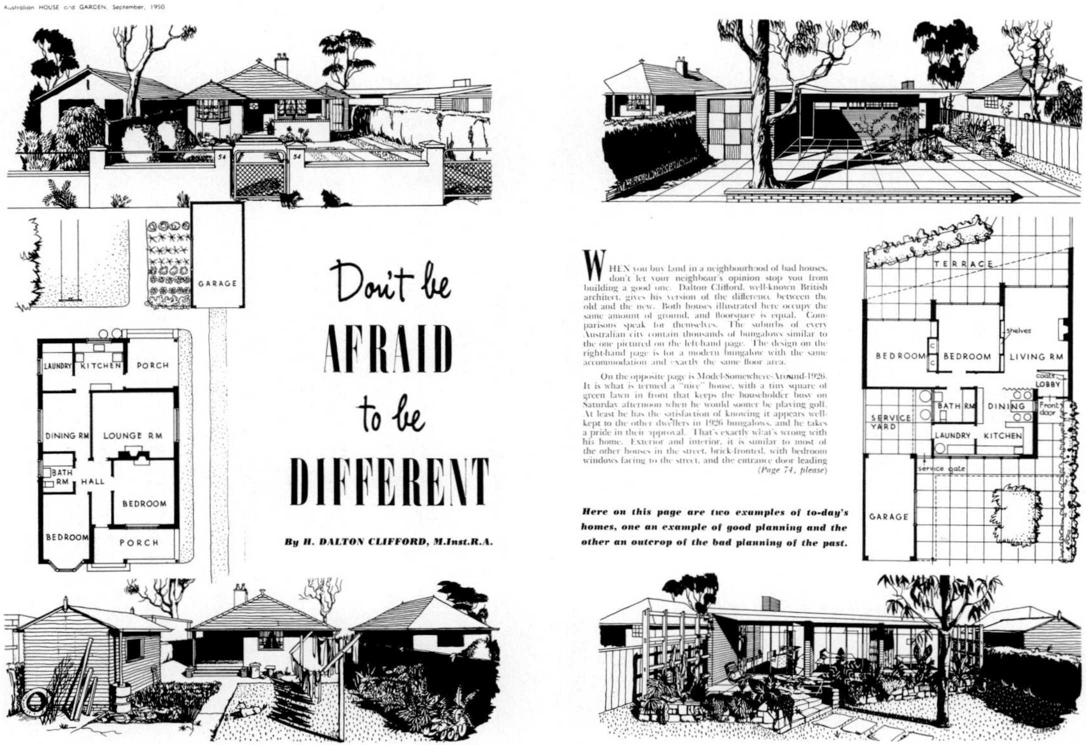

Don't be AFRAID to be DIFFERENT

By H. DALTON CLIFFORD, M.Inst.R.A.

WHEN you buy land in a neighbourhood of bad houses, don't let your neighbour's opinion stop you from building a good one. Dalton Clifford, well-known British architect, gives his version of the difference between the old and the new. Both houses illustrated here occupy the same amount of ground, and floorspace is equal. Comparisons speak for themselves. The suburbs of every Australian city contain thousands of bungalows similar to the one pictured on the left-hand page. The design on the right-hand page is for a modern bungalow with the same accommodation and exactly the same floor area.

On the opposite page is Model-Somewhere-Around-1926. It is what is termed a "nice" house, with a tiny square of green lawn in front that keeps the householder busy on Saturday afternoon when he would sooner be playing golf. At least he has the satisfaction of knowing it appears well-kept to the other dwellers in 1926 bungalows, and he takes a pride in their approval. That's exactly what's wrong with his home. Exterior and interior, it is similar to most of the other houses in the street, brick-fronted, with bedroom windows facing to the street, and the entrance door leading

(Page 74, please)

Here on this page are two examples of to-day's homes, one an example of good planning and the other an outcrop of the bad planning of the past.

Figure 17 'Don't be Afraid to be Different', 1950 (Australian House and Garden, *September*)

Figure 18 *'A house you can really build yourself!'*, 1952
(Australian House and Garden, *January*)

Figure 19 Advertisement for Triton Constructions, 1950
(Australian House and Garden, *January*)

Figure 20 The modernisation of Armstrong Siddeley
(Australian House and Garden, *January 1951, October 1951, March 1952)*

Figure 21 The modernisation of Pyrox Ltd
(Australian House and Garden, *October 1950, September 1955*)

Figure 22 Back to the future: New South Wales Housing Commission retrofit, 1993
(Development Now, *March)*

they should be applied only as a 'fallback measure' in cases of severe exploitation.

Other commentators have stressed the unique circumstances surrounding post-war housing provision as critical to the expansion of owner occupation. For example, Kass (1987) provided a complex multifaceted picture of the growth of the 'great Australian dream' during the 1950s. While the combination of depression, war, urban decay and immigration created a shortage of dwellings, one key difference between this crisis and previous crises was the coincidence of full employment and a consequent rise in demand for housing finance.

However, as Kass maintained, this affluence in itself cannot explain the emerging dominance of owner occupation. A unique combination of other variables had to be present for this to occur. First, rent control forced more and more landlords out of the rental market and their properties became part of the owner occupied stock. In addition, private landlords withdrew from the new private dwellings market. Second, this was a period of historically low interest rates for home loans and the state maintained rates at an artificially low level. Kass's conclusion emphasised the contingency of the growth of owner occupation by stating that although 'a "home of one's own" was by now more a reality, it was much less the result of the "suburban ideal" or of ideological pressure than it was the outcome of this extraordinary coalition of economic and social circumstances'.

Another variable which needs to be added to Kass's coalition of circumstances was the scarcity of building materials and building labour which promoted owner-building. Given the 'privations' and 'self-exploitation' which this form of construction often entails (Pickett 1993), this phenomenon adds further support to the claim that owner occupation was often embarked on as a last resort. Holland (1988, 10) described owner-builders during the years immediately after World War II as 'low to middle income earners building modest houses because there was little choice'.

The argument presented in this chapter suggests that the growth of owner occupation throughout the period was related more to the contingent social and economic conditions than to any universal or innate 'dream' of owner occupation or the promotion of an ideology of owner occupation. Kelly's (1957, 399–400) personal recollections give some indication of the limited options open to many post-war households with 'small capital' or 'a little savings':

> The ballots of the Housing Commission left at every drawing a disappointed majority, and the deposits required by the better-class council settlements, plus the subsequent payments, meant that many people of small capital had no hope. From this class sprang the home builder in the literal sense, the man who decided to turn his own skill and endurance to create his own dwelling. He watched the papers for the cheaper blocks of land, the division of old estates in outer Sydney, the release of areas within the green belt . . . For the most part the ensuing houses were fibro constructions, with here and there one in brick or wood. They were unpretentious, even humble.

Powell (1993, 68–72) also recalled the frenetic building activity in the outer western suburbs of Sydney during the 1950s. Her account highlighted the necessity rather than choice of owner occupation, as well as the sense of community which developed through self-help groups, the hardships many families endured, and ultimately the great sense of achievement:

> Some families lived for many years in their garage or half-house, spending their weekends painstakingly constructing the foundations and putting up the framework themselves, saving enough to get the roof tiles, then to buy the fibro for the exterior walls and the masonite for the interior walls. Then they would move into one room at a time, so the garage would become the kitchen and living quarters and the family or part of it would sleep in the new rooms. For many of the new migrants to Australia, desperate to move out of depressing hostel accommodation and without established networks of friends to support them, this was often the only way. Both husband and wife would work five or six days a week and in their spare time they and their children would build the house.

Part IV will illustrate how architects, designers and home magazines of the 1950s responded to these problems and recognised the financial and materials constraints imposed upon house consumers. Simple flexible owner-builder home plans regularly appeared in magazines guiding the amateur through the various stages of construction.

Finally, another factor often neglected in discussions of owner occupation and its relation to the spread of suburbia is the role of financial institutions. Between 1945 and 1956, the share of institutional funds for housing which went towards the construction of new dwellings increased (Hill 1959, 141). These institutions favoured new construction as it increased housing stock and thereby contributed to the alleviation of the housing shortage. However, this policy narrowed the locational choices open to households and aggravated the problems involved in securing finance for older dwellings. As a consequence, 'many people of moderate means have been forced to build or buy new houses, although a less expensive (and perhaps larger) older house would have suited them better' (Hill 1959, 141). Regardless of housing and locational preference, existing financial arrangements also contributed to push working-class households out towards the edge of the cities.

Precedents

Owner occupation grew at an unprecedented pace in Australia during the 1950s and by the end of the decade the nation had one of the highest rates in the industrialised world (Troy 1991). Social scientists tended to adopt grand theories to explain this, attributing it to the great Australian dream, the Australian character, modernisation, home-centredness, privatisation, the end of ideology and class cleavages, embourgeoisement or alienation. Most of these explanations emphasised the 'draw' or the 'pull' of this form of tenure. A number of subsequent theorists such as Kemeny have emphasised the role of the state in 'pushing' the tenure of owner occupation during the 1950s and the stigmatisation of alternatives.

The evidence presented in this chapter suggests that the state, at most, performed a 'facilitative' rather than 'generative' role in fostering high levels of owner occupation (Berry 1988, 116) and that the metaphor of an 'accelerator' is more appropriate than that of a 'trigger'. This analysis also supports Berry's claim that material rather than ideological forces encouraged the promotion of market solutions to the housing problem (Berry 1988, 121). However, while Berry focused on the structural dynamics of global and local capitalist restructuring during the 1950s, the analysis presented in this chapter makes the options available to housing consumers more intelligible. A whole range of social and economic forces coalesced during the decade to push Australia towards a more monotenural society. These particular forces often are neglected by social scientists engaged in grand theorising about social processes.

Evidence drawn from the nineteenth century suggests that these 'particular' circumstances had precedents. Discussing owner occupation in the nineteenth century, Williams (1984, 169) claimed that with 'constantly fluctuating immigration rates, housing shortages were commonplace and rents were high and as a consequence, ownership was often the only solution available to colonists'. Fry's (1972) analysis of owner occupation in Sydney during the two decades leading up to the boom of the 1880s also provides support for this comparison. Many Australians owned their house because the dwelling—often roughly and cheaply built by the owner—and the land were cheap. During this period of expanding population, housing the nation 'was a great call on Australian resources and much of this demand was to be met by owner occupiers who bought or built houses for themselves'. Other features of this earlier period of housing stress were high rents, high wages and steady employment, all of which 'provided the incentive to get a home of one's own' (Fry 1972, 10).

These features reappeared during the housing crisis of the late 1940s and throughout the 1950s. Mullins (1981b, 38) has also suggested that levels of nineteenth-century owner occupation were linked to the mercantilist form which capitalism assumed in the colony and the urban peasant form of community relationship:

> Australia's mercantile workforce did not typically live in a concentrated way around a single employer. There was a clear physical and social demarcation between work and community, with workers being scattered around the city. This lack of concentration resulted in a relative absence of investment

> in rental accommodation in Australia and workers were required instead to be more reliant upon home ownership. If they could not find rental accommodation, they were forced to buy a house, invariably single family, or to buy land and build a house. It was this forced self reliance upon home ownership which provided the basis for the rise of the urban peasantry.

Although linked to a different form of capitalist development, the post-war period provided a similar set of circumstances and a similar set of solutions, although one key difference between the two eras was that there was no developed system of housing finance leading up to the 1880s.

Examining theories of Australian owner occupation also exposes a range of popular myths surrounding the tenure such as the myth of 'consumer sovereignty'. An argument developed by Checkoway (1986) in his analysis of post-war suburbanisation in the United States can be modified to explain the growth of Australian owner occupation during this period. Consumers were 'important but not decisive actors' since the particular range of choices before them was outside their control. The role of the consumer was to make a 'logical choice among alternatives which were developed elsewhere'. Furthermore, the choices which were made 'is not proof enough that they would have chosen to do so if a different set of alternatives had been available to them' (see also McQueen 1991, 208).

Exposing the real nature of the relationship between affluence and owner occupation is also important. As Collins (1988, 153) observed, the 'myth of the "Lucky Country" has been embellished by confident pronouncements of conservative social scientists that Australia really is affluent, classless, meritocratic and egalitarian'. Chapter 2 demonstrated that this myth allowed the complacent to place blame on the victims—or at least helped them forget about or ignore the plight of those in housing need. If opportunity abounded and one didn't get much, then one deserved what one got!

In order to provide support for the view that the high rates of owner occupation were fuelled by the particular circumstances of the period, Part IV will explore one of the apparent contradictions of the post-war housing environment: why did the 'affluence', 'social mobility' and 'prosperity' which the nation was said to enjoy coincide with architectural and housing standards which were characterised by 'austerity'?

Part IV

Fulfilling the Dream?

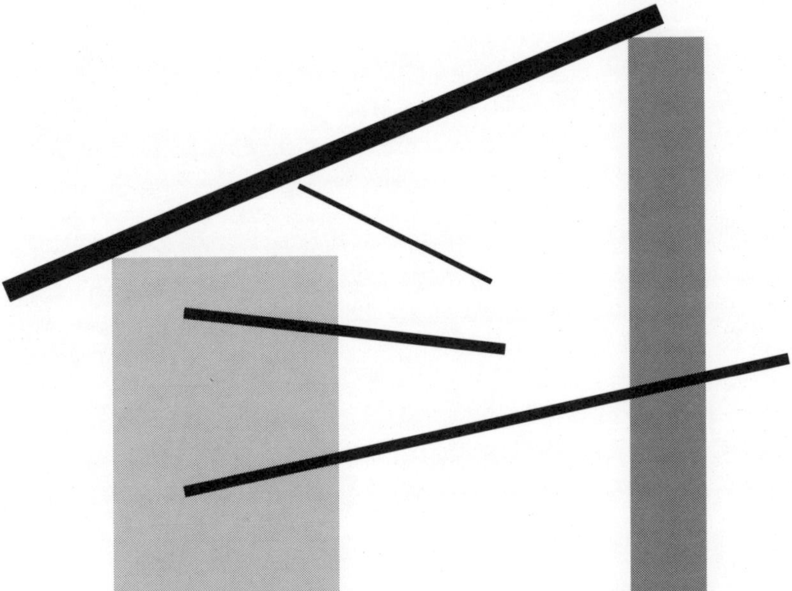

7

Austerity, Modernism and House Design

While Chapter 6 evaluated changing patterns of post-war housing consumption, this chapter explores some important transformations in housing design through returning to some of the themes of production discussed in Chapters 4 and 5. It examines how a design philosophy which had been considered 'dangerously radical' before the war suddenly 'became the norm' (Apperly, Irving & Reynolds 1989, 211). At the same time, the norm fell far short of the modernist utopia.

Inter-war modernism and housing provision

Modernism was not a product of the post-war period and its influence extended well beyond the boundaries of the architectural profession. Reiger's (1986) description of the changing nature of the Australian family and other aspects of everyday life between 1880 and 1940 illustrated the pervasive nature of modernism and its relationship to social change and modernisation in Australia prior to World War II. Architectural developments were influenced by, and helped influence, this process of modernisation. While Reiger's account of the advent of modernism and its impact upon the Australian home operated on a much lower level of abstraction than Mullins' discussion of changing community forms in post-white settlement Australia, it provided graphic domestic instances of many of the dynamic processes which transformed

Australian patterns of urban settlement from a 'urban peasant community' at the turn of the century to a mostly 'suburban community' after 1945. As noted in Chapter 1, these distinct community forms were associated with dominant trends in local capitalist development which was transformed from a mercantile basis between the 1840s and the 1940s to a monopoly capitalist basis post-1940s. Reiger (1986, ch. 2) also examined the link between changing patterns of domestic production and capitalist relations of production.

During the period from 1880 to 1940 a growing separation emerged between the public world of work and the private sphere of home. Associated with this split was the notion of the role of the 'efficient' housewife and 'scientific' methodology. This process of modernisation was fostered by a range of moral and religious reformers as well as a new specialist group of professionals and experts in such fields as housing, town planning, public health, hygiene, domestic economy and the family. These experts were dedicated to the diffusion of scientific methods and home management techniques which emphasised modern values such as efficiency and utility. The imposition of a more strictly defined and specialised division of sexual labour and the transformation of existing patterns of family behaviour were undertaken through 'a common frame of reference' linked to 'technical rationality as the dominant type of social action in modern Western society' (Reiger 1986, 55).

This relationship between the family and experts also began to influence house design during the inter-war years. The architectural profession began to experiment with the design and internal arrangement of the small servantless family home with the 'efficient mother-housekeeper at the helm' (Reiger 1986, 50). With the 'model family' in mind, architects, developers and the health profession emphasised owner occupation over rental accommodation and the small detached suburban bungalow surrounded by its own private garden over flats and multi-storey dwellings. These corresponded with modern conceptions of a healthy lifestyle as well as the environmental determinism of contemporary town planning and housing reform. This was the age of the 'Ideal Home' exhibition, dominated by images of the Californian bungalow.

Increasingly, this search for the ideal home was linked to advice on the management of domestic activities and arrangements (Reiger 1986). On the other hand, during this period many radical intellectuals criticised suburbia and 'villadom' and associated its privatisation, comforts and trappings of affluence with the decline of working-class militancy (Rowse 1978).

This process of modernisation deepened existing Australian patterns of suburbanisation evident in the nineteenth century and extended them to more well-to-do sections of the working class. This phase of suburbanisation was also associated with a process of local economic restructuring and industrialisation linked to the wider process of intensive global capital accumulation and the beginnings of mass consumption (Berry 1984, ch. 3; Connell & Irving 1986; see also Chapter 1). As car ownership became more widespread among wealthier sections of the community, suburban expansion began to extend beyond the ribbons of the railway and tram lines. The car garage became a more familiar feature of the domestic built environment from the 1920s onwards.

The status of modernist experts and professionals within the field of domestic design and architecture was also heightened by the shortage of low-cost housing immediately after World War I. This provoked a search for new, efficient and scientific solutions to the problem of obtaining space and shelter very similar to the post-World War II search described in Chapters 4 and 5.

The modern home of the 1920s featured a number of innovations, including increased window area for more light, small and functional kitchens, less ornamentation, sleep-outs, more room for appliances and less pantry space. Many of these innovations modified the housewife's domestic production duties (Cuffley 1990). Interior design also reflected these changes with the advent of modern functional furniture. The following section will describe how circumstances after World War II accelerated these trends.

Although modernism and the 'international style' only made a superficial imprint upon the Australian built environment prior to World War II (Boyd 1963; Taylor 1986; Howells 1993; Hamann 1981), its impact in the realms of design and innovative materials was important. The appearance of the jazz style or art deco in the 1920s and the plainer more functionalist style of the 1930s made modernism a more familiar option, especially in wealthier suburbs. Simultaneously, modern interior design was making progress in the pages of magazines, and during the 1930s modern domestic architecture also began to receive attention in magazines such as *Australian Home Beautiful* and *Art in Australia* (Cuffley 1990, 42). Among the features favoured by modernist trendsetters were white painted or rendered concrete, steel window frames, steel, glass, flat and low-pitched roofs, corner windows, enhanced light, an outdoor orientation, low horizontal lines and curved streamlined appearances (Cuffley 1990, 140).

Cuffley's description of inter-war modernism in architecture parallels the social changes observed by Reiger (1986, 51). Many of the stylistic trends were made possible by innovations in building materials such as advances on concrete techniques, the growing acceptance of asbestos cement, brick veneering, the growing range of wallboards and plywood, bituminous felt and concrete tiles. The latter offered distinct advantages over the Marseilles tile for those wishing to achieve the modern look, being more weather-tight and therefore more suitable for lower-pitched roofs.

However, these inter-war modern trends failed to represent more than a small proportion of the housing market and the movement only began to gain ground during the mid-1930s (Cuffley 1990, 147) after the collapse of the housebuilding industry during the depression. Its momentum was impeded by World War II and the suspension of housebuilding activity.

Two key distinctions between inter-war and post-World War II modernism were its promotion and its form of consumption. Inter-war modernism was presented as one stylistic option among many and was promoted alongside a range of other options such as Californian and Spanish mission bungalows. The inter-war era has been characterised as period of 'confusion' in style, design and architectural interpretation. According to Stapleton (1985),

> as one house rose up in the suburban landscape, stark and white and a monument to European Modernism, another would be built beside it commemorating the Georgian era, and there was no guarantee that the interior of either would reflect the tone of its exterior. The inter-war years represent a return to the precepts of the Victorian age, when abundant

> stylistic choice, confusion and a naive delight in technology, represented by Functionalism and Modernistic design notions, spread across the whole range of available housing.

The inter-war modern movement was also presented as a more exclusive fashion adopted by the progressive, cosmopolitan, well-to-do with an eye on Europe or the United States. Rybczynski (1987, 198) modified Veblen's (1970) concept of 'conspicuous consumption' among the leisure class and defined modernist design as 'conspicuous austerity'. The most important distinction is between austerity-as-choice and austerity-as-necessity. The latter only began to emerge as an important modernist challenge during the post-war housing shortage.

Post-world war II modernism and housing provision

Modernist design assumed more universal significance after World War II, since the functionalist emphasis in architecture fitted well with the severe housing shortage and building material scarcity discussed in Part II. This economic, demographic, architectural and ideological coincidence lifted modernism beyond the realms of 'mere fashion'. The modern look became associated more with necessity and science. It was also was presented as the perfect accompaniment to 'modern living'.

As Chapter 9 will illustrate, by the early 1950s the term 'modern' had become the operative word in architecture and design. In the advertising profession, the term tended to justify itself and 'everything shiny and new was infallible' (Cuffley 1990, 147). Yet post-war housing experts and professionals understood the term in a colder, more calculated, rational and 'scientific' sense than the advertising profession, which tended to emphasise instead qualities associated with fashion, entertainment and beauty. Housing experts and architects embraced modernism as a functional and expressive part of the structure of modern everyday life. From this perspective, the war represented an irrevocable split from the recent pre-war past and the memories of the depression, *laissez-faire* capitalism and decaying inner cities.

The post-war future was a clean slate to work on, erasing the accumulated decoration and decay of the past. For the modernist architect, this psychological feeling of a new beginning was heightened by the challenges of the building material and labour shortages and the cessation of building during the war (Bunning 1945, 39). Post-war modernist designs, techniques, materials and conceptions of enclosed space were experiments in search of the solution to the housing crisis. The architectural and town planning professions were fortified by the lessons of the 1930s and inspired by the hopes of post-war rebuilding, and they pencilled the contours of the future onto this imaginary clean slate. The more interventionist welfare state and full employment also increased the confidence of the architectural profession and housing experts.

Freeland maintained that the 'houses of the first five years after the war ended were minimal houses in all ways' (Freeland 1972, 271). On closer inspection the term 'minimal' is not as straightforward as it initially appears. The term can suggest either a modernist lack of decoration and pretentiousness or it can suggest quality of the most dubious standard. This can be ascertained by examining housing structure and appearance, and housing size and housing design.

Housing structure and appearance

The materials used for external cladding were the most visible transformation in the appearance of the post-war house. Brick shortages increased the share of asbestos cement and weatherboard in the new dwelling construction market. Also, timber-framed brick veneer construction expanded at the expense of double brick construction. However, the origins of this phenomenon can be traced to the middle to late 1930s. Between 1936 and 1940, timber-framed fibro or weatherboard houses accounted for 25 per cent of all building permits in Sydney and most of these permits were concentrated in the newer western suburbs (Spearritt 1978, 68; for Bankstown see Neutze 1971b, 47). According to the 1933 census, only 2.1 per cent of the total housing stock was clad with fibro-cement. By 1947 this figure had increased to 6.7 per cent and the total proportion of fibro-cement houses in the national stock reached 12.7 per cent by 1954 and climbed to 16.3 per cent in 1961. It reached a peak by the 1966 census at 17.1 per cent before progressively declining in subsequent censuses. According to the ANZ Bank, approximately one out of every four houses between 1945 and 1954 was constructed with fibro-cement outer walls (ANZ 1954, 33–4). The material was especially popular among owner-builders and prefabricating firms (see Chapters 4 and 5). A May 1955 feature in *Australian House and Garden* reported that asbestos cement accounted for more new houses in New South Wales than all other materials combined. Its popularity was due to its cost and its 'tremendous aesthetic possibilities if used with any imagination'.

Weatherboard was also used extensively as external cladding immediately after the war, accounting for 35.9 per cent of new houses in 1950 and 42.5 per cent in 1952. However, while over half (52.1 per cent) of the housing stock had timber cladding at the time of the 1933 census, the proportion progressively declined from 47.2 per cent in 1947 to 44.4 per cent in 1954 and to 41.4 per cent in 1961.

According to figures presented by the ANZ Bank (1954), immediately prior to the war 80 per cent of new dwellings in Sydney were of brick construction. For Australia as a whole, 36.3 per cent of the total housing stock had brick or stone external cladding. However, the post-war shortages of building materials and difficulties involved in attracting labour to the brick industry led to a dramatic decline in brick construction. National figures indicated that 36 per cent of houses constructed in 1950 were brick and this proportion fell to 30.1 per cent in 1952 (ANZ Bank 1954).

However, these figures mask differences between urban and rural areas and the 1954 census revealed that 51.5 per cent of dwellings within urban Australia were of brick construction. The total proportion of the housing stock with brick or stone cladding declined marginally between 1947 and 1961 from 39.4 per cent to 37.3 per cent. Furthermore, most of this change can be attributed to the sharper decline in stone cladding. These figures suggest that shortages of brick made 'timber and fibro the only economic option' (Pickett 1993, 83). As the shortages were overcome and bricks became more affordable, an increasing proportion of new housing featured brick cladding.

Other external features of the post-war dwelling were transformed by the range of new and innovative materials which flooded the market in an attempt to fill the gap created by shortages of traditional materials. As Chapter 5 noted, prefabricated housing became a more acceptable solution for many households.

Information on external cladding tells only part of the story. The shortages of materials stripped the average house to its minimum necessities. Many familiar pre-war decorative features were omitted from the plan. For many consumers, this shift was a result of financial stringency rather than a belief in architectural minimalism. Features such as verandahs, porches, eaves and fireplaces were considered a luxury by most consumers during the darkest years of the housing crisis.

Roofing was another feature which exhibited popular changes influenced by material shortages, material savings as well as minimalism and modernism. For example, the butterfly roof brought substantial savings on drainage pipes as rainwater fell into a single gutter. In addition, because the butterfly roof was hidden from ground level it was possible to cut building costs by using cheaper and aesthetically less desirable materials such as corrugated asbestos cement. Single-slope roofs and other low-pitched roofs were designed to perform the same function (Freeland 1972, 272). One important advantage of the flat roof over the hip or gable roof was that a second storey could be added more easily once building regulations or finance permitted. Another advantage of the flat roof lay in the greater freedom in planning and its provision for more variety in room shape to accommodate aspect and sunlight (see Figure 12).

There was also a close relationship between the availability of building materials, tenure choice and housing form. This relationship was evident in the early post-war decline in flat construction. There had been a boom in flat building during the 1930s, especially in Sydney. Approximately 41 per cent of all new dwellings in Sydney between 1933 and 1941 were flats (Spearritt 1978). As there was no legislation for strata titling until the early 1960s, most flats built during the inter-war period were for rental accommodation. After the war, the cost of building flats increased due to the scarcity of bricks, while rent control legislation further reduced landlords' incentive to invest in new building for rental accommodation. Between 1948 and 1953 flat construction fell to 10 per cent of new dwelling completions across the nation. This was the only intercensal period since World War I when flats failed to increase as a proportion of the total dwelling stock (Neutze 1968; Department of Housing 1968). However, concrete slab technology introduced by the Victorian Housing Commission during World War II formed the basis for innovative techniques which resulted in high-rise housing later in the 1950s (Lewis 1985).

By the time brick shortages were overcome and flat construction recommenced on a large scale during the late 1950s and early 1960s, private speculative builders were tapping a new market created by legislative changes permitting strata titling. According to Freeland (1972, 295), this building phenomenon was also fuelled by 'the general affluence' among young people with 'fat pay packets'. By the end of the 1950s, before strata title legislation, around four-fifths of private flats were rented out (Department of Housing 1968, 15–19). While rental accommodation had become relatively more expensive compared to owner occupation by the end of the 1950s, the return to flat building eased the rental supply problem and made it 'at least a viable alternative to buying a home, a situation which did not exist a decade before' (Bethune 1978, 184).

The small home and house design

House design was also affected by government regulations which restricted house size, and financial institutions further contributed to the decline in house size by imposing conservative ceilings on borrowing levels (Freeland 1972, 268). The small size of houses was another factor influencing architectural style (Pickett 1993, 80):

> Efficient use of space was a necessity at a time when house size was restricted by law (as it was until 1952) and economics. The same factors, plus materials and labour shortages, gave inexpensive materials a new respectability. As space efficiency and construction simplicity could best be achieved

in a Modernist idiom, the marriage of austerity and Modernism was consummated.

Modernism during the 1950s was as much a reflection of necessity as a celebration of the functional. Under conditions where the average house size declined from 1500 square feet to 1000 square feet between 1939 and 1950 (Boyd 1991, 83), greater attention had to be paid to the efficient use of space. In the November 1949 issue of *Australian House and Garden* (*AH&G*), W. Watson Sharpe claimed that the restrictions which the government maintained on house size would ensure that 'the elimination of all but basic essentials must continue to be the main feature of modern home layout'. However, despite the lifting of restrictions in the early 1950s, this theme of space efficiency continued to be repeated endlessly in home magazines. The 1955 *Australian House and Garden Annual* declared that 'This is the day of the Small Home!' The escalating costs of building meant that space—rather than time—was money. As one commentator stated,

> The problem of planning a low-budget home which approaches modern standards of comfort and convenience, is one which confronts all home builders. Faced with ever rising costs and material shortages, the would-be owner must plan as never before to eliminate the last little bit of waste floor space—yet not to the extent of sacrificing a feeling of airiness and space. (*AH&G* March 1951, 44–5)

The language used in home magazines reflected this marriage of modernism and austerity. Another writer stated that 'space is at a premium—houses at a minimum' (*AH&G* October 1951; see also September 1950, 36–7). Keywords included 'economical', 'functional', 'space-saving', 'built-in' and 'unit' furniture, 'informal' and 'crisp geometric lines'. Manufacturers altered their line of products accordingly. For example, during the mid-1950s Palings marketed a Minor piano 'specially designed for the small home'.

The kitchen—traditionally regarded as the woman's or the servants' area—became the focus of experimentation in an effort to reduce space to the minimum and maximise efficient movement. Even in wealthier homes, the absence of domestic help elevated kitchen efficiency to a premium. One commentator noted in the

June 1949 *Australian House and Garden* (37–8) that no other room 'has received more expert attention, produced more theories, been the subject of more advice, than the kitchen' (see Figure 13). Advertisements for houses described the kitchen as a 'factory in miniature' (MacIntyre 1991) and experts described the modern kitchen as 'a lab for the preparation of food' (*AH&G* January 1950, 34). Kitchens were planned with 'great care and thought for their working convenience' using 'scientific ergonomic studies' (Freeland 1972, 269). What they failed to stress was that the kitchen's occupant was expected to perform actions in the space designed for a robot.

Architects tried to create an artificial feeling of spaciousness out of the limited internal floorplans. Glass was more prominent and large windows provided a feeling of openness through bringing the outdoor areas into rooms. Glass also made interior spaces appear larger through 'strengthening the indoor-outdoor relationship' (*AH&G* October 1952, 19). The June 1949 *Australian House and Garden* claimed that 'the accent in modern architecture is leaning more and more towards the provision of outdoor living'. Barbecues began to appear in growing numbers in back yards—or outdoor living areas—during the post-war period (Cuffley 1993; *AH&G* September 1952, 28–9; Fiske, Hodge & Turner 1987, ch. 2). This 'bonding of the house and garden into greater living space' (*AH&G* August 1948, 28) occasionally reflected a trend for the house to become part of the site or part of the natural setting (*AH&G* October 1950, 32–3).

Interior space also became more open-plan. For example, the division between lounge rooms and dining rooms became less pronounced. Most consumers were confronted with the problem of 'making one room fulfil the functions of two' (*AH&G* August 1949, 54–5) and one commentator stated that 'modern rooms are no longer designed for single activities' due to the economics of building (*AH&G* October 1951, 25; see also 'One Room with Two Lives', February 1955, 9). However, these 'dual-purpose rooms' were sometimes regarded as a temporary phenomenon and a common feature in descriptions of 'ideal homes' was the provision for 'additional living space in the future'. By the mid-1950s countervailing trends towards house expansion began to feature more prominently. For example, in April 1955 the *Australian House and Garden* claimed that the idea 'of a family room has become very widespread in recent years'. Although extra space continued to remain a costly feature in new homes, the magazine suggested converting the garage, the verandah or the space under the house in older homes.

Changes in domestic relationships added a third dimension to the ideological/architectural and demographic/economic forces which influenced domestic design after the war. MacIntyre (1991) argued that during this period 'the role of children within the family was promoted to the extent that the suburban family increasingly became a vehicle for attending to the needs and demands of the baby-boom generation'. The 'family room' was one expression of this trend. Post-war architecture also reflected an 'acknowledgment of the housewife' through 'straight lines and corbusian functionalism' which eased domestic duties, compared to 'the fussiness of Edwardian and pre-war architecture'.

Bunning (1945, 45–7) believed that future houses would conserve the strength of the housewife through installing 'modern labour-saving devices' as well as the adaptation of 'scientific' methods which had been used to 'study fatigue problems in war factories'. According to Bunning, women would begin demanding better equipment in the home, after their experience 'in war and behind machines, where they have acquired new skills'. Finally, servantless middle-income women would also begin demanding 'a more scientific approach to house-design'.

Another novelty was the recognition that the kitchen was the 'nerve centre' of the house or the 'family social centre' (*AH&G* June 1952, 18–19) and 'the most important room in the house' where the 'family like to congregate' (*AH&G* December 1954, 22). This was probably more of a revelation to the middle class than the working class. Architects began promoting a merger between kitchen and dining/living room into one multifunctional space. The kitchen was opened to the rest of the house, as *Australian House and Garden* informed its readers in a 1956 article entitled 'Open-planning beats high building costs' (April 1956, 17). In this article Beth Bainbridge commented that kitchen planning had progressed through three phases: from the separate kitchen, living and dining rooms of the pre-war era, through the mid- to late 1940s 'gleaming, highly efficient cooking laboratory' separated from the rest of the house where the housewife spent a minimum of time, to the mid-1950s kitchen which had expanded into a large multifunctional family space for eating, cooking, living and playing.

Bainbridge offered six explanations for this shift in kitchen design: domestic servants had disappeared; the whole family began to discover the kitchen as a result of men's preparedness to do more domestic chores—no evidence was provided!—and children's desire to be closer to their mother; living rooms became less formal and kitchens became less clinical; kitchen appliances became aesthetically more pleasing and manufacturers now were producing 'such appetising tinned, frozen and packaged food' that much of the previous mess had disappeared from the kitchen area; changed social customs, leading to more relaxed informal parties which often spilled into the kitchens; and most importantly, the rise in building costs had reduced most people's housing expectations to little more than the 'minimum house' and in order to retain a sense of spaciousness 'the only possibility was to create one large room from three small rooms'.

Bainbridge acknowledged a contextual setting for this trend, though noting that 'at present' this arrangement was the most appropriate response to 'small home living'. She also was candid about the disadvantages of this design which included noise, odours, lack of privacy, the sight of unavoidable meal clutter and the difficulties involved in the co-ordination and continuity of decoration and colours.

The effect of material shortages was also evident in other design phenomena of the 1950s. The mantelpiece vanished from living rooms leaving bare—often flush—plasterboard walls. This void was often filled with a 'feature wall' which focused attention on a contrast such as a stridently coloured wall, a single brick wall or a large wall hanging. For example, although a 'featured' home in the April 1952 *Australian House and Garden* had no fireplace, 'the fireplace wall has been made a decorative feature around which adaptable unit furniture is grouped in cosy, conversational style'. These features betrayed a hankering after the past rather than a merger between modern living and contemporary design (Freeland 1972, 270).

This emphasis on picking out features was encouraged by paint manufacturers, who took advantage of chemical innovations to expand their range of colours (Boyd 1968, 43–4). According to Freeland (1972, 266–7), this plethora of colours helped disguise the 'cheap materials and rough workmanship' used to construct the post-war dwelling. However, experts were also willing to suggest how colour could solve design problems by heightening ceilings or 'camouflaging' and 'spotlighting' features.

Boyd, on the other hand, turned to 'affluence' to explain this new fetish for strident colour. It was a 'direct cultural expression of easy living' as well as 'a reflection of the money in the modern pocket . . . irrespective of practical and economic influences'. In support of this position, he drew a comparison between the 1950s and the boom of the 1880s when Victorian affluence had been reflected in 'heavier, richer wallpaper and gilded plaster'. Boyd claimed that the Australian fear of starkness had been carried through to whitegoods. Long after manufacturers in Britain and the United States changed from cream to white, separate lines of cream-coloured whitegoods were produced for the Australian market. Boyd labelled this penchant for off-white the 'cream Australia policy' (Boyd 1968, 44).

During the decade after World War II, rising building costs and material shortages provided modernism with room to experiment with innovative design. Its proponents elevated modernism to a science for modern living. As Apperly, Irving and Reynolds (1989, 217) stated, having supplanted 'historicism', it was only in hindsight that modernism—or internationalism—could be viewed as a 'style'. On the other hand, many consumers refused to fully embrace the philosophy and under austere conditions took from it only what they needed. As a consequence, the modernist revolution failed to be as comprehensive and all embracing as many architects and experts had hoped. The different bases of the appeal of modernism will be explored further in Chapters 8 and 9.

Necessity, taste and ideology

There is a bifurcation in the literature on post-war Australian modernism. On the one hand some writers have focused on the circumstances of scarcity and austerity which provided an opening for modernist ideas and made modernism appear 'necessary'. On the other hand, there are those who view 1950s modernism as a 'sham' and who focus on the circumstances of affluence and a buoyant economy which encouraged the nation to gorge itself on rich, heavy, creamy featurism.

Powell's (1993, 72) description of the expansion of Sydney's western suburbs after World War II focused on the former. The owner-builder trend and the reality of cost-cutting 'determined the type and style of housing in general'. In his explanation of post-war modernism, Pickett (1993, 80) also focused on the economics of austerity. In spite of 'a background of affluence', economic and demographic circumstances 'ensured that 1950s houses were notable for their austerity'. Producing houses that were 'austere in size and construction gained Modernism more converts more quickly than generations of architects' and builders' advocacy could have done'. Pickett claimed that modernism corresponded to the needs of the period (1993, 83):

> For the majority of home-buyers, house design had to be adapted to these cheaper materials, and to shrinking house size. It was here that the Modernist emphasis on space efficiency and construction simplicity had most relevance. Without the pressure of building industry austerity, suburban Modernism might have become just another way of decorating the street fronts and interiors of houses, a mere item in the history of style—the 1950s equivalent of pre-war fripperies like Spanish Mission or mock-Tudor.

On the other hand, architectural critics such as Boyd and Freeland emphasised the impact of the forces of affluence in their appraisal of the Australian domestic built environment during the period and the subordination of functionalist design to popular taste. According to Boyd (1968, 465), the modernism which flourished in the early 1950s was a false dawn which failed to enlighten the architectural landscape:

> The forces of [the modernist] revolution that were boiling up in Melbourne before World War II were diverted and dissipated after the apparently easy successes of contemporary

> design against pseudo-historical nonsense in the first decade after the war. Suddenly about 1955 it looked as if the revolution had succeeded and a rational architectural millennium had practically arrived. But really all that had happened was a modernisation of some building techniques combined with the adoption of another decorative period style. Certainly it was a fairly recent period. It was the International Style, barely a quarter of a century old, with Australian fruit dressings. And although the dressings varied it was just as much a superficial, decorative style as Spanish Mission, which was the last one to pass through. It is still the style of the bulk of Australian architecture. This vulgar hybrid won, and the revolution for a 20th Century architecture of integrity was frustrated.

Although less caustic in his appraisal, Freeland (1972, 280–1) was not immune to an elitist critique of the 1950s built environment and stressed the victory of the ersatz over the truly innovative:

> With all this pruning and saving the average standard house of the immediate post-war years was an unlovely thing. It was simple but because it was handled insensitively it was utterly sterile. Because of this the uniformity to which it was reduced resulted in an awful monotony rather than a gracious harmony. Restricted by circumstance from having the individuality in his home which is so important to the average Australian, he resorted to cheaply obtained effects to achieve it. Nobody but the owner was aware of them but to him they were desperately important. The pattern of the roof tiles, the colour of the front door or the weird shape of the letter box were immensely important individual distinctions to the owner but in their eye-assaulting stridency they were minor repellent prickles in a sea of sterility . . . To the spectator, which included many professionals as well as the public, it seemed that all the hectic forms and colour were ruled by nothing other than a desire to be different. In following the fashions, they strove for the novel, the startling, the unusual and different for their own sake. The disturbing confusion that tormented those who were most deeply involved with the struggle to find a new direction became a sort of carnival approach for those who merely followed the trends.

Following Boyd and Freeland, Taylor (1986, 12) has claimed that the 'austerity years' immediately after the war 'were marked by low standards of performance—the outcome of limited funds, materials and skills'. Bolton (1981, 150) also found little to praise: the 'shortage of skilled tradesmen and materials, the consequent "do-it-yourself" movement, the pressure of demand in an inflationary era, the absence of new ideas from a war-torn Europe, all made for mediocrity'. The point is often lost that the issue of mediocrity was irrelevant for thousands of young households escaping overcrowded, overpriced, substandard, accommodation.

This antipathy towards 1950s design can be traced partly to professional and expert disappointment with the discrepancy between modernist theory and what passed as modernism in the Australian built environment. Similarly, as a new generation of experts and professionals bombarded citizens in the 1980s with the message of urban consolidation, it became easier for many contemporaries to forget why the suburban block appeared so attractive and even necessary in the wake of World War II.

The 1950s is often regarded as the decade of uncontrolled urban sprawl (Collins 1993, 10). A more sensitive understanding of the magnitude of the demographic and economic problems the nation faced during the period helps explain why 'consolidation' was never placed high on the urban agenda. To sneer at the 1950s is often to betray a lack of historical imagination—not to mention a spatial and sociological imagination.

The relationship between modernism, modernisation and modernity will be explored in greater detail in the following two chapters. Chapter 8 examines Boyd's critique of the Australian landscape from a professional architectural perspective. The subsequent chapter takes a more popular approach and analyses the dilemmas of housebuilding and homemaking through the medium of a popular home magazine of the 1950s, *Australian House and Garden*.

8

The Good, the Bad and the Ugly: Boyd and the Modernist Expert

Robin Bóyd's critical evaluation of the Australian post-war built environment made him one of the most widely read and cited social commentators of his generation. His influence remains strong in the 1990s. His concepts—derived from the vantage point of the 'International School'—became part of the vernacular. For example, the term 'featurism' 'curled on many lips' as a 'national disease' after the publication of *Australia's Home* (Strahan 1984, 245). In addition, the title of Boyd's 1960 publication, *The Australian Ugliness*, became a cliche often used to characterise and explain Australian culture and attitudes.

Boyd's work contained numerous contradictions and tensions, often cloaked by his ambiguous terminology, and he rarely backed up his claims and arguments with references, preferring to rely on anecdotal evidence. In a review of the first edition of *Australia's Home*, Phillip (1952, 38–41) pointed out that this limited the force of his argument. Despite these failings, Boyd's work is invaluable as a reflection of a modernist perspective on the processes of urban change in Australia during the 1950s.

As Hugh Stretton (1991, vii) has pointed out, throughout his architectural career Boyd's overriding concern was a desire to see Australians 'build good instead of bad, beautiful instead of ugly, sociable instead of separatist habitations'. This immediately poses the problem of defining and measuring the good, the bad and the ugly.

Boyd and featurism

Milo Dunphy (1961) described Boyd's approach as 'a sort of feet on the ground functionalism'. Boyd was a modernist with an almost evangelistic belief in reason and he struggled throughout his life to convert Australians to a modernism suited to local conditions. He tried to disseminate the message of modernism at a time when its trimmings—but not its substance—were gaining ascendancy. In an era notable for its tame commercialised futurism, Boyd's good fight meant a lifetime's devotion to the battle against the evils of 'featurism'.

Featurism can be best understood through its contrast with modernist principles. According to Boyd, the 'modern movement' operated on the basis of five principles which represented an 'inviolate' architectural code of 'integrity and goodness'. A modern building should fulfil the function of the building within itself and within society; respect the nature of materials and structural realities; press technology and methodology into ever higher efficiency; renounce all historic allusions and irrelevant beautification; and give the building strong expression—but of itself, not the architect's ego (Boyd 1968, 464–5; see also 1967b, ch. 2).

The antithesis of modernism was featurism. In *The Australian Ugliness* Boyd (1968, 23–6) described featurism as 'the subordination of the essential whole and the accentuation of selected separate features'. Rather than being the manifestation of a bold idea, featurism was a 'nervous architectural chattering' completely oblivious to its surrounding environment. 'Good' (modernist) design involved creating order—or a 'whole, single, unified concept'—from a range of separate, often conflicting, functional needs in the most economic manner possible; the 'bad' (featurist) 'deliberately and proudly destroys any unified entity' through 'isolating parts, breaking up simple plains, interrupting straight lines, and applying gratuitous extra items wherever he fears the eye may be tempted to rest'. While this sin does not appear as grave in a more eclectic post-modern era, it was unforgivable to the more 'totalising' modernist. As the next chapter will illustrate, during the 1950s inter-war eclecticism became one of the symbols of all that was wrong with Australian design.

The unintended consequence of individual featurism was a suburban landscape in which each competing individual dwelling attempted to surpass its neighbour, aesthetically and materially. As a consequence, suburbia—or 'subtopia'—resembled a busy hustling shopping strip where each individual structure struggled desperately to catch the eye (Boyd 1968, 25). Once more, this characteristic which irritated the modernist Boyd would be later celebrated by post-modernist architects such as Venturi who would claim that 'Main Street is almost all right' (quoted in Jencks 1978, 35). Boyd (1968, 36) labelled this unintended consequence 'the process of uglification'. This result was unavoidable:

> even while the intentions of the early settlers towards the landscape are honourable, every one of them has different intentions. They condemn one another for spoiling the landscape, but in fact none is to blame individually while all are to blame collectively. It is not lack of imagination or sensitivity or originality which causes the spoilation, but an overabundance of these qualities without the co-ordinating discipline of traditional craft technique and, more important of course, without a common artistic aim.

Boyd was describing what some sociologists would later identify as the contradiction between 'individual' rationality and 'collective' rationality (see Boudon 1989, 5–8). One thousand individual attempts at beautification can result in uglification, no matter how aesthetically pleasing individually. These consequences form part of that general category of effects that Giddens (1987, 9) among others has labelled 'perverse consequences'.

Although Boyd painted a vivid picture of uglification and featurism, his analysis fell short on attributing responsibility. He variously blamed the conservatism of the producer, the taste of the consumer, the designer, as well as 'society'. The previous chapter noted Boyd's observation that paint manufacturers took advantage of innovative chemical processes and manufacturing techniques and eagerly promoted a riot of colour schemes which fed the featurist urge. Public and private builders and developers also contributed. The first task of a developer on a subdivision invariably was to clear the site of all natural vegetation, behaviour Boyd labelled 'arborophobia'. The desert-like aspect of the landscape would then be intensified by builders competing with one another 'to reduce the bush to a desert of terracotta relieved only by electric wires and wooden poles' (Boyd 1968, 98). The problem lay in 'the lack of any consistent aesthetic appreciation or digested artistic code permeating the building classes' (Boyd 1968, 126).

Nor did the architectural profession emerge unscathed from Boyd's assessment of the causes of uglification and featurism. The Australian architectural norm was 'enlightened eclecticism' combined with a lack of self-confidence, a trait which Boyd viewed as 'the dominant characteristic of our pragmatic, poor man's affluent society' (Boyd 1967a, 463).

In other passages, Boyd laid the blame for featurism at the feet of the community and popular taste. Builders were simply responding to public demand for featurism. Featurism could only flourish in a maladjusted community which lacked alertness and where people desire 'consciously or unconsciously to display and know not how best to display' (Boyd 1968, 66). Ironically, while featurism was the antithesis of architectural functionalism, Boyd saw featurism as 'functional' in the sociological sense. People wanted featurism because it 'fills a need': its success was 'a symptom of maladjustment in modern society' (Boyd 1968, 128–9).

Popular taste threatened the most enlightened modernist plans. Boyd found the visual effect of the post-war new towns depressing. However, this depression was induced not by the rational schemes of the town planners but by the poor taste of the housing consumer. Examining the South Australian new town of Elizabeth, Boyd (1968, 167–8) claimed that the best intentions of the town planners were being destroyed by an orgy of popular featurism:

> The visual failure of Elizabeth is not the fault of the benevolent State authority or its technicians or professional advisers. It is the choice of the majority, many old Australians and English migrants finding common ground among the cement bunnies . . . look over any low front fence and you are likely to find neatly clipped lawns and tended flower beds and a red cement urn holding a cactus, or a stork with scarlet legs, or a yellow cement bunny, or a gnome with a coat greener than anything else in Elizabeth.

What heightened Boyd's sense of irritation was the Australian public's positive attitude towards featurism. He argued that this desire reflected a national diffidence which he expressed metaphorically as the nation 'wallowing in the kennel of the cultural under-dog' or 'wallowing contentedly in her cultural backwater' (Boyd 1967a, 465; 1968, 89). Boyd (1958) labelled this condition 'austerica', which represented a way of life 'where an austerity version of the American dream overtakes the indigenous culture'.

The purveyors of featurism thus appeared to include almost everyone—manufacturing suppliers, developers, builders, designers and home buyers. As if in despair, Boyd often shook his fist at 'society' as the overarching culprit. This made the possibilities of change appear hopeless. All that could be recommended was awareness-raising on the part of the modernist vanguard dedicated to the aesthetic revolution (Boyd 1968, 146):

> The way to escape from the Featurist mess throughout the whole world of design is not to attempt the impossible task of standardising people's preferences in the atmospheric quality of the environment, by seeking a common denominator in popular tastes in living habits or materials or techniques, or by trying to find an acceptable style to which everyone is prepared to conform. The way out of the mess is not by way of taste, but by way of cultivating the quality of ideas in design. Any object lacking a strong central motivating idea must be lacking intrinsic interest and coherence, and untrained eyes will look immediately for features to add the visual entertainment.

Boyd was ambiguous about the capacity of ordinary people to understand modernism, let alone their ability to modify it to local conditions. On the one hand, members of the public were advised not to rely on their own untrained eyes; on the other hand, they were not to slavishly follow overseas trends; they should follow their own local cultural leaders. The latter could distinguish between the good and the bad. At certain moments Boyd appeared to pull back and recognise the elitism inherent in this argument:

> Here is the difficulty which arises in some form in every study of any art: should we attempt to define it, to tie down what "right" is when we say something looks right—right to whom,

> when, where? or must we leave it free? Or can we do both, define it just sufficiently for comprehension and appreciation on the widest plane but not sufficiently to dampen enjoyment of it on any plane? (Boyd 1968, 192)

However, this recognition of the problem of aesthetic appreciation and cultural reform was intermittent. Ultimately, Boyd—like Leunig's bystander—retreated to a mountain top to stare down and critique the urban chaos, confident in his understanding of the world yet powerless to change it (see Figure 14).

Featurism and housebuilding

Featurism was associated primarily with the housing consumer. However, Boyd also linked the phenomenon to the housing producer. He maintained that in the atomic age the economies of scale and other advantages of mass production had barely touched the housebuilding industry which stuck to traditional forms 'for fear of losing individuality and personality around the family hearthstone' (Boyd 1968, 134–5). In defence of mass production, Boyd contrasted the potential of standardisation and mass production with the monotony and drabness associated with the 'Australian ugliness' (see also Boyd 1953, 30). However, the agency of change was once again reified through the use of subjectless phrases such as 'housebuilding postpones'.

Overgeneralisation was a convenient means of ignoring the roles of a variety of agents of production involved in housing provision and disguised the ultimate sources of featurism and uglification. Everything was blamed for the phenomenon and, in consequence, no remedial solutions or positive direction appeared feasible. This overgeneralisation was illustrated in his 1967 Boyer Lectures where, 'mentioning no names', he stated that 'architects aren't really to blame for the gaudy indiscipline that disgraced new construction'. Neither were 'the builders, nor the estate agents, nor the amateur do-it-yourselfers, nor the Developers—but all of them, all this nation'. It was 'the taste of Australian civilisation' (1967b; 29).

Boyd never lost faith in the modernist vision of prefabrication, despite its failure to fulfil its early post-war promise when some people imagined that 'houses instead of tanks and planes would roll off the factories' production lines' (Boyd 1962, 77). Although he earlier accused the Australian housebuilding industry of being hopelessly out of date, he later argued after a visit to the United States that Australia's technological standards were 'adequate' and that 'our organisation of the building operation is not as appalling as I had imagined in comparison with America's'. Indeed, Boyd applauded the 'broad range of building techniques [Australian builders have] at their fingertips'.

The principal cause of the poor standards of the Australian product was 'the debility and uncertainty, the lack of virility in our design'. In *The Walls Around Us* (1962, 78) he maintained his faith in prefabrication, noting the advances in standardisation of materials rather than whole buildings, and only admitted that 'the thought of houses being made like cars has been *temporarily* abandoned'. Five years later, he predicted that 'the much heralded, much frustrated, prefabricated house will *surely* have arrived *at last* by the year 2000 AD' (1967b, 40; my emphases).

While Boyd's approach to the built environment has been described as elitist, it was an intellectual rather than a class elitism. Pickett (1993, 85) has also accused Boyd of elitism and 'snobbery' in relation to the average suburban builder as well as the post-war housing consumer. He cited Boyd's 1949 claim that the average builder 'tends to do the right things for the wrong reasons. If he had more money it is just possible that his building dreams might take a form somewhat less sensible and austere'. In other words, Boyd considered post-war scarcity as an architectural blessing in disguise which placed featurism beyond the reach of the average housebuyer and homemaker.

Pickett (1993, 87) also castigated Boyd and 'other architectural evangelists' for overestimating their own importance in post-war housing design and stated that 'perhaps in no other area of cultural endeavour are such crude notions of authorship and influence so prevalent'. Most architectural critics have identified the absence of architecturally designed homes as one of the key problems with the design of 1950s houses. As a contemporary example of this professional vanity, Pickett cites Taylor's claim that access to good house design was opened to new housebuyers only during the 1960s when larger project builders began collaborating with architects.

The housing literature has been dominated by this argument that the origins of appealing mass housing only began after the 1950s with the more prominent involvement of the architectural profession, and that the marriage between the architect and the mass project builder helped overcome the drabness and austerity of much 1950s design. For example, in the early 1970s, Walsh (1972, 156–7) claimed that 'a number of the larger builders employ the services of architects and as these builders tend to concentrate in the lower priced housing market, the benefits of architect designed houses are now available to a wider range of home buyers than formerly'.

In 1967, *Australian Home Beautiful* (quoted in Archer 1987, 215) interviewed architects who believed that the proportion of architecturally designed houses would increase with 'rising prosperity' and a 'cultural upsurge'. The article noted with favour the 'commissioning of many architects to design homes for repetition construction by project builders'. There was an assumption that as 'the affluent society' emerged, its taste would improve. The magazine also predicted a process of 'cultural diffusion' whereby the more culturally advanced would lead the more culturally blind: 'These [architects] have improved immensely the quality of project houses and widened the field of choice. The practice has also speeded up the rate at which architects' creative ideas, appearing first in custom-designed homes, are being spread through new houses at all price levels.'

Boyd (1963, 3) also shared the view that architects had enlightened the housing scene, although he claimed that their influence began during the 1950s when 'the more advanced ways of building and the cleaner details which had been developed by the tiny *avant-garde* of the 'forties gradually spread into the everyday practices of commercial designers and "spec" builders'. This judgement may have been influenced by the fact that Boyd was involved in the earliest project home in Australia—'the Peninsula'—built by Contemporary Homes in 1953 (Saunders 1972, 91) as well as his involvement in the Victorian Small Homes Service. Reiger (1991, 42) also commented that these architectural services began to encroach upon the traditional territory of the small local builder and allowed architects to exert more influence upon house design. Nevertheless, the prevalent view remains that the enlightened architectural profession performed a pivotal role in leading house design out of the aesthetic darkness of the 1950s.

Pickett's allegations of snobbery are only partly true. True to form, Boyd's attitude towards the average 1950s housebuilder was full of ambiguity. In *Australia's Home*, he argued that the practical simplicity of the average post-war dwelling had been 'encouraged' by functionalism, even through the motives for this were 'largely economic'. The builders' motives had yet to ascend to modernist heights, and they were 'still antagonistic to the intellectual simplicity of Functionalism', while simplicity was accepted only 'negatively' (Boyd 1991, 84–5, 96).

Yet Boyd (1968, 156–7) also had a grudging respect for the average 1950s suburban dwelling built by the speculative builder. Unhindered by competitors and advertising agents, it was usually 'non-Featurist'. Its characteristics, such as 'its materials, its brick veneer and high tiled roof, may be chosen usually for the stodgiest and most pompous reasons, but when the whole easy-going statement of the conventional Australian villa box with its projected lounge room is made in the lazy Aussie drawl of a brickie and his carpenter mate it has its own rough dignity'. In this passage, the 1950s builder is absolved from the sin of featurism.

More importantly, Boyd had a far more circumspect outlook on the growth of the project building phenomenon and its influence on design. He observed the tendency whereby 'the number of unfussed non-Featurist cottage-villas is diminishing as the small speculative builder-designers begin to succumb to organisation-builders modelled on the American image: their houses often complete with American Colonial details'. Boyd did not believe that the growth of the project builder—or even its alliance with architects—would relieve the Australian ugliness. Indeed, project builders were bypassing the opportunity—or abrogating their responsibility—to introduce genuine prefabricated solutions to the housing problem (Boyd 1968, 134–5):

> The irony is that the prefabrication of the physical matter of the house is not progressing as quickly as was expected largely

> because people objected to the idea of being regimented; yet the same people accept a much more chilling prefabricated thinking which grips the very spirit of the private home. It is not simply that the mass produced designs of many site-built houses are as impersonal as the products of any machine; the paralysis goes deeper than the thousand-fold reproduction of the conventional veneer cottage . . . At the best, architectural quality is often no more than one of a few generally accepted 'treatments'. For the convenience of the workaday designer a little unofficial stock of standard architectural characters has gradually been built up. Each standard is a more or less conscious plagiarism of one of the few spirited leaders of architecture. Select the flavour that suits you best; here is instant architecture. Your home? Simply add water to Frank Lloyd Wright. Your office? Simply add water to Mies van der Rohe.

Housing continued to be punctuated by 'inevitable decadal changes' in style whereby 'in little ways the details keep changing. But the pattern seems to continue as ever' (1991, xvii–xviii). Boyd possessed a degree of respect for the decade of the 1950s. At least there was no sense that the 1960s were any better. Like its predecessors, the 1950s might have been 'an aesthetic calamity', but it was also a 'material triumph' (1991, xviii).

Powell (1993, 24–5) also included Robin Boyd among the post-war 'snob social commentators' who dismissed the 'Australian way of life'. In Powell's account, Boyd's snobbery or elitism is portrayed as a class position. To illustrate this point, Powell pointed to Boyd's condemnation of the working-class 'Villawood Zone' in Sydney's outer west as 'dreary, ill-considered housing growth'.

However, Boyd saved his most vitriolic attack for the more prosperous suburbs. He claimed that the middle-class suburbs further south differed only in their pretentiousness while he reserved his harshest judgement for the wealthy North Shore suburbs which had destroyed the natural environment in a 'wild scramble of outrageous featurism'.

Commenting on the early post-war owner-building boom, Boyd claimed that generally 'these houses were well made and finished' (1991, 84). It would be more correct to identify Boyd's elitism or 'snobbery' as an aesthetic, intellectual and philosophic position than a class position (see Boyd 1967b, 42), although the focus on aesthetics certainly obscured issues of class and poverty (see Figure 15 for a commentary on the 1966 study by the Royal Australian Institute of Architects, entitled *Australian Outrage*: the same criticism could have been levelled at *The Australian Ugliness*). In his Boyer Lectures, Boyd (1967b, 53) ended with an uncharacteristically optimistic note of hope that perhaps the newly formed Arts Council would 'turn the cultural tide'.

Powell also claimed that Freeland was more sensitive than Boyd to the constraints which influenced the production of the built environment during the 1950s. Freeland's description of small homes of the 1950s—'sterile little boxes tinged with an anaemic echo of wrought iron and a carport'—might have captured the atmosphere of post-war scarcity, but it also betrayed a certain disdain. However, Freeland also criticised the 'better class suburbs' for 'revelling in an orgy of extroverted braggadocio'. His attitude towards the post-war housing environment mirrored rather than contrasted with Boyd's position.

It is important to acknowledge that Boyd was rare among his contemporary architectural critics in his interest in houses other than those of the exclusive and the wealthy. While he often questioned the economic efficiency and the aesthetic appeal of the standard small house on a large suburban block, he appeared to accept this as inevitable. Indeed, Rowse (1978) placed Boyd among those post-war writers who began interpreting suburbia in a more favourable light as an 'innocent utopia', and 'an authentic image of the way ordinary Australians lived'. For Boyd, Australia *was* the small house for better or worse, although more bad than good.

While some commentators have overestimated the influence of architects and their ability to overcome what was considered the sterility of the 1950s suburban landscape, it is somewhat unfair to tar Boyd with this brush. His fatalistic pessimism ran far deeper! Although it was possible to understand the problems of post-war urban Australia through modernist lenses, it was far more difficult to intervene effectively. Spearritt (1978, 112) also has claimed that this tension between philosophy and action led to a paralysis of hope: 'No suburb escaped Boyd's waspish eye: his objection to suburbia was largely aesthetic, but he had no feasible proposals for how else the urban population might be housed'.

The non-featurist future

The creation of a 'feasible' alternative eluded Boyd. While he was unable to provide a coherent account of the agents of change, on a number of occasions he provided a glimpse of his utopian 'Australia beautiful'. Naturally, it would be a future in which 'the world at long last would be free of Featurism' (Boyd 1968, 132). It would also be a world free of architects! Like Marx's state in communist society, the architect would wither away as a result of the application of modern technology and the profession would be deprived of its privileged design function: 'The great architectural significance of modern technology is that it marks the beginning of the end of the gentleman's profession of architecture which has served the world with varying success for two centuries' (Boyd 1968, 136). The old architect might be redeployed 'as one member of some large town planning organisation and his old art of space manipulation would be confined to the siting of various standard components' (Boyd 1968, 132).

Thus, the transformation of the architect's function would alter the form assumed by the profession in accordance with the onward march of reason and progress. Boyd (1968, 174–5) dreamt of the bright rational future which other industrial housing proponents envisaged:

> Industry saw its opportunity in the growing public reaction against Featurism and the growing desire for more unity and dignity in the home environment. It turned its resources to producing big sectional parts for buildings. It submitted to regimentation to the extent of recognising and adopting standard sizes. This was the big breakthrough for reason. Suddenly everything fitted together: all manufacturers' wall panels, floor and roof sections, baths, air-conditioning packages, stoves, sinks, were interrelated and interlocking. Each buyer was able to make his choice of structural units and the new

unobtrusive appliances and to arrange these, jigsaw-fashion during evenings of togetherness, into a plan suited to his family living pattern of the moment. Next year he might change the arrangement, buying a few more wall panels or an extra bathroom package.

Boyd suggested that this vision was within reach. The initial step—'the planned community with an easy acceptance of nature, mutual respect, and a common artistic aim'—had passed beyond the stage of conception, while the second step—'the sectionalised houses mass-produced at a fraction of today's costs while providing infinitely more amenities'—was also close at hand. All that was required was the final attitudinal step which could be undertaken 'pending a hint to industry that the public is ready to live in logical, realistic, honest-to-goodness shelter' (Boyd 1968, 174–5). However, the gap between the idea and the reality—or the conception and the creation—remained unbridged.

It is this idealism of the vision combined with the reality of the surrounding environment which helps explain much of Boyd's growing frustration over time. He was a disappointed rationalist. This disappointment was made more acute by his reflections that perhaps the rationalist heaven had been within reach immediately after the war when the progressive Melbourne architectural community had stormed the bastions of featurism. Boyd's nostalgia for this period between 1945 and 1955 was evident in his recollections of the period (1967a, 457–9):

For nearly ten years afterwards, until the mid-1950s, the architectural atmosphere was charged with a passion for adventures hardly less fervent than that of the Utopians of Germany—after another war and on another side. What a feeling of fight and challenge spread through Melbourne's little architectural world at the time! . . . It was the European revolution happening all over again, a generation later. What sensations, what excitement, what inexperience . . . Whatever happened to that promise?

Answering his own question, he believed that the essential components of the school—'a great structural-functional ideal carried out with an enforced austerity and a voluntary cavalier technique'—had collapsed under the weight 'of two or three new annual layers of graduates freed from the anxieties and stimulations of the post-war period'. This marriage of convenience between modernism and austerity had been destroyed by affluence. Boyd must have agreed with Galbraith's (1970, 212) sentiment that an 'austere community is free from temptation'. The austerity of the average post-war house appealed to Boyd because 'there was nothing that could have offended the cultivated tastes of the time on grounds of overexaggeration or over-adornment' (Boyd 1991, 84). The main fault with the post-war austerity house lay in the 'clumsiness and ineptitude' of its design. However, as scarcity disappeared affluence made the temptation of featurism irresistible. Freed from economic constraint, the builder would revert to 'sly little means of "relieving the plainness"' (Boyd 1991, 85).

Boyd did not believe that the post-war modernist experiment was 'a fizzle', and that the dogma of functionalism had been proved a 'false god' with 'disappointing results' (Hamann 1981, 137). According to Boyd, Australia was still waiting for the revolution, and his faith in functionalism remained 'absolute and undeviating' (Boyd 1967b, 31). The way forward was to revive the idealism of the post-war Melbourne school, to reject the impoverished offering of much that passed for architecture and to 'show some determination to build a more real and consistent architecture based on that shelved morality which we know to be valid'. This would be the victory for reason and architectural integrity (Boyd 1967b, 18). He also refused to be deflected by the new generation of historicists, including Philip Johnson—who later built the post-modern monumentalist AT&T building in New York. Boyd (1963, 6) captured the tension between modernism and post-modernism through describing Johnson's vision as 'a fine eclectic philosophy for a sophisticated New Yorker, but it reads like a broken signpost at the end of a long road which we once thought would lead to a vital, realistic architecture of this century'.

However, the key target of Boyd's bitterness was popular conservatism and this feeling increased in intensity over time. Hamann (1981, 134) has pointed out that Boyd's most optimistic work was *Victorian Modernism* (1947)—all his subsequent work contained a more 'jaundiced' view of the Australian public's openness to good design. The years before his death in 1971 were surrounded with an 'aura of despair' (Hamann 1981, 139).

In the 1967 Boyer Lectures he drew a picture of an Australian society divided into two uneven sections, with 'the great mass' of 'satisfied materialists' on one side and 'restless creators' on the other. The dominant section contained 'the modern Australian who believes in the long-established, still popular, anti-intellectual Australian values, who is convinced that the Australian state and rate of progress are satisfactory'. The minority, including Boyd, contained 'the modern Australian who sees so many shortcomings in Australian social development that he is on the point of despair' (Boyd 1967b, 3, 7, 27). This ambivalent 'love-impatience' (1967b, 8) was also evident in his scathing social critique *The Great, Great Australian Dream* (see also Bolton 1993). The 'gentle irony' and 'aloof benediction' towards suburbia which Rowse (1978) associated with Boyd was replaced gradually over the years and his work took on a harder, more cynical edge.

Boyd's critique of the built environment during and after the 1950s reflected the hopes and disappointments of the modernist expert. Nothing, except the philosophy of modernism, was sacrosanct to him. Neither producer nor consumer, the past nor present, speculative builder nor project builder, wealthy nor poor, writer nor subject could escape his criticism. This was his major strength as well as his major weakness. It gave his writing a sharp edge while at the same time endowing his critique with a static quality. It was impossible to identify either the source of the problem or any agent of transformation. Deliberately ambiguous terminology often covered his own misgivings or uncertainties. This characteristic also applied to his overall attitude towards housing in the 1950s, which acknowledged a grudging admiration for the post-war 'achievement' as much as disdain for its execution.

The Australian Ugliness bore a strong intellectual resemblance to another commentary on post-war Australia, Donald Horne's *The Lucky Country*, first published in 1964, four years after Boyd's book. Indeed, it was almost as if Horne took Boyd's architectural criticism and applied it on a broader canvas to the whole of Australian culture. *The Australian Ugliness* was cited and quoted twice in *The Lucky Country* in support of Horne's own views. The two books complemented each other. Both were products of the post-war boom, and both writers exhibited a similar intellectual elitism, although Horne was more sympathetic to suburbia (Clarke 1970, 78–9). In both works, the 'masses' appeared impenetrable to ideas, oblivious to the potential for cultural change and content to wallow in mediocrity. Boyd showed how the masses brightened what Horne (1966, 24) described as the 'sheer dullness of life'.

On the other hand, both writers aimed their sharpest barbs at the economic elite and the wealthy. Horne echoed Boyd's description of suburban class differences in asserting that the 'upper levels of society' revealed 'mindlessness triumphant' and that to a 'sophisticated observer' life at the top appeared 'depraved, a victory for the anti-mind'. However, Horne recognised the shortcomings involved in his grand sweeping statements more than Boyd did. Horne acknowledged that the lenses through which he viewed the world—his 'understandascope', as Leunig would have called it—could not provide universal vision and that the scenario could be transformed through alternative lenses. In addition, societies, 'like people, are always in a state of ambivalence, even in prevailing behaviour and attitudes: everyone of us holds beliefs and attitudes that contradict each other; our behaviour, in turn, often contradicts our beliefs—and itself. People change their "natures" from one situation to the next'. Horne acknowledged that these contradictions were reflected in his own work.

This honesty was less apparent in Boyd's work, where the reader was left to contend with a critical assault on everything, which ultimately affected the sharpness of the total picture. While he endorsed 'revolutionary scepticism' in architecture (Boyd 1963, 4), his writing possessed more of the noun than the adjective.

Boyd's evaluation of featurism was unidimensional. This criticism has also been made by Fiske, Hodge and Turner (1987, 45), who suggested a deeper reading of the 'features' which frustrated Boyd's search for the underlying order within a structure. They suggested that, perhaps 'the "features" typically express a critique of dominant structures and dominant meanings, and that what is wrong, if anything, is only that this critique is typically partial, fragmentary and unconvinced'. As a consequence, perhaps the static approach to the good, the bad, the ugly and the beautiful was the problem. Fiske, Hodge and Turner hypothesised that perhaps the features didn't 'go far enough in suggesting alternative social structures'. Rather than demanding a return to simplicity and austerity as well as embracing functionalism, a more radical architecture 'might try to create a house out of the meanings carried by the features—the critiques, the compensatory ideologies that exist to oppose the dominant ideology'.

During the 1950s, Boyd and other modernist architects were not alone in their evangelical promotion of modernism. Popular home magazines also were engaged in a struggle to turn the modernist idea into a modern reality. The following chapter reviews the decade through the lens of the *Australian House and Garden* magazine.

9

Learning to be Modern: Magazines and Modernity

According to the dominant school of thought within Western sociology during the 1950s, popular magazines performed an important function in maintaining social cohesion and socialising people into their class roles, and advertising was part of such socialisation. This perspective complemented the then fashionable explanations of 'affluence' and 'embourgeoisement' discussed in Chapter 6. According to Barber (1957, 296–7):

> The advertisements presented in the mass media have a share in their class socialising functions. The facts and attitudes conveyed by the advertisements provide people with part of what they need to know if they seek to symbolise their social class position, or to maintain or advance it . . . In a great many other areas of behaviour, advertisements serve to inform people about patterns of consumption that are required in their social class position. For example, people rising into and within the middle classes find the advertisements and articles about home decoration in magazines like *House Beautiful* or *Better Homes and Gardens* or in newspapers like the *New York Times* very useful . . . advertising, along with the other content of the mass media, has an important role in socialising Americans in the ideas, norms, and emotions required for an open-class kind of society and for their class positions within it.

Over the past two decades, numerous Australian analyses have adopted a more critical approach to the functions of popular post-war magazines. Bonney and Wilson's (1983; ch. 7) analysis of the *Australian Women's Weekly* examined how femininity was subject to modification by historically specific circumstances such as war, post-war consumerism and suburban growth. They also noted that the magazine 'exemplifies the 1950s ideology of democratisation through "levelling up", middle class and working class women being enjoined to imitate ruling class manners' (Bonney & Wilson 1983, 240).

More recently, Blackburn's (1992) analysis of the advertising industry noted the important role performed by home magazines during the period of post-war consumerism (see Chapter 1). The advertising industry propagated a 'new ideology of consumption' or a 'consumers' ethic' which was used by mass manufacturers to educate young families into the lifestyle of mass consumption and post-war prosperity.

According to Blackburn, popular magazines were willing promoters of this message. He identified the *Australian Woman's Weekly* and *Home Beautiful* as 'major agents of the consumer faith'. The latter magazine 'developed a format in which most of its articles and all of its advertisements were directed to the promotion of products that embellished the home'. The message carried throughout the magazine was that a successful marriage was based on the purchase of a range of new consumer durables. Advertising and feature articles became less distinguishable 'as large amounts of advertising money and improved techniques meant that advertisements could be more frequently integrated into the text'.

Blackburn, Bonney and Wilson each see the function of popular magazines as being tightly bound to the logic of post-war capital accumulation and mass consumerism, and link it to the promotion of specific forms of patriarchy, femininity and consumption. However, they did not discuss in any detail the forms in which housing was consumed, despite acknowledging the importance of the 'suburban container'.

In contrast, Cuffley (1990, 38) has conducted extensive surveys of *Australian Home Beautiful* in his analyses of Australian housing between 1920 and 1960 and has noted that although 'we might miss some of the nuances of ordinary day-to-day life in the selective and often glamorised view presented in the popular magazines, they are an invaluable source of information to the social historian'. However, Cuffley's reading of home magazines tended to be descriptive and largely uncritical; he described the 'manifest' functions of home magazines, while ignoring the 'latent' functions uncovered by critics such as Blackburn, Bonney and Wilson. On the other hand, the latter analyses were unable to express in any detail the manifest form in which home magazines promoted the post-war product; therefore the relationship between architecture and capitalist modernisation remained obscure.

Home magazines, heavily dependent on advertising, were obviously promoting forms of mass consumption and capital accumulation. It would be surprising if they acted otherwise. However, they were also promoting ideas about everyday life which had a certain autonomy from the structural dynamics of capitalist expansion. The texts in home magazines can be seen as an intricate fabric which interwove the threads of capitalist modernisation, patriarchy, modernist design and the experience and mood of post-war modernity. Pulling out and examining an individual thread is far less useful and rewarding than the making sense of the whole pattern. Post-war modernism and capitalist modernisation should be considered as both autonomous and intricately interrelated structures and ideologies.

During the early post-war period, Australian home magazines performed a number of manifest functions, high among their priorities being the dissemination of housebuilding information and the interpretation of the latest trends and designs. However, they also performed a didactic role through introducing Australians to modernist concepts and ideas on design. Although it is possible to read a latent promotion of an ideology of 'classlessness' or 'middle classing', the promotion of modernism was a much more salient aspect of the magazine. Furthermore, from the late 1940s until the mid-1950s modernism was associated most directly with the 'small' or 'minimum' home and this modest dwelling was promoted extensively. This 'socialising' role represented particular artistic and aesthetic values as much as class mobility and reflected universal conditions of material restrictions and government building controls.

After the war, the media, retailers and professional groups took advantage of the public's hunger for adequate shelter by involving themselves closely in housing provision. In Victoria, the Royal Victorian Institute of Architects and the *Age* sponsored the Small Homes Service Victoria. From its shopfront in the State Electricity Building in Flinders Street, Melbourne, the Service provided architectural advice to prospective housebuilders for a small fee. In the early 1950s, the New South Wales chapter of the Royal Australian Institute of Architects in association with *Australian Home Beautiful* opened a similar service called the Small Homes Service (NSW). Stock house plans could be viewed and obtained for a small fee from the venture's shopfront in David Jones' George Street store in Sydney. The *Australian Women's Weekly* also established its own Home Plan Service in conjunction with a Melbourne architectural firm, Borland and Trewenack, with shopfronts throughout eastern Australia including McWhirter in Brisbane, Anthony Hordern in Sydney, Myer in Melbourne and Geelong, Fitzgerald in Hobart and Piggott in Toowoomba (*Architecture in Australia* June 1962).

Other magazines frequently provided plans and advice to prospective owner-builders and homemakers. This chapter is based on an analysis of one such magazine, *Australian House and Garden*, between 1948 and 1961. This particular journal was selected for a number of reasons. First, as it was established in 1948 it was a product of the post-war world. Its best-known competitor in this market, *Australian Home Beautiful*, was well established prior to the war. Another popular home magazine, the *Australian Women's Weekly*, covered many other matters as well as housebuilding, design and decoration. Other magazines established during the post-war period failed to survive past the 1950s—*Australian Homemaker*, for example, was incorporated into *Australian House and Garden*. Furthermore, these magazines were more accessible to the general public than specialist journals such as *Architecture in Australia*. *Australian House and Garden* best reflected the post-war environment and has the added advantage of surviving in an unbroken series throughout the period under scrutiny. In addition, its ownership structure and editorial board remained unaltered throughout the period.

Australian House and Garden was first published in December 1948 by K. G. Murray. The magazine's first editor was Beryl Guertner, and the board of associate editors consisted of

W. Watson Sharpe, Laurence Le Guay, John Nisbett and Edmund Dyker. Murray had earlier tested the home magazine market through publishing a number of Watson Sharpe's booklets on post-war housing. The venture marked a shift upmarket for the publisher, who had launched *Man* in December 1936. *Man* was devoted to smutty jokes, nude photographs and Australasiana, although it also featured foreign affairs commentary and a 'sociology department'—which was more than could be said for any Australian university at the time (Greenop 1947; Lindesay 1983; Zubrzycki 1970).

According to Lindesay (1983, 139), Murray encouraged 'lowly paid amateur writers', although another observer closer to Murray did point out that unlike many other Australian publications of the era it *did* pay its writers and artists (Greenop 1947, 259). By the end of the war Murray had established a chain of magazines including *Man Junior*, the short-lived *Insider*, *Cavalcade*, *Digest of Digests*, and the wartime publications *South West Pacific*, *Army* and *Action*. Searching for unexplored post-war avenues, the Murray organisation released *Adam* in 1946 before entering the home journal arena in 1948 with *Australian House and Garden*.

The magazine attracted contributions from an impressive range of experts. Some contributors—such as Frank S. Greenop, the editor-in-chief of a string of Murray publications—wrote for *Man* as well as *Australian House and Garden*, but the new magazine also featured articles from renowned architects such as Robin Boyd and landscape gardeners such as Edna Walling. Although it was peppered with tame family-centred jokes, the overall tone of the texts was serious. During the early years this tone verged on the educational.

Reading post-war design

During its formative period (1948–52) *Australian House and Garden* passionately propounded the superiority of a modernist design philosophy, with advice on house design and rather heavy-handed didactic efforts to purge Australian homemakers of their 'stuffy' conservatism.

Appropriately, Robin Boyd wrote an article in an early issue (July 1949) publicising the Victorian Small Homes Service. He took a characteristic swipe at 'our house' which was 'in a rut' due to the fact that most examples had been 'designed by amateurs'. Boyd boasted that this era was passing and that the Small Homes Service was penetrating and colonising the outer suburbs which had previously been almost the 'exclusive domain of the designer-builder' rather than the architect. Boyd's claim helps explain the discrepancy between himself and other architectural historians concerning the origins of the influence of architects in the suburbs.

The architect Eva Buhrich (September 1952), relentlessly played the Boyd theme, declaring that Australian suburban houses were 'aesthetically, unsatisfactory' and lacking in unity. She also defended the much maligned processes of prefabrication and contrasted the industrialised vision with the monotonous reality of pre-war hand-built suburbia. In a regimented manner, the pre-war bungalows stood side by side 'a dutiful six feet apart, not far enough to allow for any privacy, not close enough to form any sort of unit, but loudly proclaiming their differences which are for the most part quite superficial, [claiming] an individuality which they cannot hope to possess'.

According to Buhrich, tomorrow's home would emphasise the virtues of simplicity and restraint including features such as simple roofs, simple floor plans, expanses of solid wall and large glass window walls. These features were more than the latest 'aesthetic whim'. They corresponded with the needs of modern living and there were technical developments capable of meeting these needs. Buhrich also questioned the building industry's ability to embrace the spirit as distinct from the content of modernism. For example, 'the thoughtless application of corner windows that permit a view into the neighbour's bathroom, of large openings that have to be permanently screened, of glass bricks and circular windows are only a fashion introduced for sales appeal by the speculative builder'. Boyd's later reflections that modernism became another fashion were clearly a possibility foreseen by writers such as Buhrich during the early post-war days.

Other more elitist articles admonished the public—or the reader—rather than the building industry. Peggy Gaynor (June

1951) used the second person and the first-person plural in order to add dramatic force to her argument that the time had finally arrived for her readers to reconsider their conservative attitudes towards house and interior design (see Figure 16). All the evidence suggested that the majority of Australians failed to appreciate good design: 'We don't seem to have a national tendency for home planning or exploiting our natural advantages. Only encouragement of the men who do have this ability and appreciation will bring us even into line with building developments abroad'. There was an sense of impatience at Australia's failure to embrace this revolution from above and outside. The readership had failed to take advantage of the advice presented by experts: 'Despite articles and magazine pictures, have we learnt anything? . . . Why can't we bring a fresh approach into our own homes? . . . Personally, I think it's a lack of courage'.

The attack then began to get personal: 'The other things you've read about dozens of times in this magazine or similar ones, aspect, furniture scale and arrangements aren't eyewash—they are worth considering if you want attractive rooms'. Readers were then invited to peek through the cream-coloured lace curtain net into the average Australian sitting room: it contained a round coffee table in front of the couch, a standard lamp, wedding silver perched on top of a china cabinet, the wedding clock in the middle of the mantelpiece with a glass vase at one end and a bevelled glass mirror above, chenille or velvet curtains with a cream-coloured net in between. The colour scheme was green or rust, blue and gold or fawn and brown. The scene became more cluttered as further ornamentation, children and money were accumulated. 'Do you recognise your room anywhere there?' asked Gaynor. 'If you do we don't condemn you for it. But don't you think it amazing that we can picture your room without knowing you, your interests, your likes and dislikes? . . . If our homes are dull and uninteresting—awful thought! we might be too'. She continued to admonish the reader:

> these have been harsh words—but they could be harsher. If they get you het up, then protest back. It will show that some of us, have been stirred out of the lethargy that is a killer of home planning progress. We have our feet planted in a new

> half-century. Are we as advanced in home planning? America, England, Europe have all made honest national attempts to build round the people's needs. But in Australia? No, we haven't.

A stuffy Edwardian or Victorian straw man had been assembled and subsequently demolished by the confident polished glass and steel man of modernism. In addition, this direct attack on the taste of the consumer also delivered a glancing blow at Australian furniture manufacturers and retailers who—with a few exceptions such as Namco, Kalmar and Snelling—remained tied to pre-war fashion concepts. However, a magazine which relied on advertising revenue from these sources could hardly mount a direct attack on *their* taste!

Other articles during this period took a softer approach to the alleged conservatism of the reader. In an article entitled 'Have it modern—your way' (March 1952), Frank Greenop discussed the failure of retailers to stock adequate supplies of modern furniture. Once again, the blame lay at the feet of the public: 'If Australian tastes are conservative, or old-fashioned, or timid, or lacking in art and imagination, it is ultimately not because the store buyer has refused to take a risk, but because the purchaser has been too easily satisfied'.

Adopting Gaynor's tactic of launching a personal assault on the aesthetic senses, he asked: 'Have you ever seriously asked yourself if you are conservative?' Too many people simply assumed that they were modern without looking for any evidence. For example, too many people were simply puzzled when confronted by new design and were unsure whether it was good or bad: 'Now that is no way to get along and keep pace with modernity'. Greenop then explained some of the rules of modernity. The first rule demanded 'complete harmony between furniture and furnishings and room decoration, so that the finished room is a neat, harmonious whole'. A 'good modern room' necessarily required some knowledge of 'modern things' and this explained the popularity of interior decorators and designers in the post-war period. The second rule was to shop around. This rule was especially important in the current building climate where a house could take up to a year to build.

As the house reached completion stage, people had a tendency to be impatient and buy anything as long as they could move in. The best method was to look at all stores and make a catalogue of available items with the help of experts. However this 'doesn't mean that you are going to take whatever is dictated to you as modern whether you like it or not: but it does mean that you are going to buy what you like with the expert's guidance, and consequently you will be pleased and assured in what you do'. The third rule also involved guidance and professional advice through bringing in a designer or an architect 'so you know before you buy just what the finished result will be'.

In an earlier article (November 1951), Greenop had also claimed that simplicity (of glass, steel frames, polished wood and simple colours) 'makes the modern home'—despite the fact that this simplicity appeared to require the assistance of an awful lot of experts!

This promotion of the experts—interior designers, architects, designers—was a recurrent theme during the early years of the magazine. The author of 'Better Living in a Well Planned House' (June 1950) believed that most 'modern homemakers' were caught in a conflict with their own feelings. In contrast with modernist rationality, feelings were 'born of sentiment and prejudice'. These articles reveal another struggle between the ideas of the public and the ideas of the magazine experts. Readers were also offered compromises: 'No one would say you aren't entitled to charm and a house you may be proud of' but the plan had to take priority over the appearance.

An open mind was advised because the old pre-war solutions to housing were no longer appropriate under post-war conditions and it fell upon the shoulders of the architect to discover new solutions. The consumer was advised to remain calm and retain confidence in the expert, because the solution 'may involve materials, appearance, and room arrangement somewhat unfamiliar to you. Only if you keep an open mind towards the process, can your architect do the best for you'.

Another early article (August-September 1949), this time unsigned, was entitled 'Be Kind To Your Architect'. This advice on the crucial role of the specialist expert brought in to control the consumer's irrational and sentimental instincts, was an extension of the process of modernism Reiger (1986, 51–2) described. The question was 'What is to be done?' The answer was—ask the expert!

Most writers were aware that their readership remained somewhat wary of modernism. P. Hull (October 1949) attempted to allay these fears of the unknown by pointing to the historical precedents of 'functionalism and simplicity' in Australian history. The early pioneers 'were knocking up functional furniture from local timber that was the last word in simplicity'. However, this was usually a stopgap until money and availability allowed them to live in a more familiar comfort reminiscent of England. Thankfully, fashion had burst out of the 'Victorian clutter' and the world of design had reverted to the catchcries of the pioneering days. Hull's article was aimed at overcoming readers' wariness of modern design and its pre-war revolutionary connotations:

> 'Modern' became the starkly interesting word of the 1920's synonomous [*sic*] with bare walls, geometric lines and little comfort. During the 1930's the tubular steel chairs and futuristic furniture twisted themselves into shapes designed to fit the body,—revolutionary designs as well fitting but as uninspiring as surgical corsets. But after this 'modern adolescence' designers have evolved a maturity in furniture design that combines all the simplicity they strove for in the 20's with a beauty of style and line that was lacking then.

After the 'shock of the new' it was now safe to purchase these new 'domesticated' and 'unthreatening' modern products (see White 1993). In true Hegelian style, Hull believed that modernism would transcend the spirit of fashion. Proclaiming 'the end of furnishing history', he reassured his readers that if 'our modern outlook remains uncluttered and simple' then the cycle of fashion would grind to a halt. 'Furniture', he stated, 'is as indicative of a nation's moods and moments as the history that the nation makes'. Cuffley also noted that functionalist architects during the 1950s announced the 'end of architecture' and were 'convinced that stylism was dead and that future generations would recognise their wisdom in this matter' (Cuffley 1993, 112).

H. Dalton Clifford also adopted the technique of historical comparison in order to contrast pre-war conservatism with the modern outlook. In 'Don't be afraid to be different' (September 1950) Clifford attacked popular conceptions of house design and planning. His technique of 'constructive destruction' involved setting up a design stereotype popular with the previous generation and mercilessly pointing out its flaws in contrast to contemporary design. The new beginning and modernity were regularly emphasised through holding up the tastes of one's aunt or grandmother for ridicule (see Figure 17).

The object Clifford chose to highlight bad taste was the 'Californian bungalow' or the 'Model-Somewhere-Around-1926'. It was described as a 'nice' house, with a small square of well-kept lawn. It resembled other houses along the street, which were brick-clad with the bedrooms looking onto the street and a narrow, draughty hallway which served no useful function. While the front windows provided a pleasant appearance, the late afternoon sun made the front rooms hot and stuffy and the proximity to the street made them noisy. The faults multiplied, from the dining room which received the sun all day to the views into the neighbour's living room, from the lack of consideration of site and location to the dingy lounge—'a musty, dim museum of a room'.

The owner of this bungalow, so the story went, enjoyed looking over his fence at the Model 1950 which resembled a goldfish bowl, full of glass, yet without a window onto the street, without a proper hall, dining room or sleep-out. The owner of the 1926 bungalow was thankful for his conventional home and could not understand how the moderns next door manage to live in such a peculiar and unfamiliar abode. And if Mr 1926 'built a house like That, what would the neighbours say?' Everything wrong with the pre-war residential environment was contained in the story; the primacy of ornamentation, conservatism bred through familiarity, thoughtless design which ignored function, and fear of neighbourly sanctions.

Clifford then examined the modern home through the practical lens of its modern-minded owner. Model 1950 was built for comfort and individuality. Predictably, the owner first consulted an architect, recognising that this would eventually save him money because the architect's life work is based on 'keeping abreast with the latest trends in planning [and on studying] new materials, and domestic apparatus so that he can design a house for maximum comfort'.

Accepting the architect's expert advice, he replaced the tiny square of lawn with a flagged yard and substituted the backbreaking afternoons of weeding for a quick hose-down once a month. Blinds and curtains could be drawn over the large windows while still allowing a good view. The bedrooms at the back were protected from street noise, even though the house might 'look back-to-front'. The garage was located at the front of the block and this modern concept of 'space-saving' also allowed for a terrace which functioned as an open-air living room. Furthermore, Model 1950 abandoned the separate dining area 'which is a survival from the days when most sizeable households had at least one servant'.

Space-saving also dictated the disappearance of the hall, the elimination of numerous walls and the sleep-out, while providing more built-in cupboards, cupboards forming partitions between rooms, and the grouping of plumbing. The 'goldfish bowl' was not cold in winter, because double glass and a sealed vacuum cavity between the panes provided the insulating value of brick: 'It's used a lot in America'. These historical contrasts between the new and the old illustrated the difference between the 'good' and the 'bad' and the functional and the ill-conceived.

Many feature articles were supported by stories of the experiences of post-war families. It mattered little whether these families were real or fictitious, although scepticism must have gradually grown among readers because during the late 1950s and early 1960s the magazine would stress that they were discussing an 'authentic family'.

A typical theme concerned the once-wary family which had successfully negotiated the difficult and uncharted path to modernity, and loved it! Frequently, stories provided glimpses of modern living in the United States or Canada. Better still an American family—embodying all that was modern—could set up home in Australia. The Rose family ('Transformation Job', January 1952) arrived in Sydney to settle but were bitterly disappointed when they discovered that they would be unable to find a home 'with all the comfort and color' which characterised homes on the west coast of the USA.

The shortage of building supplies and the general housing shortage forced the Roses to 'accept a drab black-bricked house tucked away on the flats of an outer suburb of Sydney'. This house, 'one of the 1920s building era', was another much maligned Californian bungalow. Bringing their bright 'up-to-the-minute' streamlined ideas from the USA, the Roses finally transformed their utterly, drab, stifling depressing bungalow into a bright fresh home decorated with modern furniture—which Mrs Rose brought over from the United States. It was quite a battle for the couple as they were fighting material shortages and the conservatism of local tradesmen—some of whom refused to touch the job!

By personifying imported modern ideas, the article made the Australian environment and attitude look even shabbier. Unlike Australian families, this American family didn't need an architect. Presumably, they were modern to the core. Bonney and Wilson (1983, 240–2) observed a parallel phenomenon in the construction of post-war femininity, whereby the local was denigrated and the imported—especially the American—was worshipped. From 1951, homes from the west coast of the USA—often described as 'ultra-modern and functional'—began making regular appearances in the magazine. These homes taught Australians 'a lesson' on 'versatile contemporary ideas' (July 1952).

In the case of the Roses, the irony that a Californian family had destroyed a Californian bungalow appeared lost on the editors. In retrospect, it is also ironic that Boyd (1967a, 463) noted how the dominant Sydney architectural school of the mid-1960s had 'much in common superficially with, if you can remember it, the Californian Bungalow style of the 1920s; the same rugged ragged clinker bricks and earthy colouring and nutty-crunchy textures'. During the late 1940s and early 1950s readers of home magazines were unable to forget the Model-Somewhere-Around-1926.

The Queen Anne villa—or the Federation house—popular at the turn of the century, was also dismissed by modernists for its late-Victorian and Edwardian fussiness. In an article entitled 'Before—and After', the Hayes family were far from enamoured with their dull-looking, dingy and depressing house. It was 'similar to many old-time Queen Anne style villas in our metropolitan areas, solid but no longer attractive by modern standards'. The ugly and unoriginal home was transformed into a 'distinctive, original and attractive' dwelling through removing the Dutch gables and heavy verandah and replacing them with a streamlined roof and a pergola. However, the Queen Anne/Federation home received lighter treatment than the Californian bungalow. One possible explanation for this is that the post-war home bore a closer resemblance to a naked Queen Anne, 'sans the verandahs and decoration that during the Federation period had reached their peak of refinement' (Riddel 1993, 120).

By 1952 there were signs that 'the modern' was becoming more pervasive and acceptable. A survey conducted at the 1952 home exhibition held by the New South Wales Chapter of the Royal Australian Institute of Architects showed that three-quarters of the visitors wanted a house that 'looked modern' (Cuffley 1993, 122). While, as Cuffley pointed out, there are problems with the representative nature of such a sample as it was possibly the more 'interested and better-informed' who attended, the sample also probably contained a higher proportion of the population seeking to build a house.

By September of the same year the *Australian House and Garden* could confidently state that the 'modern trend in home decoration has clearly influenced many practical home owners who now favour the utilitarian comfort of contemporary design [over] the more elaborate style of traditional decoration'. By May 1955, the magazine could publish an article on an eccentric man who 'lives with antiques—and loves it!' The modern house had secured its minimalist programme.

These texts from *Australian House and Garden* illustrate the very strong and unified position adopted in favour of modernist design. It stood for the functional and the prefabricated, it promoted a range of experts and professionals and it looked beyond Australia towards the United States for assistance in the struggle against the conservatism of local tradition. The texts also betray a certain tension between the editorial line and popular taste, and a good deal of indirect criticism of many of the local manufacturers and retailers who provided the advertising for the magazine. As the 1950s progressed, the tone of the magazine became less didactic and the editors assumed that readers had absorbed the mood of modernity. Another pervasive issue during the period was the adaptation of the modern to the material constraints of the era.

Reading the basic house

Despite its editorial elitism and the professional self-advertising, the magazine was also responding to a set of real needs dictated by post-war social, economic, political and administrative changes. The magazine believed that traditional housing solutions were inadequate given the strains of the post-war crisis and that the consumer could no longer 'cling to the past any more and get the best house for [his/her] money'.

One commentator, in 'Outlook for Moderns' (October 1951), pointed out that house design had to be reconciled with social changes such as the 'lack of domestic help, the fact that money won't buy half its pre-war value, that social life must necessarily be more informal'. Rising to meet these post-war challenges, the experts emphasised to their readers that a 'modern' house should be distinguished from simply a 'new' house. While a modern house was new, a new house was not necessarily modern. Concepts such as light, convenience and comfort which had become all-important in 'modern' house design were a response to real needs. Building regulations combined with the 'general economic situation' led 'without question to the building of smaller homes' (October 1951). Glass walls, split levels, dramatic use of colour and the placing of furnishings were only some of the concepts employed to conceive and create a feeling of spaciousness.

The magazine emphasised that the small house did not necessarily imply the 'cramped house'. Architects—the scientists of enclosed space—were now capable of opening rooms before their clients' eyes with streamlined efficiency. Indeed, the small house made architectural advice even more important, especially as socio-economic conditions dictated changes which emphasised function rather than fashion (May 1951):

> There is no doubt that the modern trend towards open planning is more than a fashion or a phase. Rising building costs

> and material shortages will continue to limit the size of our houses for many years to come, and unless we reduce the number of rooms by eliminating partitions between hall and living room, living room and dining room, dining room and kitchen, our houses will become too cramped and pokey to be habitable. We need spaciousness and airiness in Australian homes to suit our climate and our way of life.

Although architectural historians and critics such as Boyd and Freeland have labelled the post-war dwelling the 'austerity' house, contemporaries did not use this term to describe the average post-war home. An architect in the November 1949 issue described his plan as a 'commonsense' house designed to meet the needs of the post-war family. It was not 'a luxury house nor an austerity house but one within the means of the average income group'. In November 1951 Greenop calculated £2250 was insufficient to fulfil your dream and would probably buy you 'a fibro house designed on austerity lines', excluding land. The term 'austerity' was associated more with emergency housing and temporary housing than the average new-built dwelling.

Architects and writers in these early post-war magazines performed an important role channelling relative deprivation into spatially acceptable forms. The texts acknowledged that the aspiration of the average reader was still a three-bedroom house, with separate living and dining room.

In September 1950 Birrell warned the reader that this aspiration remained beyond current means. For the foreseeable future, members of the public would have to suppress their pre-war expectations and wartime plans. Readers were encouraged to review their needs realistically and build a 'basic house'. This tightly planned 'basic house' was a complete dwelling suitable for families and newly weds (September 1950). Houses which were basic but also capable of expansion were labelled 'nucleus' houses. Other architects described the post-war home as the 'minimum house', designed for two people and amenable to future expansion or transfer into a future garage-workshop (March 1951). The minimum house contained all the practical ideas of modernism such as in-built cupboard space and large areas of glass. Some plans also assumed that no main services would be available. A house featured in December 1954 was '8 square—and modern to the minute', a common phrase used to emphasise that this was the 'day of the small home'.

During the late 1940s and early 1950s, the majority of plans displayed in the magazine were variations on this 'minimum' or 'basic' dwelling. The functional home for the hard-pressed family or young worker dominated the architects' contributions. One story from 1951 ('One-room house from a two-room garage') told of Peter and Polly who had fled their inner-city flat and bought a block of parcelled land. There was a garage on the block which the enterprising couple—with the help, of course, of an interior and architectural design team—remodelled into a one-room house capable of future expansion. These designs fell far short of a projected middle-class lifestyle. In the March 1951 issue Gaynor acknowledged this:

> You are the one who must adjust your thinking to this substitute dream house and decide whether his [the architect's] drafted plan is going to please you when it's built. It's hard, for many of your cherished dreams have been wiped out with 'That's unobtainable at the present', or 'That would mean going over the price you want to pay'. 'You have to be thankful for anything nowadays' is poor compensation when a home is the one lifelong possession we really aim for.

Other articles showed readers how to achieve such 'Compromises in Space' (May 1951). These compromises included forgoing the hallway, the rumpus room, the wife's sewing room and the guest room; eating in the living room; furnishing bedrooms as children's sitting rooms; creating space by illusion using different colour schemes; painting woodwork to blend with the walls; using a straight streamlined plan; abandoning meaningless decoration; leaving materials in their natural state where possible; and above all else keeping the design and the plan simple.

On the one hand, many experts recognised that this *was* a compromise for many consumers by stating that 'the role of dreamer must give way to that of practical philosopher, wherein we admit the need for compromise and confess that the "little house" of today is cut to fit the pocketbook and has no frills and ambitious folderols'. Artificial sweeteners were occasionally added, as suggested by the title of a November 1951 feature entitled 'Where Modern Means Beautiful'.

On the other hand, these compromises often appeared as the victory of modernism or at least as the architect's and interior designer's challenge! The minimum house might have been a product of unforeseen and contingent economic circumstances, but this provided modernism's advocates with an unprecedented opportunity to display the practical virtues of their knowledge.

The magazine also provided advice on the advantages and disadvantages of renting and buying a home. During the period 1947–54, when owner occupation rates rose most dramatically in Australia, the texts provided a balanced analysis of tenural issues. The magazine was no crude forum for the 'ideology of home-ownership'. In June 1950 W. Watson Sharpe ('shall we Rent or Buy?') claimed that 'the odds are about even'. The difficulty in finding rental accommodation, exacerbated by the tendency for older houses to be purchased for owner occupation and the fact that 'it is so uneconomical to build a house now as an investment, that it is unlikely any new houses will be available for renting for a long time to come', plus the sense of security in ownership, tipped the scales in favour of purchasing.

There was no need for the magazine to provide support for owner occupation, however; few readers had any alternative. In a mid-1958 editorial on the housing shortage, the magazine drew attention to the lack of rental accommodation and the possibility that rent control had forced many households to buy 'inappropriate housing' on the fringe of the cities.

During the early post-war period the magazine did feature stories of interior decorating successes in rental accommodation. Articles featured young newly-weds who had previously lived with in-laws or friends and focused on the interior design problems of their rental accommodation—often a garage or a flat. Beth and Bill Coleman, newly-weds on a modest income, were unable to purchase their own house 'nor pay the exorbitant price demanded these days even to rent a comfortable cottage'. They overcame the housing shortages and spiralling prices by renting a converted double garage (see also September 1950, 63). However, one tenure which remained conspicuous by its absence in the pages of the magazine was public housing.

During the late 1940s and early 1950s, the magazine was directed mostly at the consumer of the basic/small/minimum/little home. There is only limited evidence that the magazine aimed to familiarise its readers with a 'middle-class' lifestyle. However, it did tend to homogenise suburban life; there was no indication in its pages that suburban life on Sydney's North Shore differed from that in the western suburbs, and feature houses were chosen disproportionately from areas such as Pennant Hills, St Ives, Roseville, Lindfield in Sydney and Balwyn or the Mornington Peninsula in Victoria. Nevertheless, the designs which were promoted did not correspond to any pre-war class images.

True to the idealism of much post-war modernism, *Australian House and Garden* promoted a new style of living and a corresponding design which was supposed to reflect the mood of post-war modernity. However, there are grounds for claiming that *it was almost as if* the modernism promoted in the magazine was a means of channelling wartime dreams into feasible housebuilding and homemaking realities. In this limited metaphorical sense it can be argued that the magazine functioned as a safety valve, releasing some of the sense of housing deprivation experienced by post-war housing consumers by showing them how a small house could be made desirable, rather than being just a makeshift or compromise.

Reading bricks

The magazine in its early years also devoted considerably more space to housing production than later in the 1950s. Through time, house production became a more incidental and peripheral part of the magazine while interior design became more central. The magazine's formative years corresponded with the increase in owner-building and this trend was reflected in the magazine. Housing economics featured in early articles such as 'What of the Home-Building Future?' (October 1949) and 'Shall We Build Now?' (November 1949). Other articles provided advice on buying a block of land such as 'A Block of One's Own' (January 1950),

'Land-ho' (November 1950) and 'The Case of the Difficult Site' (December 1951). This era pre-dated house and land packages.

Other articles were directed at the enthusiastic or romantic owner-builder and the frustrated house-seeker who might be considering building. Numerous articles focused attention on the difficulties involved in the task of construction or the unexpected future limitations which amateur designs and plans might pose. In November 1952, Buhrich summed up the frustration many households faced in the midst of 'a housing shortage that has improved very little since the end of the war'. The realistic options often narrowed to either shared accommodation—'strangers in the best case, in-laws in the worst'—or the building of a temporary dwelling to weather the worst of the housing storm. Buhrich warned that although the latter option was tempting, a temporary structure could swallow future resources and even become a substandard permanent home with little value or appeal.

Other articles were designed to remove any illusion that owner-building and owner-contracting were easy options. For example, both Burnett ('So You Think It's Easy', June 1949) and Bernard ('Facts You Will Face', August 1952) set out meticulous organisational schedules for the housebuilding process and a long list of problems which would be confronted due to inexperience, the economic climate and material and labour shortages.

Despite these warnings, the magazine provided invaluable practical support and encouragement for the owner-builder. In February 1952 the magazine embarked on a four-part series on 'The House You Can Really Build Yourself' designed by associate editor W. Watson Sharpe (see Figure 18). This two-bedroom house could be built without any professional assistance (except for a plumber and electrician, as stipulated by building regulations). Other stories described owner-building successes ('They Built Their Own Home in 156 days', July 1952).

For the less adventurous, there were also articles on the latest advances in prefabricated houses such as 'Let's Pre-Fabricate' (October 1950) and 'Facts About Factory-Made Houses' (July 1952). The articles were supportive of pre-cut and prefabricated houses not only as a means to 'offset the long lag in homebuilding' but also as tomorrow's 'efficient and economical' housing solution. Other articles helped the owner-builder or renovator with information about the latest materials ('Ways with Wallboards', November 1952), warnings and advice on avoiding 'unscrupulous contractors' in the timber trade ('What Do You Know About Timber', January 1950) or advice on the advantages and disadvantages of different roofing materials ('The Roof Over Your Head', July 1951).

Attention to the needs of the owner-builder was maintained throughout the mid-1950s. The magazine continued to provide a wealth of straightforward advice for both producers and consumers. However, building conditions were improving and these changes were reflected in the articles, information and advertisements found within the magazine.

One November 1955 article which assessed the advantages of three ways to build—subcontracting, building oneself, and borrowing to build—provided some indication of the changing economic climate. One family recalled that in 1951 'the building situation was almost the reverse of what it is today; supplies were hard to come by, but loans to the private builder were relatively easy to get'.

These conditions were reflected in the magazine's new owner-builder venture which was one step up from the 1952 two-bedroom home—'the most successful, big-scale handicraft ever'. The 1955 model was a 13-square, three-bedroom house which could be built by the amateur for £2050. This was substantially bigger than the 1952 model and reflected the easing of supply problems within the building industry. The tighter financial conditions were also taken into account in the planning of the house which could be erected in three separate stages—'pay-as-you-go and do-it-yourself! This is the byword of most people today, particularly of potential homemakers determined to become home-owners'.

The homes promoted in the mid-1950s were similar to those promoted in the early 1950s. In a November 1955 article, the modern small home was described as 'a place of pleasant comfort, spaciousness—despite its size—and easy living'. Although the small house continued to receive much attention, larger homes were beginning to appear more regularly. Greater emphasis was placed on comfort and the promotion of a relaxed lifestyle and less emphasis was devoted to functionality. One June 1955 article featured an 'uninhibited' three-bedroom house complete with 'a finely proportioned entrance hall'—a feature looked upon darkly a few years before.

Another change in emphasis was the move away from multi-functional rooms towards the creation of grouped or 'distinct' areas serving different needs. The trend in contemporary house design was towards 'planning the living room and formal meals into one zone, with the kitchen alongside; next comes the sleeping area, created around a bigger, more useful bathroom; third is the playroom zone, where the family can enjoy informal leisure hours, or where intimate parties of a few close friends can be staged'. Despite this trend, the magazine continued to be dominated by 'minimalism', such as ideas 'on what people want in tomorrow's minimum homes' (April 1955). In the regular 'Advise Please' column, readers—real or fictitious—'anxious to modernise the front' of their 'colonial type house' would seek expert assistance (April 1956).

The magazine also continued to publish articles on the latest advances in housebuilding techniques and evaluations of the advantages of new materials. For example, in an article entitled 'Here's How the Owner-Builder can Save Pounds', Vance Amory examined nine new wall covers such as Gyprock, Weldex and Masonite. The author pointed out that owner-builders required materials with 'simplicity of handling'. He also claimed that manufacturers had recognised this market and were developing products which could be handled by both tradesfolk and handyfolk. This saved the owner-builder considerable expense on trades labour. Numerous publications exploited the owner-builder and handyman phenomenon during the mid-1950s. For example, by 1955 *Man* had established a 'handyman' section.

Thus, while the magazine continued to emphasise the small home and the need to get value for the building pound, by the mid-1950s the contemporary home the editors promoted was a more comfortable and more spacious house reflecting a society enjoying both full employment and a higher level of affluence. Modernism had become all-pervasive, although its early 1950s emphasis on functionalism was disappearing. It was now possible to appeal to readers who appreciated 'contemporary architecture and furnishings but hanker after the softness of traditional decorating'. This observation supports Boyd's description of the metamorphosis of modernism into simply another period style during the 1950s.

The emphasis on the owner-builder had declined somewhat by the early 1960s. This decline was associated with the changing relations of housing production discussed in Chapter 4. Post-war modernist philosophy was emphasised most in articles on home design for owner-builders. However, throughout the rest of the magazine's regular features, modernism was only one among a number of ways to express contemporaneity. For example, in April 1961 the magazine embarked on the 'easiest-ever Build-it-yourself house', a three-bedroom expandable timber home. Fully expanded, this 11.1-square house could be built on an 8-square plan and 'reflected the modern trend for functional design with simple clean-cut lines'. It was targeted at 'the couple starting out, a place for retirement, or a super weekender'. The magazine described other 8-square, one-bedroom 'starter plans' which would eventually grow into 'a full-sized dream house'. W. Watson Sharpe also continued to give modernist 'Help for handymen home builders' or remodellers (February 1961).

By 1960 it was possible to refer to a three-bedroom 16-square design as 'small home living on a *grand* scale' (December 1960). The keywords used to describe the 1960-Model-Modern included 'gracious', 'elegance', 'glamorous', 'privacy', 'charm', 'sublime beauty', 'de-luxe', 'luxurious', 'every living comfort' and a 'modest castle'. In addition, the early 1950s emphasis on 'a feeling of space' or 'the search for space' gave way to a different mood, the 'space-age'. 'Spacious' now meant having a lot of room rather than a rational ordering of scarce space according to function.

Modernity gradually began to lose its close connection with modernism. The more eclectic atmosphere was reflected in a December 1960 statement that all good kitchens should incorporate the best ideas of 'modern and traditional planning'. Homes also began to appear for the 'traditionally-minded' that didn't sacrifice 'good design' (March 1961). Readers were now informed in a non-judgemental manner that there were 'plenty of people who like a traditionally comfortable brick house with tiled roof and three full bedrooms'.

The early 1960s also witnessed a revival of the colonial style, described as 'modern colonial' (May 1961) and the combination of 'modern planning with old style charm' became acceptable. Colonial kitchens were described as 'friendly, they're fun to work in and they're a welcome change from strictly utilitarian kitchens'. These kitchens could be decorated with display shelves, gingham as a frill over the windows, frilly tops for kitchen stools and pelmets around the windows. Other touches mentioned were the warmth of timber finishes and panelling or a natural timber finish on cupboards. The writer added in parentheses that 'I don't mind if I cheat a little', betraying a lingering sense of modernist guilt. These ideas would have been consigned to the 'bad', the 'fussy' and the 'ornate' a decade before. A remodelled home in the May 1961 issue featuring 'timber panelled walls, old-style colonial lights, chintz and warm colour schemes' was described as being 'packed with colonial appeal'. By 1962 the South Australian Housing Trust was describing its largest standard house—15.5 squares—for sale as the 'American Colonial' (Marsden 1986, 233).

By the early 1960s modernism had retreated from its vanguard status among designers and was merely another choice of style available to the homemaker. The heroic days of the late 1940s and early 1950s, when conditions had forced the streams of modernism and modernity to flow together, had all but passed. The 'end of fashion' had become merely another faded fashion. Between 1950 and 1960 the imperative had changed from 'I need' to 'I like'. By the end of the decade Aberdeen Blinds were asking readers 'Which Design Is Yours?', featuring a range of different house styles. In June 1950 a Kalmar Interiors advertisement asked the reader 'Do you need modern furniture?' By 1955, it was assumed you wanted it. By 1960 it depended on your preference.

This transformation in the tone and content of the magazine reflected the move away from linking austerity with function towards linking abundance with personal choice and desire. It was hardly surprising that Boyd fired his most powerful volley against featurism, *The Australian Ugliness*, in 1960. The battle had clearly turned against his professional army of modernist experts.

Reading advertisements

Between the late 1940s and the early 1960s advertisements within *Australian House and Garden* followed a similar pattern to the changes in housing provision described throughout this book. The exploitation of austerity gradually gave way to a less functional and more luxurious emphasis and the term 'modern'—which had become all-pervasive by the mid-1950s—gradually lost its position as the principal keyword unlocking the savings of the 'affluent' consumer.

Scarcity featured prominently in a range of advertisements during the late 1940s and early 1950s. The most consistent use of the theme appeared in advertisements for Masonite, the wall-board firm which bought a full-page coloured space every month throughout the period. The advertisements changed regularly, but were often in the form of short scripts featuring a foreman or an architect advising a young newly-wed couple. During this period of general shortages and building inflation, the advertisements boasted that Masonite 'pioneers the reduction of Home Building costs!'

However, the impact of this economic breakthrough was diminished by the conditions of scarcity. Up until 1953 Masonite had to insert an 'author's note' at the end of every text explaining that although Masonite reduced costs, it was almost impossible to obtain the product. By the mid-1950s—with twelve different Masonite products on the market—these qualifications ceased (see Chapter 5). During this period, consumer durables such as the Thor Automagic combination clothes/dishwasher also stressed that 'The little wait . . . is well worthwhile' (November 1952). The long lead times involved in housebuilding were also exploited by innovative building firms such as Triton which offered a one-bedroom 'modern villa' 'built *quickly* on your own land' for £620 (see Figure 19).

As noted in Chapters 4, 5 and 7, advertisers also targeted owner-builders throughout the period. Pre-cut or ready-cut house packages regularly appeared in the magazine, while other innovative manufacturers targeted the handyman by using different packaging: Rawlplugs released its fasteners under the 'popular outfit', the 'household outfit', 'the handyman' and 'the craftsman' labels. Innovative products stressed their ease of use and handling. Naco Air Control Windows adopted this technique, featuring a contented owner-builder 'without any previous carpentering experience' installing his Naco self-mullion windows 'using only a screwdriver and a pair of pliers', saving him 'pounds in installation costs!' (1951).

By 1952, the advertising world had discovered the power of the 'modern'. Modernity and modernism formed a united front in the advertising industry's 'cash struggle' against the post-war consumer. While the word 'modern' had always been a powerful phrase for the advertising industry, from around 1952 until the mid- to late 1950s it assumed an unprecedented prominence. Modernism 'became the advertising industry's favourite word' (White 1993, 20; O'Callaghan 1993; 161). A number of examples illustrate the pervasiveness of the word and its assumed subliminal power:

1) Early post-war advertisements for the Armstrong Siddeley Whitley sports saloon used terms which suggested exclusivity and wealth, such as 'prestige', 'like a thoroughbred horse or a class yacht', 'pride' and 'painstaking craftsmanship'. By 1951 this exclusivity was still conveyed in phrases such as 'how to steal the show', 'comfort', 'spacious luxury', although the description now mentioned the car's 'fine modern lines'. By 1952, the same car was 'designed for modern living' and pictured outside a highly modernist home—which had featured in the magazine a few months previously (see Figure 20).

2) In June 1949, Colas bitumen, by the Shell Company, was marketed for laying driveways 'without using materials in short supply'. By May 1951 advertisers labelled the product the 'easy economical way' to lay garden paths. By May 1952, Colas had also pointed out that 'Colas is the modern way of making paths'.

3) In October 1951 a home was 'only half a home without Pyrox Instantaneous Gas Hot Water Service'. By the mid-1950s the emphasis had changed: 'Why spoil Modern Architecture? Ugly

water storage tanks mar modern flat-roof design and weaken roof structures. Be Wise, install a Pyrox' (see Figure 21).

4) While Insulwool insulation products emphasised comfort during the late 1940s and depicted a man cheerfully rising from bed 'on a cold and frosty morning', by December 1954 Insulwool helped you to 'be in the fashion' and 'modernise the comfort of your home'.

The lure of the modern appeared in some unlikely places. In September 1950 the case for a decorative screen was made through emphasising its ability to give 'character to a room'. By April 1952 the importance of a screen was justified on modernist grounds. The large open flexible areas which characterised the 'modern house' were divided into 'zones of activity' in place of small space-wasting separate rooms.

This modernist feature now led 'to a revival of that favourite equipment of grandmother's time: the movable screen'. Old practices and grandmothers' tastes could reappear in modern disguises. Wallpaper manufacturers such as Crown, Sanderson and Shand Kidd joined the modern procession. Consumers were told to 'Be smart, be modern, choose wallpaper'. This authoritative statement was backed up by 'famous overseas designers'. Gaynor (November 1949) also asked readers to reconsider wallpaper:

> Exciting patterned wallpaper? Did you say no? Well, well, we thought you would. Aunt Minnie's faded gargoyles and sorry little nosegays trailing round the walls killed your interest dead. No wonder you kalsomined them over when you inherited the house. 'Clean modern walls for me', you said. Yet here we are to lure you back—to stripes and spots and polka dots, to flowers and leaves and landscape scenes and every other fantasy wallpaper designers can dream up. For despite your cry for the modern, you are really out of date.

Toeing the modernist line could be difficult! In August 1951, readers were informed that dark walls were returning, but this time 'they have a modern interpretation that is dramatic and interesting'. Unfortunately, for many people 'the thought of dark red or brown walls conjures up a mid-Victorian atmosphere'. The writer never indicated where this perception might have come from! The term 'modern' was used to catch the reader's eye, even if the advertisement had little to do with the concept. Sundour Fine Furnishing Fabrics caught the readers' attention with the bold title: 'Contemporary or Modern? There are two schools of thought. Some say "modern" and some say "contemporary". We can leave those differences to architects, critics and the lexicographers. Our contribution to the discussion is a wide range of Sundour Fabrics . . . and that seems to satisfy both schools of thought' (December 1954). Clearly there were no other schools of thought worthy of consideration.

Jeldi, a manchester manufacturer, claimed to be 'first with a modern contemporary chenille bedspread' (November 1955). Ormonoid pointed out that 'the most modern roof is the easiest to construct' thanks to Ormonoid roofing and asphalt. Ford commended the Zephyr-Six to readers on the grounds that it was 'so far ahead in design that it will stay modern for years ahead: Zephyr-Six be modern, buy Zephyr—by Zephyr, be modern' (April 1956). E. G. Glass & Co. in George Street Sydney was the 'shop for young moderns' (February 1955).

By the mid-1950s, other terms began to appear as keywords. Thor's automatic washing machine was 'famous in America as in 69 countries'. A glamorous Miss America stood proudly beside her machine and a caption which read: 'When Miss America becomes Mrs, she doesn't sacrifice her glamour to wash day drudgery' (May 1955). The mid-1950s also witnessed the first underground sprinkler systems for handyfolk such as Watermatic by Moldex. This was marketed as 'the very latest idea from America' (September 1955). Jayworth Block Masonry were available in a comprehensive range 'which includes the latest designs from America' (February 1961; see also O'Callaghan 1993, 161).

Designers and advertisers were also quick to recognise a market in new furniture 'planned for televiewing' (April 1956). CSR's Timbrock anticipated future demand from television and pulled out all cliches in its May 1955 advertisement: 'Modern, space-saving built-ins like this TELEVISION WALL are easy for the handyman, easy on the pocket' and 'relieve your room of that crowded look before television comes'. Television chairs like the Fler TV Armchair for 'watching television when you get it' began to appear during the mid-1950s (April 1956). These advertisements represented the 'austerican' phenomenon observed by Boyd.

By the late 1950s the term 'modern' had become overexposed and had lost some of its evocative power. Fewer advertisements emphasised the modern attributes of a product. The term 'beautify' began to appear more regularly during the mid- to late 1950s as functionalism became less of a requirement in the larger houses. An early 1950s advertisement such as 'Equip it with Modern Whitco window fittings' now emphasised the 'comfort and beauty' of the product (January 1961). Furthermore, 'affluence' encouraged the revival of mature products. As noted in Chapter 7, the Fibrous Plaster Association felt confident enough to place double-page advertisements which stressed how the product could 'express your own ideas of beauty' in features such as ceilings, walls, pelmets, cornices, overmantels, fire-surrounds and bookcases.

Products which retained the modernist signature were innovative or space-saving, such as Modernfold folding concertina doors which 'solve space problems so beautifully' (April 1961). Other products which retained the term 'modern' stressed that it did not necessarily imply austerity. Tylor sanitaryware products had 'never been so attractive, so completely functional . . . Go gay and modern' (March 1961).

Ironically, as the housing product was transformed from the austere, the functional and the modern to the more decorative and whimsical, advertising agents began to design more austere, abstract, modernist advertisements. In addition, photographs were replacing sketches and drawings. Masonite provided an interesting example of this shift in design. The early post-war illustrations of smiling owner-builders, foremen and architects along with a wordy script which cluttered the page had disappeared by 1961. Instead, most of the space was filled with wood panelling, demonstrating one of the many choices of colour and texture available to the consumer.

More and more advertisements began using symbolism and association at the expense of information. Modernist advertising design had arrived and was promoting products which had outlived the era of post-war modernism, austerity and shortages in housing provision.

During the early post-war era, *Australian House and Garden* reflected and influenced many of the changes in housing provision analysed in this book. For example, the magazine performed a far more important role in the production side of housing during the 1950s than after 1960. By the early 1960s, as owner-building declined and project building increased, home magazines began to emphasise interior decoration more than building techniques. While interior design had always featured in earlier magazines, it became more prominent as the years progressed.

The articles also reflected and encouraged the trend towards modernism during the early post-war period. The magazine targeted a wide—almost universal—audience and provided practical advice to deal with the climate of austerity. As the 1950s progressed, the texts also reflected the lifting of housing restrictions and the easing of the housing shortages.

There is little evidence to support a functionalist argument that home magazines performed an important class socialising role. However, the early texts did betray a certain tension between the magazine's philosophical aims and the readership. This tension could be felt less by the early 1960s as the magazine dropped its earlier manifest aim of dictating and transforming the tastes of the nation and increasingly began to describe latest trends. However, it could be argued that this merely represented a less explicit way of achieving the same goal.

As the decade came to a close, *Australian House and Garden* addressed a readership which was enjoying the fruits of a more affluent climate. Contextually divorced, a stranger reading the magazine in 1960—it had become rather glossier by then—would have been forgiven for believing that the comforts represented in the magazine represented 'the norm'. By this stage, the magazine primarily reflected and influenced that section of Australian society discussed in Chapter 2 which believed that the nation had all but solved the housing crisis. Progressively, it had less to say to the reader that did not conform to the mythical norm.

10

Speculating Beyond the 1950s

Throughout these chapters the theme of modernism has linked the various changes in the post-war provision of housing in Australia. However, an evaluation of the modernist vision is complicated by the different meanings which were attached to the concept by experts, producers and consumers. For some, modernism was the application of the scientific method to the production and design of housing; some limited modernism to the application of Fordist industrial techniques and the use of more inanimate power; others viewed modernism as a temporary expediency for overcoming the acute housing shortages experienced in the wake of World War II; others saw modernism as the adaptation of housing to post-war lifestyles; and others simply saw it as a fashion choice, from which they could select what they liked. These meanings often conflicted and often contradicted one another. They were also subject to change as social, economic, technological and ideological circumstances dictated. Modernism remained a multifaceted, complex and dynamic concept. However, by the end of the 1950s it was beginning to lose its appeal.

In 1945 Walter Bunning had outlined a modernist vision of post-war Australia which he acknowledged might sound utopian to some readers. However, he was confident that a unified, democratic and determined community could build this dream, which he set out in *Homes In The Sun*. Indeed, he ended the book with a quote from Le Corbusier which rang with optimism: 'What gives our dreams their daring is that they can be realised' (Bunning 1945, 99). Fifteen years later, more Australians had realised 'the great Australian dream' than at any other era in the nation's history. However, this dream bore little resemblance to Bunning's planned, state-facilitated, social-democratic vision for reconstruction and town planning. By 1960 fellow modernists such as Robin Boyd were fighting a rearguard battle in defence of good design against the forces of featurism.

A great distance lay between the reality-model 1960 and the vision-model 1945. The post-war modernists had all along been warning politicians, producers and consumers alike that they were on the wrong path, and by 1960 Boyd was wringing his hands and pointing to the ugly terrain which had been reached. It bore no resemblance to the good plan.

Nevertheless, the 1960 built environment was markedly different from that of 1945, and Boyd had to admit that it was an 'achievement' that the nation had succeeded in travelling so far. In some areas of housing provision, Progress-with-a-capital-P had been slow, yet in other places the tempo of development had been unprecedented. The map which the modernists had set out so confidently with in 1945 had failed to include a number of obstacles blocking the path to utopia, and other obstacles had appeared on the road which hardly could have been foreseen.

The year 1961 is a useful place to take stock and reflect on the post-war transformation in Australian housing provision. In some cases the beginning of the 1960s marked the end of the road, while in other respects it indicated a turning point. The coalition of social, economic, demographic and ideological forces which had shaped the housing environment immediately after the war was beginning to disintegrate and new forces were emerging. New questions were being asked about the path ahead and speculations were being voiced over future directions.

Many building firms which had contributed to the pace of post-war housing recovery suffered during the 'crash' of 1961. The economic downturn of 1961 was not the first occasion since the war that housing completions had fallen. As pointed out in Chapter 3, the industry was notorious for its cyclical fluctuations.

However, the post-war shortages of housing ensured rising demand and in 1961 a record 94 500 dwellings were completed despite sluggish growth rates throughout the latter half of the 1950s. The downturn of 1961 was severe enough to cause the total value of all new building to decline for the first time since the war. The 1961 credit squeeze affected every sector of the building industry, especially the residential sector, which suffered from the government's decision to tighten housing finance (Hutton 1970, 2). The slump in housing construction was also due to a rate of output in new dwellings which had been outpacing demand since early 1959 (Hall 1961, 14). Speculative activity in housing had been fuelled by cheap 'fringe' finance institutions.

This lengthy period of oversupply deepened the subsequent decline in activity after 1961. The severity of the slump forced many speculative builders out of the housing field or alternatively encouraged them to reorganise. In October 1961, Hall (1961, 15) predicted that 'the speculative elements' which had fuelled the flames of growth during the late 1950s and early 1960s had spent their force for the time being and that government action should strongly discourage their re-emergence into the housing market. He also observed the adverse affects upon the industry of abnormally high fluctuations in building activity (Hall 1961, 15):

> A whole host of delicate inter-relationships develop during a period of growth. It is difficult to re-establish many of them after they have, almost inevitably, been broken when the industry is forced into a recession of the magnitude of that which occurred in 1961. This is especially the case when there were strong speculative elements in the preceding boom.

Other indicators suggested that an era was coming to a close. One such was the decline in owner-building. After peaking at almost 40 per cent of completions in 1954, owner-building had declined to one-quarter of completions by 1961, and continued to decline while contract-built and speculative housing by private firms increased. These changes in production and demand also contributed to the industry's growing instability. Owner-builders tended to construct one dwelling for personal consumption, or else groups of owner-builders built a dwelling per household. Such activity did not contribute to oversupply and acted as a stabiliser counteracting potential instability.

As the housebuilding industry became dominated more by private firms—especially speculative companies producing a commodity for the market rather than for a specific individual—the dangers of instability increased and the industry began to assume its traditional cyclical characteristics, which had been less evident during the housing crisis of the early post-war years.

Another feature which suggested the end of a road was the emergence of project builders. Although a number of project builders had emerged prior to the 1960s, their profile gradually heightened after the 1961 recession and their emergence left a permanent impression on the structure of the housebuilding industry (Hutton 1970; Greig 1992a). They included firms which had established successful relationships with state governments during the early post-war period and attempted to exploit the growing private market, small speculative firms which had established a reputation for quality and saw an opportunity for growth and security, and a number of vertically integrated companies seeking to complement their land development, finance, material supply or non-residential construction activities.

Project builders brought to the residential construction industry the economies of scale which Bunning, the Commonwealth Housing Commission and the post-war modernists saw in their industrialised vision. As noted in Chapter 8, many project builders employed architects to design a range of standard dwellings. The larger scale of operation tended to result in a more segmented division of managerial responsibility; the all-purpose builder who arranged construction and administration from the back of the truck was being replaced by a complex organisational structure with full-time salespersons, accountants, construction managers and supervisors—some of whom might never have been engaged in the physical process of housebuilding.

Although the average size of firm remained small after 1960, the proportion of houses constructed by large-scale building firms increased markedly. By 1967, the Housing Industry Association (1967, 13) estimated that the largest thirty firms produced 20 per cent of the nation's houses (or 15 per cent of all dwellings), while the largest 250 firms constructed 40 per cent of all houses (or 30 per cent of dwellings). On this basis the HIA estimated that the remaining 10 000 firms produced an average of seven dwellings per annum, and many of them would produce under three per year. Significantly, the economies of scale failed to encourage industrialised housing, although increasingly more components were being fabricated off-site. The traditional skilled trades were slowly changing but remained important in on-site construction.

Another significant change at the turn of the 1960s—also associated with the growth of the project builders and their more standardised product—was the introduction of more sophisticated marketing techniques like the 'display village' or the 'demonstration village' where potential consumers could 'test drive' or experience the new product. At first, many local councils and consumers found this concept—which has subsequently become part of every outer suburban landscape—puzzling. One manager at A. V. Jennings recalled the problems associated with introducing the concept of the display home: 'The council said to me, "You either sell in it or you live in it. What do you mean you display it?" They had never heard of that. People used to take their shoes off outside the door and ask, "Can we come in?"' (quoted in Garden 1992, 175).

Although many project builders eliminated an element of risk through securing advance orders and finance for homes and attempted to offset their higher overheads through economies of scale, the practice also raised the spectre of further instability in the market now that the potential for overproduction had been established (Hall 1961, 7). Underlying demand counteracted this possibility throughout the 1960s, but when this demand began to level off during the early 1970s the industry entered a period of higher volatility. Cyclical fluctuations have become more pronounced since the early 1970s (Bureau of Industry Economics 1990).

Other important shifts in the organisation of housing provision were discernible at the end of the 1950s. Government housing commencements had been regarded as an important instrument for technological change and overall industry stability by the Commonwealth Housing Commission at the start of the post-war road, and had been expected to account for half of all new dwellings. This target was never reached, and by 1957/58 government commencements had fallen below 20 per cent. By 1958/59 they dropped to 15 per cent. In the 1960s, the yearly proportion of government commencements to total commencements continued to decline steadily despite lengthy waiting lists for government housing.

As the quantity of dwellings continued to rise, more attention began to focus on another important goal of the CHC's 1944 report. Since the end of the war the plan to clear inner-city areas had remained beyond the capacity of the state and most of the areas which had been cleared had been transformed for non-residential purposes. Architects and economists began reminding governments of their responsibilities and promises to improve inner-city areas (see Winston 1962, Hill 1959, Hall 1961).

Many post-war migrants had gathered within these areas and by the early 1960s pressure was being put to bear on authorities to improve migrants' housing conditions, both within the inner city and in hostels. As economic conditions began improving in Europe and as Australia faced competition from other migrant-seeking nations, it was becoming more difficult to attract and retain migrants at the level considered necessary for further economic growth. It became increasingly clear to many authorities that changes in immigration and settlement policy were required and that it could no longer be taken for granted that migrants would be as accommodating in their acceptance of substandard housing (Collins 1988; Jordens 1994).

One of the most visible changes at the turn of the decade was the dramatic growth in the production of flats and dwellings other than detached houses. The rate of production of these 'other dwellings' had remained subdued for most of the immediate post-war era and still comprised under four per cent of total completions before 1957. In 1959, the proportion of 'other dwellings' had reached almost 6.5 per cent and rose sharply to over 14 per cent in 1961 and 1962; by 1965, 'other dwellings' accounted for one in four completions and remained above this level for the next decade. Most of these dwellings were flats constructed by small speculative builders for rental purposes.

This increase in flat building should be placed in historical perspective. Flats had increased as a proportion of the total housing stock during the 1920s and 1930s, but declined between the war and the late 1950s. At this stage, a number of factors coalesced to provide a new impetus to flat building. According to Neutze (Department of Housing 1968, 5), contributing factors included 'developments in the economy of construction, the rising cost of urban land and developments in the age composition of the population that result from the depression of the 1930s and the second world war'.

Other factors contributing to the dramatic increase of flats were the physical deterioration of the inner-city housing stock (and the beginning of the slum clearances which had been postponed during the housing shortages of the early post-war era) and 'the fact that the sprawl of the major cities is now such that, for many people, the attraction of a home unit within easy access of the city proper well outweighs the relative cheapness (to the individual through by no means necessarily so to the community) of construction on the fringe of the expanding cities' (Hall 1961, 5). Other factors included further easing of rent control legislation, the increase in availability of structural materials necessary for flats which had previously been in short supply and the appearance of strata title legislation in 1961 which made owner occupation more widely available for flat-dwellers. Although most flats continued to be built for rental accommodation, this legislation began to erode the popular image or myth of home ownership as a term applicable only to possession of a detached dwelling on a quarter-acre block.

The 'great Australian dream' of home ownership itself had reached a turning point by the late 1950s and early 1960s. The dramatic growth in owner occupation between the intercensal periods 1947–54 and 1954–61 discussed in Chapter 6 appeared in retrospect as a massive leap between two plateaux. From the turn of the century until the end of World War II, approximately one in two households owned or were buying a house. Home ownership rates leapt from 52.6 per cent in 1947 to 62.9 per cent in 1954, before climbing to 69.9 per cent in 1961. Since 1961, owner occupation rates have remained approximately at this level, although rates per adult have risen as the average household size has declined.

This stability, which has been maintained despite government and industry efforts to further promote the tenure, has led some authors to suggest that this rate represents the limit which a capitalist society such as Australia can absorb. This figure remains relatively fixed despite the fact that around 90 per cent of Australians at one point or another in their housing career will own or be purchasing a house (Troy 1991, 43). This also lends support to the view that rates of owner occupation are influenced by more than government housing policy and/or ideology (see Bourassa, Greig & Troy 1994).

As the nation reached this plateau, housebuilders appeared to become more conscious of style and product differentiation. Paradoxically, this search for differentiation occurred within an atmosphere of growing standardisation as seen in the use of a range of standard designs by project builders and the greater use by project builders and small builders alike of off-site, factory-controlled standardisation of building materials. Project building thus began erode the individualist rock upon which 'the great Australian dream' had been built. Project builders standardised their houses and added cosmetic touches to hint at individual style.

Within these standardised dwellings stood the serialised consumer durables of post-war Fordism. As Dovey (1992, 186) has observed: 'The dream is for a house that reflects one's authenticity and uniqueness, yet this is to be achieved with a package of meanings that are mass-marketed'. In this respect, it could be argued that during the 1950s the closer relationship between production and consumption—manifested in high rates of owner-building—allowed greater scope for individuality. As Pickett (1993, 87) maintained, 1950s consumers 'were uniquely placed to select not just a predetermined package, but also the design elements relevant to their needs and budget'.

Part IV of this book illustrated the modifications which the concept of modernism underwent during the late 1940s and throughout the 1950s. Promoters of modernism within a range of disciplines began the post-war era conscious of their *avant-garde* status, yet confident of their inevitable ascendancy. The challenges of post-war housing, the general economic climate, the housing shortages, the experience of post-war living and the forces of reason and progress would assure modernism its ultimate success. As a consequence, modernism often appeared to its supporters as the 'end of style' and modernist design was elevated to the status of a 'science'. By the end of the 1950s, modernism had lost this pre-eminent status in design philosophy and was beginning to acquire a slightly tarnished reputation. It retained fervent disciples, yet fewer people than previously were inclined to follow the functionalist leaders and into the voices of this modernist choir crept an element of despair.

After 1960, it became increasingly difficult to identify any one suburban style as predominant. A more eclectic approach to style began to manifest itself and the modernist design stood side by side with the 'contemporary', the 'American range' style, the 'colonial', 'modern colonial' or 'modern gable'. The functional modernist disapproved of such featurist touches and gaped in horror as the modern became nothing more than another decorative touch. Project builders took this phenomenon to its ultimate expression in their attempt to satisfy an impersonal market.

This eclecticism continued into the 1970s and by the 1980s builders were borrowing from the historical styles which the early post-war modernists had so vehemently rejected, such as the Californian bungalow and the Queen Anne revival. This modern Queen Anne revival was renamed the Federation house. Some state housing commissions began remodelling some of their early post-war rental accommodation, whose design Boyd had considered clumsy but honest. He would have been much less tolerant of the 'Federated' and 'Californicated' bungalows which the state housing commissions were retrofitting and offering out for owner occupation (see Figure 22). The irony in this cycle of style was complete.

Other factors hastened the decline of modernist ascendancy in house design by the late 1950s and early 1960s. As noted in Chapter 1 the greater affluence of the majority during the long post-war boom allayed fears of another depression. The recession of 1961 brought with it a credit squeeze, but the resulting hardship could not be compared to the experiences of the early 1930s. A more austere society was free of the temptations of featurism, while affluence and Fordist mass production encouraged more conspicuous styles of consumption. The link between necessity and modernism had been broken and the advertising industry was quick to run with the tide of affluence. The scientific experiments with interior space which many post-war modernists had marketed tarred the modern house with the brush of a less prosperous era.

This book has documented the rise and subsequent decline of modernism in a variety of fields and has contrasted the grand post-war vision with the reality of 1960. A superficial conclusion could be reached that the gap between vision and reality was so great that post-war modernism was a failure. However, this ignores the innovative and often practical solutions adopted by modernist design. It would be more correct to state that modernism rose to the challenges presented by the unique and difficult material conditions of the period.

From a 'value-neutral' stance, it can be argued that modernism during the early post-war era was neither good nor bad but necessary, given the shortages of materials, space and labour. A similar position can be adopted towards early post-war owner occupation, which must be understood within the context of the limited options available to housing consumers. While useful, such a judgement tends to ignore some of the key aspects of the modernist outlook. Despite its intellectual pretensions and the elitism of some of its adherents, much of post-war modernism was egalitarian; more importantly, it advocated change, even if this change was more ameliorative than transformative. While the post-war modernist vision failed to change the world in its image, it advocated values which are possibly more necessary in the 1990s as the 'politics of domestic defence' unravel than they were in the 1950s.

The book is structured around familiar analytical distinctions in housing studies between production and consumption. However, from the beginning it was stressed that theoretical priority could not be assigned to either concept. I have acknowledged the contribution to social theory of the regulation school and more specifically Ball and Harloe's 'structures of housing provision', which stress the interaction of both production and consumption with other factors. The utility of these approaches was revealed in each section of the book. No aspect of housing provision—whether production, consumption or design—can be explained without reference to the others, as well as to wider processes of social change. Furthermore, the book provides evidence that post-war housing provision cannot be regarded simply as a slice of longer linear historical processes. In order to explain housing outcomes, it is necessary to appreciate how the force of contingency can bend 'the master key of a historico-philosophical theory whose supreme virtue consists in being suprahistorical' (Marx, quoted in Shanin 1984, 136). Ultimately, this book has been as much about using the history of post-war housing to critique the use of social theory as it has been about applying social theory to explain housing provision in the post-war period.

Bibliography

Abercrombie, N., Hill, S. & Turner, B. (1980), *The Dominant Ideology Thesis*, London, Allen & Unwin.

Aglietta, M. (1979), *A Theory of Capitalist Regulation: The US Experience*, London, New Left Books.

AIPS [Australian Institute of Political Science] (1947), *The Housing Problem in Australia*, Papers read at the winter forum of the Australian Institute of Political Science, held in Wollongong, 20–22 June 1947, Sydney, Angus & Robertson.

Albon, R. (1980), 'History and Overview', in R. Albon (ed.), *Rent Control: Costs and Consequences*, CIS Readings 2, Sydney, Centre for Independent Studies.

Allport, C. (1985), 'The Unrealised Promise: Plans for Sydney Housing in the Forties', in J. Roe (ed.), *Twentieth Century Sydney: Studies in Urban and Social History*, Sydney, Hale & Iremonger in association with the Sydney History Group.

Alomes, S., Dober, M. & Hellier, D. (1984), 'The Social Context of Postwar Conservatism', in A. Curthoys & J. Merritt (eds), *Australia's First Cold War 1945–53: Vol. 1, Society, Communism and Culture*, Sydney, Allen & Unwin.

Anderssen, H. & McEvoy, J. (1990), *Instability in the Australian Residential Construction Industry*, Bureau of Industry Economics Research Paper No. 2, Department of Industry, Technology and Commerce, Canberra.

ANZ [Australia and New Zealand Bank Limited] (1954), *Australian Housing Survey*, Melbourne, ANZ Bank Ltd.

Apperly, R., Irving, R. & Reynolds, P. (1989), *A Pictorial Guide to Identifying Australian Architecture*, Sydney, Angus & Robertson.

Appleyard, R. T. (1963), *Low Cost Housing and the Migrant Population*, n.p., Committee for the Economic Development of Australia.

Archer, J. (1987), *Building a Nation*, Sydney, Collins.

Arndt, H. W. (1949), 'Book Review: Housing and Employment', *The Economic Record*, vol. 25, June.

Atkinson, J. (1987), 'Flexibility or Fragmentation? The United Kingdom Labour Market in the Eighties', *Labour and Society*, vol. 12, no. 1.

Australian Bureau of Statistics (1991), *Construction Industry Australia: Summary of Private Sector Operations 1988–9*, cat. no. 8771.0, Canberra, Australian Government Publishing Service.

Australian House and Garden (various).

Austrin, T. (1980), 'The 'Lump' in the UK Construction Industry', in T. Nichols (ed.), *Capital and Labour: A Marxist Primer*, Glasgow, Fontana.

Ball, M. (1983), *Housing Policy and Economic Power: The Political Economy of Owner Occupation*, London, Methuen.

——— (1988), *Rebuilding Construction: Economic Change and the British Construction Industry*, London, Routledge.

Ball, M. & Harloe, M. (1992), 'Rhetorical Barriers to Understanding Housing Provision: What the 'Provision Thesis' Is and Is Not', *Housing Studies*, vol. 7, no. 1.

Ball, M., Harloe, M. & Martens, M. (1988), *Housing and Social Change in Europe and the USA*, London, Routledge.

Bank of New South Wales (1953), 'Implications of Rent Control', reprinted in R. Albon (ed.), *Rent Control: Costs and Consequences*, CIS Readings 2, Sydney, Centre for Independent Studies.

——— (1958), 'Rent Control and Property Investment', reprinted in R. Albon (ed.), *Rent Control: Costs and Consequences*, CIS Readings 2, Sydney, Centre for Independent Studies.

Baran, P. & Sweezy, P. (1977), *Monopoly Capital: An Essay on the American Economic and Social Order*, Harmondsworth, Penguin.

Barber, B. (1957), *Social Stratification: A Comparative Analysis of Structure and Process*, New York, Harcourt Brace & World.

Barnett, F. O. & Burt, W. O. (1942), *Housing the Australian Nation*, Melbourne, Left Book Club.

Barnett, F. O., Burt, W. O. & Heath, F. (1944), *We Must Go On: A Study in Planned Reconstruction and Housing*, Melbourne, Book Depot.

Bassett, K. & Short, J. R. (1980), *Housing and Residential Structure: Alternative Approaches*, London, Routledge & Kegan Paul.

Beer, A. (1993), 'A Dream Won, a Crisis Born? Home Ownership and the Housing Market', in C. Paris, *Housing Australia*, Melbourne, Macmillan.

Bell, D. (1958), *The End of Ideology*, New York, Free Press.

——— (1973), *The Coming of Post-Industrial Society*, New York, Free Press.

——— (1976), *The Cultural Contradictions of Capitalism*, New York, Basic Books.

Beniger, J. R. (1986), *The Control Revolution: Technological and Economic Origins of the Information Society*, Cambridge, Harvard University Press.

Berger, P. (1979), *Facing Up To Modernity*, Harmondsworth, Penguin.

Berman, M. (1983), *All That Is Solid Melts Into Air: The Experience of Modernity*, London, Verso.

Berry, M. (1984), 'The Political Economy of Australian Urbanisation', *Progress in Planning*, vol. 22, no. 1, Oxford.

——— (1988), 'To Buy or Rent? The Demise of a Dual Tenure Policy in Australia 1945 60', in R. Howe (ed.), *New Houses for Old: Fifty Years of Public Housing in Victoria 1938–1988*, Melbourne, Ministry of Housing and Construction.

——— (1990), 'The Politics of Australian Cities', *Arena*, 91.

Bethune, G. C. (1978), Home Ownership in Australian Capital Cities With Particular Reference to Melbourne and Sydney, PhD thesis, Australian National University, August 1978.

Bettelheim, C. (1978), *The Transition to Socialist Economy*, Hassocks, Sussex, Harvester Press.

Blackburn, K. (1982), 'The 'Consumers' Ethic' of Australian Advertising Agencies 1950–1965', *Journal of Australian Studies*, vol. 32.

Bolton, G. (1981), *Spoils and Spoilers*, Sydney, Allen & Unwin.

——— (1993), *The Middle Way: 1942–1988*, Oxford History of Australia vol. 5, Melbourne, Oxford University Press.

Bonke, S. & Goth, S. (1982), 'The Labour Process in the Construction Industry', in *Proceedings of the 1982 Bartlett International Summer School*, University College, London.

Bonney, B. & Wilson, H. (1983), *Australia's Commercial Media*, Melbourne, Macmillan.

Boudon, R. (1986), *Theories of Social Change: A Critical Appraisal*, Oxford, Polity Press.

——— (1989), *The Analysis of Ideology*, Cambridge, Polity Press.

Bourassa, S., Greig, A. W. & Troy, P. N. (forthcoming), 'The Limits of Housing Policy: Home Ownership in Australia', *Housing Studies*.

Bourke, J. M. (1960), 'Social and Economic Aspects of Government Housing', *Journal of the Australian Planning Institute*, December. Reprinted in J. Roe (ed.) (1976), *Social Policy in Australia: Some Perspectives*, Sydney, Cassell.

Boyd, R. (1952), 'The Architect and the Anchor, *Meanjin*, Autumn, vol. XI, no. 1.

——— (1953), 'Australian Towns and Cities', in W. V. Aughterson (ed.), *Taking Stock: Aspects of Mid-Century Life in Australia*, Melbourne, Cheshire.

——— (1957), 'The Future of Design Practice', in *Architecture in Australia*, vol. 46, no. 3, July/September.

——— (1958), 'Look Back in Apathy', in *Meanjin*, vol. xvii, no. 2, Winter.

——— (1962), *The Walls Around Us*, Melbourne, Cheshire.

——— (1963), *The New Architecture*, Melbourne, Longman.

——— (1967a), 'The State of Australian Architecture', *Architecture in Australia*, June.

——— (1967b), *Artificial Australia*, Boyer Lectures 1967, Sydney, ABC Publications.

——— (1968), *The Australian Ugliness*, Melbourne, Penguin.

——— (1972), *The Great, Great Australian Dream*, Sydney, Pergamon.

——— (1991), *Australia's Home*, Melbourne, Melbourne University Press.

Boyer, R. (1988), 'Technical Change and the Theory of Regulation', in G. Dosi et al. (eds), *Technical Change and Economic Theory*, London, Pinter Press.

Braine, J. (1968), *Room at the Top*, Harmondsworth, Penguin.

Brett, J. (1984), 'Menzies' "Forgotten People"', *Meanjin*, vol. 43, no. 2.

Brown, W. J. (1954), 'Mass Migration - Menace to Australia', *Communist Review*, October 1954.

Bukharin, N. (1965), 'Notes of an Economist (The Beginning of the New Economic Year)', in N. Spulber (ed.), *Foundations of Soviet Strategies for Economic Growth*, Bloomington, University of Indiana Press.

Bunning, W. (1945), *Homes In The Sun: The Past, Present and Future of Australian Housing*, Sydney, W. J. Nesbit.

Bureau of Industry Economics (1990), *Instability in the Australian Residential Construction Industry*, Discussion Paper 10, Canberra, Australian Government Publishing Service.

Bures, S. (1987), *The House of Wunderlich*, Sydney, Kangaroo Press.

Burkitt Report (1974), *Modern Housing Techniques*, A Report to the Minister for Housing and Construction by the Australian Government Taskforce to Investigate Modern Housing Techniques, Canberra, Australian Government Printing Service.

Burnley, I. (1985), 'Cities of Immigrants: Migration, Growth and Heterogeneity', in I. Burnley & J. Forrest (eds), *Living in Cities*, Sydney, Allen & Unwin.

Burns Commission (1981), *Report by Mr G. A. Burns of the Commission of Inquiry into the Nature and Terms of Employment in the New South Wales Housing Industry*, Parliament of New South Wales, Sydney, Government Printer.

Butler, D. E. & Rose, R. (1960), *The British General Election of 1959*, London, Macmillan.

Butler, G. (1992), *The Californian Bungalow in Australia*, Melbourne, Lothian.

Camilleri, J. A. & Falk, J. (1992), *End of Sovereignty?: The Politics of a Shrinking and Fragmenting World*, Aldershot, Edward Elgar.

Capling, M. A. & Galligan, B. (1993), *Beyond the Protective State: The Political Economy of Australia's National Industry Policy*, New York, Cambridge University Press.

Caplovitz, D. (1963), *The Poor Pay More: Consumer Practices in the Lower Income Families*, New York, Free Press.

Castells, M. (1977), *The Urban Question: A Marxist Approach*, London, Edward Arnold.

Castles, F. G. (1988), *Australian Public Policy and Economic Vulnerability: A Comparative and Historical Perspective*, Sydney, Allen & Unwin.

CHC [Commonwealth Housing Commission] (1944), *Final Report: 25th August 1944*, n.p., Ministry of Post-War Reconstruction.

Checkoway, B. (1986), 'Large Builders, Federal Housing Programs, and Post-War Suburbanisation', in R. G. Bratt, C. W. Harman & A. Meyerson (eds), *Critical Perspectives on Housing*, Philadelphia, Temple University Press.

Clarke, G. (1970), 'Urban Australia', in A. F. Davies & S. Encel (eds), *Australian Society: A Sociological Introduction*, Melbourne, Cheshire.

Collins, J. (1988), *Migrant Hands in a Distant Land: Australia's Post-War Immigration*, Sydney, Pluto Press.

Collins, T. (1993), *Living for the City: Urban Australia: Crisis or Challenge?*, Sydney, ABC Publications.

Commonwealth of Australia (1990), *Official Year Book, Australia*, Canberra, Australian Government Publishing Service.

Connell, R. W. (1977), *Ruling Class, Ruling Culture: Studies of Conflict, Power and Hegemony in Australian Life*, Cambridge, Cambridge University Press.

Connell, R. W. & Irving, T. H. (1986), *Class Structure in Australian History: Documents, Narrative and Argument*, Melbourne, Longman Cheshire.

Copland, D. B. (1944), 'The Change-Over to Peace', in D. A. S. Campbell (ed.), *Post-War Reconstruction in Australia*, Sydney, Australasian Publishing Co./Australian Institute of Political Science.

Crisp, L. F. (1973), *Australian National Government*, Melbourne, Longman.

Cuffley, P. (1990), *Houses of the 20s & 30s*, Melbourne, Five Mile Press.

——— (1993), *Houses of the 40s & 50s*, Melbourne, Five Mile Press.

Davison, G. (1993), 'Virtual Reality', *Arena Magazine*, no. 6, August/September.

Department of Housing (1968), *Flats: A Survey of Multi-Unit Construction in Australia*, Canberra, Australian Government Publishing Service.

Department of Information (1946), *Australia Pocket Book*, Melbourne, by authority of the Commonwealth Minister for Information and for Immigration.

Department of the Interior (1961), *Australia: Official Handbook*, by authority of the Minister of the Interior, the Hon. Gordon Freeth, Melbourne, A. E. Keating.

Department of National Development (1956), *The Housing Situation*, prepared under instruction from the Honourable the Minister for National Development, Canberra, December.

Dovey, K. (1992), 'Model Houses and Housing Ideology in Australia', *Housing Studies*, vol. 7, no. 3, July 1992.

Downing, R. I. (1948), 'Housing and Public Policy', *Economic Record*, vol. 24, June.

Dunphy, M. (1961), 'Review of *The Australian Ugliness*', *Architecture in Australia*, March.

Ehrensaft, P. & Armstrong, W. (1978), '"Dominion Capitalism": A First Statement', *Australian New Zealand Journal of Sociology*, vol. 14, October.

Elam, M. (1989), 'Puzzling Out the Post-Fordist Debate: Technology, Markets and Institutions', *Industrial and Economic Democracy*, vol. 11, no. 1.

Fischer, K. F. (1984), *Canberra: Myths and Models: Forces at Work in the Formation of the Australian Capital*, Hamburg, Institute of Asian Affairs.

Fiske, J. (1989), *Reading The Popular*, Boston, Unwin Hyman.

Fiske, J., Hodge, B. & Turner, G. (1987), *Myths of Oz: Reading Australian Popular Culture*, Sydney, Allen & Unwin.

Flower, C. (1993), 'Veneer Years', *Bulletin*, 14 December.

Freeland, J. M. (1972), *Architecture in Australia: A History*, Melbourne, Penguin.

Freeman, C. & Perez, C. (1988), 'Structural Crises of Adjustment: Business Cycles and Investment Behaviour', in G. Dosi et al. (eds), *Economic Theory and Technical Change*, London, Pinter Press.

Fry, E. C. (1972), 'Growth of an Australian Metropolis', in R. S. Parker & P. N. Troy (eds), *The Politics of Urban Growth*, Canberra, Australian National University Press.

Galbraith, J. K. (1970), *The Affluent Society*, Harmondsworth, Penguin.

Garden, D. S. (1992), *Builders to the Nation: The A. V. Jennings Story*, Melbourne, Melbourne University Press.

Gawler, J. S. (1963), *A Roof Over My Head*, Sydney, Lothian.

Gazzard, D. (ed.) (1966), *Australian Outrage: The Decay of a Visual Environment*, a study by the Royal Australian Institute of Architects, Sydney, Ure Smith.

George Wimpey & Co. Ltd (1965), *Submission to Joint Committee on the Australian Capital Territory Parliament of the Commonwealth Investigating the Question of the Adequacy of the Supply, in Relation to Demand, of Residential Blocks Offered for Leasing in Canberra*, Canberra.

Giddens, A. (1987), *Social Theory and Modern Sociology*, Cambridge, Polity Press.

Greenop, F. S. (1947), *History of Magazine Publishing in Australia*, Sydney, K. G. Murray.

Greig, A. W. (1992a), *Structure, Organisation and Skill Formation in the Australian Housing Industry*, background paper no. 13, National Housing Strategy, Commonwealth Department of Health, Housing and Community Affairs, Canberra, Australian Government Publishing Service.

——— (1992b), 'Subcontracting and the Future of the Clothing Industry', *Journal of Australian Political Economy*, vol. 29, May.

Groenewegen, P. (1972), 'Consumer Capitalism', in J. Playford & D. Kirsner (eds), *Australian Capitalism: Towards a Socialist Critique*, Melbourne, Penguin.

Gropius, W. (n.d.), *The New Architecture and the Bauhaus*, London, Faber & Faber.

Gunn, P. (1991), 'Frank Lloyd Wright and the Passage to Fordism', in *Capital and Class*, no. 44, Summer.

Hamann, C. (1981), 'Grounds, Romberg and Boyd', in H. Tanner (ed.), *Architects of Australia*, Melbourne, Macmillan.

Hall, A. R. (1961), *Housing Trends and Economic Growth*, Melbourne, Committee for Economic Development of Australia.

Harloe, M. (1981), 'The Recommodification of Housing', in M. Harloe & E. Lebas (eds), *City, Class and Capital*, London, Edward Arnold.

Harvey, D. (1989), *The Condition of Postmodernity: An Enquiry into the Origins of Cultural Change*, Oxford, Basil Blackwell.

Hay, C. (1992), 'Housing Policy in Transition: From the Post-War Settlement Towards a "Thatcherite" Hegemony', in *Capital and Class*, no. 46, Spring.

Hayward, D. (1986), 'The Great Australian Dream Reconsidered: A Review of Kemeny', *Housing Studies*, vol. 1, no. 4.

Hill, M. R. (1959), *Housing Finance in Australia: 1945–1956*, Melbourne, Melbourne University Press, on behalf of the Australian National University.

——— (1964a), 'Housing—Twenty Years After', *Australian Quarterly*, vol. 36, September.

——— (1964b), 'Housing Finance Institutions', in R. R. Hirst & R. H. Wallace (eds), *Studies in the Australian Capital Market*, Melbourne, Cheshire.

Hilton, W. S. (1968), *Industrial Relations in Construction*, London, Pergamon.

Hindess, B. (1971), *The Decline of Working Class Politics*, London, Merlin Press.

Holland, G. (1988), *Emoh Ruo: Owner Building in Sydney*, Sydney, Hale & Iremonger.

Home Beautiful (various issues).

Horne, D. (1966), *The Lucky Country: Australia in the Sixties*, Melbourne, Penguin.

Housing Industry Association (1967), A *Survey of the State of Housing in Australia*, Canberra, Economic Research Committee of the Housing Industry Association.

——— (1990), *Our Homes Towards 2000: 1990–1991 Edition*, Canberra.

Howard, M. (1981), Beyond Full Employment: The Nature and Scope of Commonwealth Intervention in the Building Industry During Post-War Reconstruction, 1941–49, Paper delivered to the Post-War Reconstruction Seminar, Research School of Social Sciences, Australian National University, September.

——— (1987), *State, Business and Unions in the Restructuring of the Building Industry in Australia, 1939–52*, Industrial Relations Papers, Research School of Social Sciences, Australian National University.

Howells, T. (1993), 'The Morning After', in T. Howells & M. Nicholson (eds), *Towards the Dawn: Federation Architecture in Australia 1890–1915*, Sydney, Hale & Iremonger.

Hutton, J. (1970), *Building and Construction in Australia*, Melbourne, Cheshire.

Ifould, W. H. (1947), 'Solutions of the Australian Housing Problem', in *The Housing Problem in Australia*, papers read at the winter forum of the Australian Institute of Political Science, held in Wollongong, 20–22 June 1947, Sydney, Angus & Robertson.

International Labor Organisation (1948), *Instability of Employment in the Construction Industries*, Geneva, ILO, Building and Civil Engineering and Public Works Committee.

International Labor Office (1948), *Housing and Employment*, Studies and Reports, new series no. 8, Geneva, ILO.

IPA Review (1954), 'Rent Control', July-September 1954, reprinted in R. Albon (ed.), *Rent Control: Costs and Consequences*, CIS Readings 2, Sydney, Centre for Independent Studies.

Jackson, R. & Bridge, H. (1987), 'Housing', in W. Vamplew (ed.), *Australians: Historical Statistics*, Sydney, Fairfax, Syme & Weldon Associates.

Jencks, C. (1978), *The Language of Post-Modern Architecture*, London, Academy Editions.

Jessop, B. (1990), *State Theory: Putting Capitalist States in their Place*, Cambridge, Polity Press.

——— (1991), 'The Welfare State in Transition from Fordism to Post-Fordism', in B. Jessop et al. (eds), *The Politics of Flexibility: Restructuring State and Industry in Britain, Germany and Scandinavia*, Aldershot, Edward Elgar.

Jones, M. A. (1972), *Housing and Poverty in Australia*, Melbourne, Melbourne University Press.

Johnson, C. (1966), *Revolutionary Change*, New York, Little, Brown.

Johnson, K. (1972), *People and Property in North Melbourne: Development and Change in an Inner Suburb of Melbourne, in the Nineteen Fifties and Sixties*, Urban Research Unit, Research School of Social Sciences, Australian National University.

——— (1979), *People and Property in St Kilda: Development and Change in an Inner Suburb of Melbourne, in the Nineteen Fifties and Sixties*, Urban Research Unit, Research School of Social Sciences, Australian National University.

Johnston, R. & Lepani, B. (1993), 'Innovation and the Australian Housing Industry', *Urban Futures: Issues for Australian Cities*, vol. 3, no. 1, March 1993.

Jordens, A-M. (1994), 'On Accommodating Migrants', *Compliance, Governability and Administration Working Paper*, no. 19, January 1994, Research School of Social Sciences, Australian National University.

Jupp, J. (1966), *Arrivals and Departures*, Melbourne, Cheshire.

Kass, T. (1987), 'Cheaper Than Rent', in M. Kelly (ed.), *Sydney: City of Suburbs*, Sydney, University of New South Wales Press.

Kelly, G. (1957), 'Portrait of a New Community: A Personal Impression', *Meanjin*, vol. xvi, no. 4, December.

Kemeny, J. (1981), *The Myth of Home-Ownership: Private Versus Public Choices in Housing Tenure*, London, Routledge & Kegan Paul.

——— (1983), *The Great Australian Nightmare: A Critique of Home-Ownership Ideology*, Melbourne, Georgian House.

——— (1986), 'The Ideology of Home Ownership', in J. B. McLoughlin & M. Huxley (eds), *Urban Planning in Australia: Critical Readings*, Melbourne, Longman Cheshire.

Kemp, D. A. (1978), *Society and Electoral Behaviour in Australia: A Study of Three Decades*, Brisbane, University of Queensland Press.

Landis, J. (1981), 'Why Homebuilders Don't Innovate', *Built Environment*, vol. 8, no. 1.

Lewis, M. (1985), 'The Portable House', in R. Irving (ed.), *The History and Design of the Australian House*, Melbourne, Oxford University Press.

Lipietz, A. (1985), 'Building and the Crisis of Fordism', in *Proceedings of the 6th Bartlett International Summer School 1984*, London, Organising Committee of the Bartlett International Summer School.

——— (1987), *Miracles and Mirages: The Crisis of Global Fordism*, London, Verso Books.

——— (1988), 'New Tendencies in the International Division of Labour: Regimes of Accumulation and Modes of Regulation', in A. J. Scott & M. Storper (eds), *Production, Work Territory: The Geographical Anatomy of Industrial Capitalism*, Boston, Unwin Hyman.

——— (1993), 'From Althusserianism to "Regulation Theory"', in E. Ann Kaplan & M. Sprinkler (eds), *The Althusserian Legacy*, London, Verso Press.

Lindesay, V. (1983), *The Way We Were: Australian Popular Magazines 1856–1969*, Melbourne, Oxford University Press.

Low, N. P. (1994), 'Growth Models and Regulation Theory: The Institutional Dimension of the Regulation of Space in Australia', *International Journal of Urban and Regional Research*, vol. 18, no. 3.

McDonell, G. (1956), 'Book Review: Australian Building Industry Productivity Report, 1954', *Architecture in Australia*, January-March.

McGregor, C. (1966), *Profile of Australia*, Melbourne, Penguin.

MacIntyre, C. (1991), '"now you're in the family zone": Housing and Domestic Design in Australia', *Journal of Australian Studies*, no. 30, September.

McLoughlin, J. B. (1993), *Shaping Melbourne's Future: Town Planning, the State, and Civil Society*, Cambridge, Cambridge University Press.

McLuhan, M. (1964), *Understanding Media: The Extensions of Man*, London, Routledge & Kegan Paul.

McQueen, H. (1991), *Social Sketches of Australia*, Melbourne, Penguin.

Marosszeky, M. (1982), Guiding Change in Housing Production, paper presented at the Commonwealth Department of Housing and Construction seminar 'Manufactured Housing', University of New South Wales, 20 April 1982.

——— (1991), International Trends in Building Construction and Materials, an address to the senior staff of the Tian Jin Building Materials Industrial Bureau, August.

Marsden, S. E. (1986), *Business, Charity and Sentiment: The South Australian Housing Trust 1936-1986*, Adelaide, Wakefield Press.

Martin, J. I. (1970), 'Suburbia: Community and Network', in A. F. Davies & S. Encel (eds), *Australian Society: A Sociological Introduction*, Melbourne, Cheshire.

Mathews, J. (1989), *Tools for Change: New Technology and the Democratisation of Work*, Sydney, Pluto Press.

Mendelsohn, R. (1945), 'The Housing Problem', *Australian Quarterly*, vol. 17, June.

——— (1982), *Fair Go: Welfare Issues in Australia*, Melbourne, Penguin.

Merton, R. K. (1967), *On Theoretical Sociology*, New York, Free Press.

Morris, J. & Winn, M. (1990), *Housing and Social Inequality*, London, Hilary Shipman.

Mullins, P. (1981a), 'Theoretical Perspectives on Australian Urbanisation: I. Material Components in the Reproduction of Australian Labour Power', *Australian and New Zealand Journal of Sociology*, vol. 17, no. 1, March.

——— (1981b), 'Theoretical Perspectives on Australian Urbanisation: II. Social Components in the Reproduction of Australian Labour Power', *Australian and New Zealand Journal of Sociology*, vol. 17, no. 3, November.

——— (1988), 'Is Australian Urbanisation Different?', in J. Najman & J. Western (eds), *A Sociology of Australian Society*, Melbourne, Macmillan.

Murphy, M. (1984), *Challenges of Change: The Lend Lease Story*, Sydney, Lend Lease Group.

National Housing Strategy (1991), *Framework For Reform*, background paper no. 1, Department of Health, Housing and Community Services, Canberra, Australian Government Publishing Service.

Needleman, L. (1965), *The Economics of Housing*, London, Staples Press.

Nelson, G. (1957), *Problems of Design*, New York, Whitney Publications.

Nelson, H. (1980), 'The Politics of Decontrol in New South Wales', in R. Albon (ed.), *Rent Control: Costs and Consequences*, CIS Readings 2, Sydney, Centre for Independent Studies.

Neutze, M. (1968), 'Flat Building in Australia', paper presented to the Economic History/Urban Research Unit Seminar, Research School of Social Sciences, Australian National University, June.

——— (1971a), *People and Property in Randwick: Post War Changes in the Population and their Dwellings in an Eastern Suburb of Sydney*, Urban Research Unit, Research School of Social Sciences, Australian National University, September.

——— (1971b), *People and Property in Bankstown: Recent Property Developments and Changes in the Population of a Middle-Distance Western Suburb of Sydney*, Urban Research Unit, Research School of Social Sciences, Australian National University, December.

——— (1972a), *People and Property in Liverpool: Changes in the Population and Developments in the Property Market During the Growth of a Fringe Sydney Suburb*, Urban Research Unit, Research School of Social Sciences, Australian National University.

——— (1972b), *People and Property in Redfern: Post-War Changes in the Population and the Properties in an Inner Suburb of Sydney*, Urban Research Unit, Research School of Social Sciences, Australian National University.

——— (1978), *Urban Development in Australia: A Descriptive Analysis*, Sydney, George Allen & Unwin.

Nielsen, K. (1991), 'Towards a Flexible Future — Theories and Politics', in B. Jessop et al. (eds), *The Politics of Flexibility: Restructuring State and Industry in Britain, Germany and Scandinavia*, Aldershot, Edward Elgar.

O'Callaghan, J. (1993), 'The Australian Interior: The Importance of Being Contemporary', in J. O'Callaghan (ed.), *The Australian Dream: Design of the Fifties*, Sydney, Powerhouse.

O'Connor, J. (1973), *The Fiscal Crisis of the State*, New York, St James Press.

Paris, C. (1987), 'Housing Issues and Policies in Australia', in S. Hamnett & R. Bunker (eds), *Urban Australia: Planning Issues and Policies*, Melbourne, Nelson Wadsworth.

——— (1993), *Housing Australia*, Melbourne, Macmillan.

Phillip, F. (1952), 'Australia's Home', *Meanjin*, vol. XI, no. 1.

Phizacklea, A. (1990), *Unpacking the Fashion Industry: Gender, Racism and Class in Production*, London, Routledge.

Pickett, C. (1993), 'Modernity and Austerity: The 1950s Home', in J. O'Callaghan (ed.), *The Australian Dream: Design of the Fifties*, Sydney, Powerhouse.

Powell, D. (1993), *Out West: Perceptions of Sydney's Western Suburbs*, Sydney, Allen & Unwin.

Pugh, C. (1976), *Intergovernmental Relations and the Development of Australian Housing Policies*, research monograph no. 15, Centre for Research on Federal Financial Relations, Canberra, Australian National University Press.

Ramsay, A. M. (1945), 'Housing Problems', *Australian Quarterly*, vol. 17, December.

Reiger, K. M. (1986), *The Disenchantment of the Home: Modernizing the Australian Family 1880–1940*, Melbourne, Oxford University Press.

——— (1991), *Family Economy*, Melbourne, McPhee Gribble.

Riddel, R. (1993), in T. Howells & M. Nicholson (eds) *Towards the Dawn: Federation Architecture in Australia 1890–1915*, Sydney, Hale & Iremonger.

Roobeek, A. (1987), 'The Crisis of Fordism and the Rise of a New Technological Paradigm', *Futures*, April.

Ross, L. (1944), 'A New Social Order', in D. A. S. Campbell (ed.), *Post-War Reconstruction in Australia*, Sydney, Australasian Publishing Co./Australian Institute of Political Science.

Rostow, W. W. (1960), *The Stages of Economic Growth: A Non-Communist Manifesto*, Cambridge, Cambridge University Press.

Rowley, K. (1972), 'The Political Economy of Australia Since the War', in J. Playford & D. Kirsner (eds), *Australian Capitalism: Towards a Socialist Critique*, Melbourne, Penguin.

Rowse, T. (1978), 'Heaven and a Hills Hoist: Australian Critics on Suburbia', *Meanjin*, vol. 37, no. 1.

Rybczynski, W. (1987), *Home: A Short History of an Idea*, New York, Penguin.

Sandercock, L. (1977), *Cities for Sale*, Melbourne, Melbourne University Press.

Saunders, D. (1972), 'Retrospective: Robin Boyd', in *Architecture in Australia*, February.

Scase, R. & Goffee, R. (1982), *The Entrepreneurial Middle Class*, London, Croom Helm.

Schlesinger, T. & Erlich, M. (1986), 'Housing: The Industry Capitalism Didn't Forget', in R. G. Bratt, C. W. Harman & A. Meyerson (eds), *Critical Perspectives on Housing*, Philadelphia, Temple University Press.

Shanin, T. (1984), *Marx and the Russian Road: Marx and 'the Peripheries of Capitalism'*, London, Routledge & Kegan Paul.

Shelter (various issues).

Smart, B. (1993), *Postmodernity*, London, Routledge.

Soja, E. W. (1989), *Post-Modern Geographies*, London, Verso Press.

Spearritt, P. (1978), *Sydney Since the Twenties*, Sydney, Hale & Iremonger.

Stapleton, M. (1985), 'Between the Wars', in R. Irving (ed.), *The History and Design of the Australian House*, Melbourne, Oxford University Press.

Strachey J. (1956), *Contemporary Capitalism*, London, Gollancz.

Strahan, L. (1984), *Just City and the Mirrors: Meanjin Quarterly and the Intellectual Front 1940–1965*, Melbourne, Oxford University Press.

Stretton, H. (1978), 'A. M. Ramsay and the Conventional Wisdom', *Australian Quarterly*, vol. 50, no. 3, September.

——— (1991), '"Introduction" to Boyd's *Australia's Home*', Melbourne, Melbourne University Press.

Stubbs, J. (1966), *The Hidden People*, Melbourne, Cheshire.

Taylor, J. (1972), *An Australian Identity: Houses for Sydney 1953–63*, Sydney, Department of Architecture, University of Sydney.

——— (1985), 'Beyond the 1950s', in R. Irving (ed.), *The History and Design of the Australian House*, Melbourne, Oxford University Press.

——— (1986), *Australian Architecture Since 1960*, Sydney, Law Book Co.

Toffler, A. (1970), *Future Shock*, London, Bodley Head.

Troy, P. N. (1991), 'The Benefits of Owner Occupation', *Urban Research Program Working Paper No. 29*, Research School of Social Sciences, Australian National University, December.

——— (1992), 'The Evolution of Government Housing Policy: The Case of New South Wales 1901–1941', *Housing Studies*, vol. 7, no. 3, July.

van de Ven, A-M. (1993), 'Images of the Fifties: Design and Advertising', in J. O'Callaghan (ed.), *The Australian Dream: Design of the Fifties*, Sydney, Powerhouse.

van Tulder R. & Ruigrok, W. M. (forthcoming), The Ideology of Interdependence: The Link Between Restructuring, Internationalisation and International Trade, University of Amsterdam.

Veblen, T. (1970), *The Theory of the Leisure Class: An Economic Study of Institutions*, London, Unwin Books.

Walsh, R. (1972), The Housebuilding Industry in New South Wales, M Com. thesis, University of Newcastle.

Ward, R., (1977), *A Nation for a Continent: The History of Australia: 1901–1975*, Melbourne, Heinemann.

Watson Sharpe, W. (1945), *Your Post-War House*, Sydney, K. G. Murray.

Weber, M. (1949), *The Methodology of the Social Sciences*, New York, Free Press.

——— (1978), *The Protestant Ethic and the Spirit of Capitalism*, London, Allen & Unwin.

Westergaard J. & Resler, H. (1977), *Class in a Capitalist Society: A Study of Contemporary Britain*, Harmondsworth, Penguin.

White, R. (1981), *Inventing Australia: Images and Identity 1688–1980*, Sydney, Allen & Unwin.

——— (1993), 'The Shock of Affluence: The Fifties in Australia', in J. O'Callaghan (ed.), *The Australian Dream: Design of the Fifties*, Sydney, Powerhouse.

Whitwell, G. (1989), *Making the Market: The Rise of Consumer Society*, Melbourne, McPhee Gribble.

Williams, P. (1984), 'The Politics of Property: Home Ownership in Australia', in J. Halligan & C. Paris (eds), *Australian Urban Politics*, Melbourne, Longman Cheshire.

Williamson, D. (1993), 'The Golden Age of Conformity', in *The Australian Magazine*, special issue 'The '50s: Why They Weren't So Bad', 18–19 September.

Wilson, M. (1993), 'Housing – An Export Industry', in *Development Now*, March.

Wilton, J. & Bosworth, R. (1987), *Old Worlds and New Australia: The Post-War Migration Experience*, Melbourne, Penguin.

Winston, D. (1962), 'The Problem', *Architecture in Australia*, June.

——— (1966), 'The Urban Explosion: The Nature of the Australian Problem', in Australian Institute of Political Sciences (ed.), *Australian Cities: Chaos or Planned Growth*, Sydney, Angus & Robertson.

Woodhead, W. D. (1978), 'The Sub-Contract System in Housebuilding', in *Housing Victoria*, special supplement, Melbourne, an article prepared by CSIRO.

Wright, Frank Lloyd (1963), *The Natural House*, New York, Mentor Books.

Yates, R. (1986), *Revolutionary Road*, London, Methuen.

Zubrzycki, J. (1970), 'The Teaching of Sociology in Australian Universities, Past and Present', in J. Zubrzycki (ed.), *The Teaching of Sociology in Australia and New Zealand*, Melbourne, Cheshire/Sociological Association of Australia and New Zealand.

Index to Authors

General Index